the
KING AND I

HERBERT BRESLIN

AND

ANNE MIDGETTE

BROADWAY BOOKS

NEW YORK

the
KING AND I

THE UNCENSORED
TALE OF
LUCIANO PAVAROTTI'S
RISE TO FAME BY
HIS MANAGER,
FRIEND, AND SOMETIME
ADVERSARY

PRINTED IN THE UNITED STATES OF AMERICA

BROADWAY BOOKS and its logo, a letter B bisected on the diagonal, are trademarks of Random House, Inc.

Visit our website at www.broadwaybooks.com

Book design by Laurie Jewell

The Library of Congress catalogued the hardcover edition as follows:
Breslin, Herbert H.
The king and I : the uncensored tale of Luciano Pavarotti's rise to fame by his manager, friend, and sometime adversary / by Herbert Breslin and Anne Midgette.—1st ed.
p. cm.
Includes index.
1. Pavarotti, Luciano. 2. Breslin, Herbert H. 3. Tenors (Singers)—Biography.
I. Midgette, Anne. II. Title.

ML420.P35B74 2004
782.1'092—dc22
[B]
2004045508

ISBN 0-7679-1508-9

1 3 5 7 9 10 8 6 4 2

FOR THE FAMILY

THE BRESLINS
CAROL, ERIC, CLEMENTINE, CAMERON

THE JAFFES
ANDREA, TOBY, ALEXANDER, ISABELLE

CONTENTS

introduction

OPENING MONOLOGUE

Herbert Breslin on Luciano Pavarotti

He's been called the world's greatest tenor, the King of the High Cs, one of the twenty-five most recognizable people on earth. I call him Signor Cervello. Mr. Brain.

Luciano Pavarotti, you see, is one of the world's leading experts on everything. He knows more about music, medicine, dentistry, the prostate, child care, legal matters, and so on and so forth than anyone else alive. The rest of us are mere incompetents. At least, that's how he sees it.

"The fish in Pesaro are the best in the world," he'll say. It doesn't matter if he's talking to someone from the North Sea, who might reasonably beg to differ. Pesaro has the best fish. That's that.

Got a medical problem? Only Luciano knows what doctor you should go to. But when you do go to the doctor, don't listen to him. Luciano knows much better than the doctor what medicine you should take.

I say, "Oh, Signor Cervello, excuse the rest of us for being so ignorant."

He calls me "*stupido*." But that's not a special accolade. He calls everyone that.

Who am I? Call me Herbert, or Herbertino, as Luciano does when he's feeling more affectionate—which is, these days, not often. If you're not in the classical music business, you may not have heard of me. People in my line of work—artist management and publicity—don't always get a share of the limelight. It's our business to stay behind the scenes and create limelight for other people. We're the movers and shakers, the people who make things happen, but not necessarily the people to whom things happen. At least, not from the public's perspective.

If you are in the business, you may have heard terrible things about me. I'm supposed to be brash, rude, mercurial, ruthless, money hungry. I squeeze people for every penny I can get out of them, throw terrible screaming tantrums, send devastating one-line put-downs to business associates through the fax machine. For all I know, I eat babies for dinner. When you're successful, people say all kinds of things about you.

Well, screw them. Let them talk. For your purposes, all you really need to know about me is that I'm one of the best managers and publicists in the business. Nobody knows classical music, and the business of classical music, better than I do. If I do say so myself.

You want proof? I guided Luciano Pavarotti's career, the greatest career in classical music, for thirty-six years. Never mind the dozens of other major artists I advised, steered, and counseled: that alone should be enough to make my point. Not many opera singers penetrate to the consciousness of the general public. Most big celebrities have movie studios or networks behind them, with armies of employees pounding away at promotion and public relations. Luciano, at the beginning, had none of that. He had me.

When Luciano and I started together, I was a simple publicist who had never managed an artist's career and he was a promising young tenor from Italy. I had done publicity for a number of important artists and he had appeared in some major opera houses. I met this young, eager, warm singer, and I believed he had the potential to be something huge. So did he. Neither one of us could have imagined where it would lead.

But I did see that this was somebody who could transcend the limits of the opera world. And I acted accordingly. I got him out of the opera house and into the concert hall. I kept him in front of the public with one performance, one event, one "first" after another. First U.S. recital, first "Live from the Met" broadcast, first solo recital from the Metropolitan Opera stage, first American Express commercial, first solo concert in a 20,000-seat arena. When Luciano first came along, sopranos ruled the opera world: Callas, Tebaldi, Sutherland. I shifted the attention of the opera world from rampant diva-dom to a tenor. Then I brought that tenor out of the opera house and into the arms of an enormous mass public. Those were my ideas. Nobody else had ideas like that. And Luciano was very happy to go along with them. Together, we changed the landscape of opera.

The story of Luciano Pavarotti is the story of a very beautiful, simple, lovely guy who turned into a very determined, aggressive, and somewhat unhappy superstar. It's the story of a man who came from a small town in Italy, from a family without a lot of money or education or privileges, and, against all odds, turned into one of the most famous people in the world. It's the story of the price of that success. I accompanied that journey every step of the way. I watched it all unfold. Hell, I unfolded some of it myself.

There were three stages in my relationship with Luciano. In the beginning, there were the years of closeness, collaboration, and excitement, as we became close friends—indeed, almost like family—and laid the foundations of the edifice we were building. In those years I knew a burly, clean-shaven young tenor, a little callow, a little awkward, thrilling to the joy of what he was doing and the excitement of all the wonderful things that were happening to him. That excitement was my excitement, too, as I took my dream client and tested myself to find out what could be done with him. We were a team; we planned together. If I said, "Jump," Luciano, with a huge grin splitting his face, would jump. And the crowd would go wild.

Then there were the middle years, when my client and I were at the top of our professions, learning how to deal with the realities of success. There was the constant adulation. There were the female fans flinging themselves into his dressing room; there were the "secretaries," the long-term loves who were part of Luciano's entourage when he was on the road and who discreetly and oh so professionally vanished into the woodwork whenever his wife showed up. There was the money. Money beyond our wildest dreams. Luciano Pavarotti made me a rich man. I didn't do so badly for him either.

I learned a lot, in those years, about the Italian mentality. Never say anything too directly is the first rule. If something good happens, don't congratulate an Italian outright. Drawing attention to good fortune may be dangerous.

"Luciano, that was a great concert!"

"Agh." He makes a face and a dismissive gesture of the hands. "It was so-so."

Or, "Luciano, I hear you're expecting a child. Congratulations!"

"*Malocchio!*" he'll hiss, and grab for his balls. That's a way of warding off bad luck. Italian men have no doubt where the seat of their luck lies.

But it can be hard to make plans if you can't say anything directly. "Do you want to do this project at the Metropolitan Opera, Luciano?"

"Yes, yes, yes. Absolutely." So you can be sure that in the end that project is never going to get off the ground.

Unless, of course, he says, "No, never. What a terrible idea." That's the project he's going to wind up doing.

Then there was the final stage in our relationship, the last decade or so. To be frank, this period got to be pretty tiresome after a while. One arena concert after another, always with the same program; The Three Tenors in every city, town, and country in the world; tinselly pop concerts in which he mouths his way through songs he has no idea how to sing; phoned-in performances of operas he should know by heart; a messy, sad, and very public divorce. All of it, in my opinion, tarnishing the reputation of a man whose name used to be a synonym for excellence.

By this final stage, I didn't advise Luciano anymore. Nobody could advise Luciano, because nobody could tell Luciano anything. As I said, Luciano knows everything better than anyone else.

"Luciano," I'd say, "don't you think it's time to consider retiring?"

"Pff," he'd say, with another of his dismissive hand gestures. "You don't talk." It was a command. "I want to sing a *Tosca*."

So I would shut up and find an opera house that was willing to put him on in that. It wasn't too hard. However well or badly he sings on a given night, Pavarotti can always make a theater a lot of money. When Pavarotti sings, ticket prices go up. And the house is sold out.

After thirty-six years, I probably know Luciano as well as anyone else in the world. And yet sometimes I wonder if I know him at all. It's very difficult to know what Luciano is thinking. I would love to talk to a psychologist about what makes him tick. I wonder where it all came from: his foibles and superstitions, his driving talent and his laziness, his incredible force of personality that bends everyone around him to his will. I wonder if he loved the women who shared his life or simply appreciated their convenience and usefulness and the reflected glow cast on him by their beauty. I wonder if he was happy with the money we made or if it became a kind of addiction among many others—like the addiction to food that keeps him in his distinctive physical shape or the addiction to the adulation of the crowd, bathing him in applause. Now, as he drags his unwilling body from performance to performance, requiring a whole staff of assistants to attend to his needs, I wonder if he's happy.

I asked him that the last time I saw him.

"Pff," he growled. "I am very happy."

He didn't look happy. But I hope he is.

Luciano Pavarotti was my client, my greatest singer, my superstar, my cross to bear—and my friend. For thirty-six years, we were together through many successes and a few failures—actually, hardly any failures—through sickness and health, incredible closeness to and slightly embittered distance from each other, all in the course of the greatest opera career we'll ever see in our lifetimes. I helped make Luciano Pavarotti. But I couldn't make *another* Pavarotti. It takes a Pavarotti to make a Pavarotti. And no other Pavarotti is going to come along.

What was it like to work with Luciano? There's no simple answer. The question summons up a whole spectrum of memories. There's the strapping young singer I met in New York in 1967, when I rode out to the airport with him in a taxi to discuss taking him on as a public relations client. There's the sweating tenor in massive evening dress, clutching a creased handkerchief and basking with shut-eyed relief in the applause at his first U.S. recital. There's the voice I would hear on the phone many times a day, wanting to talk about the next concert or ask if someone in my office could please run over to his apartment with a pound or two of fresh tomatoes. There's the figure in full Arab garb in the Arab quarter of Jerusalem, beaming like a child on Halloween, as if the burnoose and kaffiyeh he had just purchased could actually disguise the unmistakable Pavarotti profile. There's the self-satisfied star in the front of the limo after a concert, quizzing us in the back about the details of his schedule for the coming weeks, delighted every time he's able to catch us out. There's the thwarted lover, threatening suicide after the decampment of one of his girlfriends, and the shrewd businessman whom I tutored in the importance of a dollar, holding out for another half a million for some glamorous television project. There's the potentate on his throne backstage at an arena concert, hair sloppily colored jet black, snapping his fingers to command a member of his entourage to bring him his preperformance consommé.

I've been a fan of music and musicians all my life. I've seen many of my idols get older, waver, and reveal feet of clay under their gowns. From Judy Garland to the great Italian soprano Renata Tebaldi, I saw singers I'd worshiped in their youth turn in mediocre performances in their later years. But I still went to hear them and basked in the five glorious minutes they gave me, and willingly overlooked the other, indifferent hour or two. What remain, in the fan's mind and heart, are the good memories of someone who was truly great.

I worked with Luciano Pavarotti, the greatest tenor in the world, for thirty-six years of my life. Sometimes he was a great, great client. Sometimes he acted like he ruled the world around him and everyone in it, including me. Sometimes he was a close and generous friend. Sometimes he was a real pain in the ass.

But all in all, we had a pretty good run.

Chapter I

FROM CHRYSLER TO CARNEGIE HALL

Midlife Crisis: My Start in the Business

Here's how not to begin your brilliant professional career. In 1957, I was thirty-three years old. I was married, with a child on the way. And I was working as a speechwriter for the Chrysler Corporation. In Detroit, Michigan.

Detroit, Michigan. Who would even want to think about it? Misery.

People suppose that to succeed in the classical music business you should be very highly directed. You should have experience as a performer, so you know what it's like on the other side of the footlights. You should get your foot in the door early and work in a number of different areas so you get to know all sides of the performing arts. Ultimately, you'll gather the experience you need to set up your own company and manage top-level artists.

Well, that's all bullshit.

I came out of nowhere. I was smart. I was full of energy. And

I had no idea what I wanted to do with my life. All I knew was that I loved music.

How much did I love music? I'd been obsessed with opera since I was eight years old. The beauty, the glamour, the excitement, and the tremendous voices pulled me into another world. I had a huge collection of records I listened to constantly. I had scrapbooks of the performances I'd seen and the artists I loved. Whatever else was going on around me, opera served as my own private support system and gave me tremendous sustenance. So much sustenance, in fact, that it became my life.

The problem I had when I was thirty-three was that it had nothing to do with my life. Especially not my life in Detroit. There's a little bit of music in Detroit, but nothing you would really want to seriously consider. I'm a New Yorker. I was starved for opera. I would get the *New York Times* and wistfully scan the cast lists at the Metropolitan Opera, which the *Times* used to print every Monday, for the two weeks ahead.

One week I saw that Renata Tebaldi was scheduled to sing *Tosca*, and I couldn't help myself. Tebaldi was one of the greatest sopranos singing. People portrayed her as a rival of Maria Callas: Tebaldi's pure vocal beauty against Callas's dramatic brilliance. Myself, I liked Callas fine, but I was a fierce fan of Renata Tebaldi. Intoxicating things happened when the woman opened her mouth. It was enough to make you fly to New York. I said to my wife, Carol, "We're going to see that *Tosca*," and I bought tickets.

Carol is a New Yorker, too, so she was game for a weekend in the city. She herself was prone to making dramatic pronouncements that she didn't want our first child to be born in Detroit. She was no happier living there than I was. She didn't completely share my passion for opera, but she was certainly happy to go, especially to see a performance as great as I promised her this one was going to be. By the time we walked into the old Met on Thirty-ninth Street, I was beside myself with excitement.

Imagine my feelings when I saw a notice in the lobby announcing that Madame Tebaldi was indisposed. Tosca would be sung by Antonietta Stella.

I went cold with disappointment. By today's standards, Antonietta Stella is nothing to sneeze at; but I hadn't flown in all the way from Detroit to hear Antonietta Stella sing Tosca. I couldn't believe my plans had been thwarted so cruelly, and I didn't want to accept it. I completely lost my temper. I said, "I do not want to hear this performance."

Opera houses, of course, don't refund a patron's ticket money if an artist cancels. Cancelations are practically part of opera routine. A singer's instrument—as any singer will be the first to tell you, and the second to tell you, and the last to tell you, so often do they reiterate it—is extremely fragile. A mild cold, a touch of allergies, a dry hotel room: any one of these things, and a thousand more, can keep them offstage. If opera houses refunded ticket money every time a big singer got sick, they'd all be even more broke than they already are.

I knew this, or some of this, at the time, but I didn't care. I let the box office know it. I said, "I do not want to hear anybody else. I do not want to have anything to do with this performance. I want my money back."

"We can't give you your money back," said the man at the box office window.

"I want my money back!" I said. By this point, I was raving like a banshee. Nobody knew what to do with me. My wife was standing by, looking a little bewildered at my behavior.

I made such a stink that they finally summoned Francis Robinson, who was the head of the box office in those days, to come out and deal with me. Francis was a lovely guy and extremely knowledgeable about all things operatic; he wrote a lot about the opera, and he ran the Met's public relations department. But I barely knew who he was that night, and he sure as hell didn't know who I was. I wasn't even in the music business. I was just some crank from Detroit making a ruckus in the lobby.

"How can I help you?" said Francis.

I said, "Mr. Robinson, I am not as insane as I may sound, but the fact of the matter is that I came in from Detroit to hear Madame Tebaldi, and I was looking forward to it so much. I know that she's sick. But I do not want to go and listen to this."

"Well," Francis said with a smile, "unfortunately there's not much we can do to bring Madame Tebaldi to tonight's performance. Listen. Go to the performance now, and we'll see about getting you a pair of tickets to Madame Tebaldi's next appearance."

He did, too. He was a lovely guy.

Later in my life, I always remembered that incident whenever fans got upset at a Luciano Pavarotti cancelation. You come all that way for something you're really excited to see, and then your hopes are dashed. It's like having the rug pulled out from under you. I knew exactly how they felt.

Not that I ever gave any of them a free pair of tickets as compensation. I'd be in the poorhouse.

Little did I know that night at the Met that within a few years I would be Renata Tebaldi's press agent. I might have felt better.

As I said, I was hooked on opera from childhood—from the day my father took me to see *Carmen* at the New York Hippodrome, on Sixth Avenue at Forty-fourth Street. I don't know exactly why he took me; it wasn't as if we went to performances all the time. We were not people of great means. But he did love music. And *Carmen*, with its rousing tunes and gripping drama, was a great first opera. My father couldn't have suspected what he had started.

By the time I was a teenager, every spare penny I had was going for opera. From our home in the Bronx, I'd take the subway down to Manhattan and wait on the line for standing-room tickets. There was a real camaraderie on that line in those days. My friend Myron Egan, who was killed in the war, and I went together and saw everything and everybody that we could. After the show, we'd wait for the artists to come out and get their autographs. And what artists. In those days, it was the ladies who ruled opera: we went to hear the sopranos. Grace Moore, the glamorous American soprano, killed in a plane crash at age forty-eight: I heard her debut as Tosca. Zinka Milanov, the Yugoslavian who looked like a potato and sang like a goddess: somewhere I still have a picture that she autographed for me sixty years ago.

I fantasized about being a singer myself. But since I didn't have a lot of financial resources, I also had to pay close attention to what was practical. To help pay for all of my opera activity, I occasionally took a job in opera itself—as a supernumerary in the big operas, like *Aida*, that call for a lot of warm bodies onstage. In those days, you got paid something like two dollars for being a super. I got a little extra, because I always tried to take home a piece of my costume as a souvenir. I soon added a wig, a helmet, and a number of other items to my collection of opera memorabilia. I saw myself as a self-supporter, which was something that turned out to be very useful to me.

When I look back, all the dates in my life are marked by the music I heard. Well, nearly all. When I first went into the army in 1943, I was stationed in Nebraska, and there was no music there at all. My job was to guard the German and Italian POWs as they worked in the fields. My great contribution to the war effort was overseeing the harvest of the sugar beet crop in western Nebraska. The Italians were very lazy; you had to push them to get the work done. Come to think of it, this first exposure to the Italian mentality may have stood me in good stead in my professional life.

Later in the war, I did get music. In 1944, I was transferred to Camp Crowder, Missouri, and I went to Joplin, Missouri, to hear a recital by a wonderful soprano named Miliza Korjus, a lovely looking woman, if a little zaftig, who had starred in the film *The Great Waltz*, about Johann Strauss. It should have been called *The Great Schmaltz*, but she sang well. She could venture into a stratospheric range to which few singers could aspire.

In 1945, I went to Europe as a cryptographer with the army signal corps, following right behind Eisenhower. Army HQ was in Reims, France, and I took a day trip to Paris and went to the Opéra-Comique, where I heard Puccini's *Madama Butterfly* with a soprano named Jeanne Ségala. Eisenhower moved on to Frankfurt, where all the theaters were bombed out; they were putting on opera performances in the basement of the Börsensaal, the stock exchange, and I attended a *Tosca* and Mozart's *Nozze di Figaro* down there. On my furlough, I went to Rome, where at the Teatro Reale I heard Maria Caniglia, the soaring Italian soprano, in Verdi's *La Traviata*. I adored Europe. I even found a voice teacher in Reims named Madame Patou, who gave me lessons once or twice a week in exchange for money, as well as coffee and sugar and other things I brought her that were very hard to get in those days. I would say I was a tenor of some kind. I was a rather immature student; I had never studied music, and I couldn't read music. She tried to teach me solfège, the art of sight-reading with musical syllables, and I didn't know what the hell she was talking about. But I still remember some of the songs she taught me.

In 1948, I heard Giuseppe di Stefano, the great Italian tenor, and the mezzo-soprano Risë Stevens in Ambroise Thomas's sentimental opera *Mignon*. That was back in New York. I didn't necessarily want to be back in New York, but when the war ended, I was twenty-one years old and I didn't know what to do with my life. I was so full of drive and energy that I knew I wanted to do *something*, but I had no marketable skills. I wasn't an artist, I wasn't a writer, and I didn't have much experience doing much of anything. I was just a person, with no way to express myself. I tried to tell my parents that all I wanted to do was stay in Europe, but they wouldn't hear of it. What would I do in Europe? they wanted to know. I didn't really have an answer to that, other than "Sweep the streets," so I got on a boat and sailed back to the States, with no idea what was going to be happening to me. I was completely lost. I stood on the upper deck of the ship—the *Ernie Pyle*—as it was pulling out of Le Havre, and I looked out over the port, and at France behind it, and I said to myself, "I'm coming back." It was my first concrete ambition.

And I achieved it. In 1949, I heard the German soprano Maria Reining, a fantastic singer, as the Marschallin in Richard Strauss's *Der Rosenkavalier*. I was back in Paris. In New York, I had gotten my college degree in business administration from the City University of New York and had taken a job in an import-export company. From my princely salary of $35 a week, I saved $10 a week, religiously, and at the end of two years I had $1,000 and was ready to go back to Europe. I still didn't have any idea what I was going to do when I got there, but I learned that the GI Bill would pay you $75 a month if you went to school, so I decided to enroll at the Sorbonne and take a course in *la civilisation française*. I didn't speak any French, but I didn't let that worry me. I figured I would pick it up. So I sailed back to Europe in June of 1949 on the *George Washington*, an old troopship that had been reconverted for passenger use. It wasn't that easy to find passage in those days—a lot of people wanted to go, and the possibilities were limited—but I did. I think I would have swum if I'd had to. When I got on that boat, I was in a state of excitement and anticipation that words can hardly bring across. I was beside myself. Until that point in my life, I had never had exactly what I wanted, but I knew that this, now, was the real me, going where I wanted, and I had made it happen.

My stay in Paris was everything I'd hoped for. I found lodgings at the Maison Française at the Cité Universitaire, where all the students lived; I hung out at Le Select, the famous café in Montparnasse; I went to some of the political rallies that were going on in France at that very turbulent time, led by people like Maurice Thorez, the head of the French Communist Party. I felt I was in the thick of things, which was a place I was very anxious to be in those days, even though I never was actually in the thick of anything. But once my time was up, I had to go home again— and think of another way to get myself back.

I decided I'd become a teacher. That way, I would have long vacations and be able to travel to Europe every summer, and every Christmas, and possibly at Easter. Obviously, I was being completely unrealistic. I got a degree in education from Columbia—

still under the GI Bill—and began teaching history at a high school in New Rochelle, New York. The first year was all right. One day during my second year, I said something to the class, and when I heard myself say it, I realized I had said the exact same thing the year before. I had a sinking feeling: would this be my life for the next thirty years, saying the same thing at the same time every year, year in, year out? Teaching wasn't for me after all.

My problem was that while I was quite clear about what I didn't want, I had no idea how to figure out what it was that I *did* want. I began working for the National Association of Manufacturers, an extremely right-wing organization, writing pamphlets and the like. It didn't necessarily reflect my own political views, but I needed a job. I was essentially a great whore; I would do anything for money.

And anything to get to Europe. I came up with all kinds of ways to go over. In 1952, three very rich kids engaged me to take them to Europe as their chaperone. Their parents didn't want them to go alone, so they decided that I would be able to protect them. That could have been a truly colossal mistake on their part; but it turned out all right. One kid thought he had picked up gonorrhea, but it was a false alarm.

And when I was crossing over with those kids, there was a fire drill on the boat and, coming back from the drill, I met this girl, and she turned out to be the woman whom I asked to marry me. We've been married for fifty years.

CAROL BRESLIN

My life with Herbert began with a phone call. Herbert had gotten my name from a friend, who said, "Call this girl," so he called me. I assumed, of course, that he was calling me for a date. As we talked, we found out that by a funny coincidence we were both sailing on the same boat for Europe. We chatted for a long time, and then he said, "Well, it was nice talking to you," and hung up, and that was the end of that.

I sailed for Europe a few weeks later. Of course, I had no idea what he looked like, and I didn't know if he was on the boat or not. I was in the lowest class of the boat that you could possibly be in, and the state-rooms didn't have their own bathrooms; whenever you wanted to take a shower you had to go to the bath steward and make an appointment. Every time I tried to make an appointment, somebody was in there, and when I passed by the shower stall I could hear him bellowing opera. It was extremely annoying.

One day, there was a fire drill on the ship, and as we were filing back to our rooms afterward a man walked up to me and said, "Are you Carol?" I have no idea how he picked me out. We started to talk, and we decided to get together and have cocktails. More for lack of anything to say than anything else, I started to tell him how I could never get into the shower because this person was singing, or rather bellowing, opera. Just as I said it, I saw the expression on his face, and I thought, Oh, my God, guess who it is. He was not amused at all.

When we got to Europe we went our separate ways. I think we were supposed to get together for dinner, but it never happened. And then we all came back to the States in August or September. And Herbert called me up again. But he called the following April. It was not a swift beginning.

Carol, my wife, was very helpful to me, because she knew what I wanted, even though she didn't know any better than I did how to get it. She also knew that when I wanted something, I was good at it. When there was a retrenchment at the NAM and I found myself out of a job, she and I took turns typing up letters of application for every kind of employment you can imagine. Except anything in the music business. For all my love of music, it hadn't occurred to me to look for work there. I had only a vague notion of what the music business actually was.

One day, I got a letter asking whether I'd be interested in coming to Detroit to work for the Chrysler Corporation. The honest answer to that question was, "No, not particularly," but after all, I didn't have a job. I flew out for an interview and met a really wonderful guy who was the head speechwriter, which was part of the public relations department. He was also interested in music, and in history, as I was, and we talked for a couple of hours. We never got around to discussing the job, though. After I left his office, I realized I knew no more about the company than when I'd started.

"How did it go?" asked Carol when I got home.

I said, "I have no idea."

I guess it went well. I got the job. We moved to Detroit. And we were miserable.

As I said, there wasn't a lot of music to hear in Detroit. They did have a recital series at the Detroit Museum of Art, where I heard Mattiwilda Dobbs, one of the first black sopranos to make a career in classical music, and the first to sing at the Met, a year after the contralto Marian Anderson broke the color barrier for singers there in 1955. Her concert was a lot of fun.

But that recital was a rare high point in a very bleak landscape. My job was awful. I had to write speeches for all the different departments in the company, which gave me some experience in a number of fields, but I had to write them for people like the vice president of industrial relations at Chrysler. I remember one time when he was giving a speech to honor the fiftieth anniversary of an important black fraternity. "Give them a lot of Gospel references," he advised me. "I'm sure they'll like that." This was not my world. I would come home every night and listen to my record collection and think, How the hell am I going to get out of here? Carol wasn't happy, either. She had a decent job at the natural history museum at Cranbrook, but she missed New York, too. It was back to the application letters with a vengeance.

Many letters later, I landed a job interview with the executive vice president of the Bulova Watch Company, which is based out in Queens, on the way to LaGuardia Airport. "Oh," he said, "you're exactly what we wanted." The Bulova Watch Company wasn't exactly what I wanted, but it did offer one overwhelming advantage: it was in New York. So I took the job. We closed up our house in Detroit and flew back and moved in temporarily with my wife's parents while we looked for an apartment.

On the Thursday before I started work, I got a phone call from Bulova, asking if I would be kind enough to come in.

I said, "Why? I start work on Monday."

"No," they said, "we need to see you tomorrow."

What they wanted to tell me, it turned out when I got there, was that the executive vice president who had liked me so much was no longer with the company. As a result, there was no job left for me to take. The company would honor its commitment to me until I found something else to do, but I had better get looking.

My wife was pregnant, we were living with my in-laws, I was out of a job, and I had no financial resources to fall back on. Disaster.

Disaster, my ass. It turned out to be the best thing that ever happened to me.

One thing was clear: I wasn't leaving New York again in a hurry. By that point, I had also figured out that there *was* such a thing as the music business. Names like Columbia Artists and Sol Hurok and NCAC, the National Concert Artists Corporation, had finally penetrated my consciousness. So I hit the sidewalk and went to see all of them. Unfortunately, I couldn't offer them anything that was useful to them, because I didn't know anything. At least Bulova was going to keep paying me for a while.

Finally, one day, I went and interviewed at the Metropolitan Opera Guild, which, among its other functions, publishes *Opera News*, the leading opera magazine in America. At that time, the director of the Guild was a man named Richard Leach. I talked to Richard, and he changed my life.

I said, "Mr. Leach, I would love to work for *Opera News*. I know more about opera than anybody you know. I don't know if I have skills as a magazine writer, because I've never tested them. But I know that I know a lot about opera."

Richard, of course, could have laughed me out of his office.

But he didn't. And instead of telling me that my chances of land-ing anything in the field were slim, he encouraged me.

"Well," he said gently, after we had talked for a while, "I don't think we have anything for you. But I suggest that you call John Crosby, who has just organized an opera company in Santa Fe."

It was only a single lead, but it was a totally new sensation to have someone encouraging me to follow my dreams. No one had ever done anything like that for me before. I never forgot it.

I left Richard Leach's office and headed for the nearest pay phone to call John Crosby. I said, "Mr. Crosby, my name is Her-bert Breslin, and Richard Leach gave me your name, and I would like to come up and talk, because I would like to work for the Santa Fe Opera."

"All right, come up," said Crosby.

John Crosby had just founded the Santa Fe Opera in 1957. The story is that he went out into the hills north of Santa Fe with a gun and fired it off until he found a place where the echoes, and therefore the acoustics, were optimal, and that's where he built his open-air opera house. At that time, the idea of opera out in the middle of nowhere seemed more quixotic than exotic, but John, who had studied music and composition and later jobbed around as a music arranger and performer in the New York opera scene, was determined as hell. He quickly built up his enterprise into a serious opera company, with a summer-only season. His very first year, he brought in the composer Igor Stravinsky, who became a regular guest. The company became known for impor-tant American premieres—like the first U.S. performance of Al-ban Berg's *Lulu*, one of the greatest operas of the twentieth century—and American debuts of singers who went on to have major careers, like José van Dam, Kiri Te Kanawa, and, much later, Bryn Terfel. When the theater burned down in 1967, John rebuilt it within a year. He was a much better administrator than he was a conductor. In spite of that, he insisted on conducting at least one opera every year—usually a lesser-known work by Richard Strauss, a composer he adored. Whatever Santa Fe might offer in a given season, there was always one Strauss opera on the program. The Santa Fe Opera became the most important summer opera festival in the United States. John died in 2002, but his company is still going strong.

John was also known as something of a difficult character, but then again, I was to be known that way, too, later in my career. Whatever the reason, we got along fine. We talked for a while about his new company, which he ran from New York except for the summer months, when there were actually performances.

Finally I said, "I would love to work for you."

"Well, I would love for you to work for me, too," he said. "Except, of course, I can't afford to pay you anything."

"I would proofread for nothing," I said.

It was the first and last time I ever offered to work for nothing. But it was the only way I could get my foot in the door.

So that's how I started in the music business.

Every morning, I would work with John Crosby, learning everything I could learn about the Santa Fe Opera, doing press and publicity and just getting to know people in the music world. It was invaluable experience, and exactly what I wanted.

And every afternoon I would service my other accounts. Although I had been very unhappy working at Chrysler, I had gathered a lot of experience while I was there in all aspects of publicity: consumer publicity, industrial publicity, financial publicity. So I had the wherewithal to put together my own one-man public relations office.

Since I had to earn money, I would take just about anything. I had a group of engineers who specialized in automated materials handling. I had a firm that had invented some kind of new dry cleaning process. I had a piano company. I had a hat company. That was Mr. Arnold, over on Fifty-seventh Street. He created a hat collection inspired by the châteaux of France. I knew shit from Shinola about hats, but I knew about publicity. I printed up stationery in a kind of a beige color, to give the impression that it was coming from château country, and I went to an architecture book and looked up the names of parts of buildings that might or might not be like châteaux and named every one of his hundred hats after them. There was the Flying Buttress hat, the Drawbridge, and the Moat. The Moat, for example, would have a round brim all around it. You get the idea.

That was the kind of imagination that was necessary to make it in publicity in those days. Just taking a picture of a hat or of a piano wasn't going to get a product into the newspapers. And the companies were paying for whatever it took to get them into the newspapers, in whatever way possible. Whether or not you happen to think this is an honorable profession is really quite immaterial.

Because of all my professional activity, I needed to have an office, but at that point I couldn't afford the expense of actually leasing my own. I therefore approached a woman named Mildred Chagall, an artists' manager who happened to be a distant relative of the painter and who had an office on West Fifty-seventh Street. I proposed to Mildred that she receive my mail. She didn't have to do anything, just get my letters and let me pick them up once a day. For that, I would pay $15 a month.

Mildred was amenable. My next step was to put my home telephone on an answering service. When anybody called, they were greeted, "Herbert Breslin's office," and they could leave a message.

Then I printed up letterhead for myself. I was very proud of the design, a trumpet at the top of the page, next to my name. Finally, I had a way to tell the world who I was: Herbert Breslin, Public Relations. The letterhead had my business address, which was Miss Chagall's address: 119 West 57th Street. I'm at the same address today. And my employees still say "Herbert Breslin's office" when they answer the phone. And I'm still using the same trumpet on my letterhead.

I tried to make the most of my Santa Fe connection. Every time I got a mention in the paper about the company, I would copy it and send it out to a whole host of people in the music management world, to demonstrate what I could do as a publicist. I didn't get a lot of response. And unfortunately, my job was short-lived: at the end of the summer, it ended, too. My thanks for working for free for the Santa Fe Opera was that the following year, when John Crosby had enough money actually to pay a publicist, he engaged someone else. I didn't hold it against him. I think he wanted someone with more experience. And he had already given me what I wanted.

One night a few months later, my home phone rang at about six o'clock. It was a woman by the name of Agnes Eisenberger, who worked for an organization called Colbert Artists' Management. Henry and Ann Colbert didn't have the largest agency around, but they were well respected. They were from Berlin— Ann kept her German accent all her life—and they maintained strong ties to Europe. Ann was a fascinating woman who was very, very knowledgeable about music. Many managers are handicapped by not knowing enough about the repertory or about what might be good for their singers, which means that ultimately their singers fail. But Ann was extremely savvy. Her clients weren't necessarily the most famous artists in the music business, but they were very high quality. She did a lot of work with chamber music and more elite things like that. And a couple of those clients, after they signed with her, went all the way to the top.

"Oh, Mr. Breslin," Agnes Eisenberger said to me on the phone, "we received some of your materials."

I said, "Mrs. Eisenberger, you received my materials six months ago; you're only just calling me now?"

"We'd like you to come in and see us," she said, undaunted.

Of course, I wasn't about to say no. So I went in and met them, and we all got along very well. It turned out that Ann had a client for whom she thought I might be the perfect person to do publicity. It was the soprano Elisabeth Schwarzkopf.

The likelihood is that Ann had her because no other agency would touch her. Schwarzkopf was one of the greatest German sopranos around. She did a few opera roles and did them superbly: works by Mozart, Richard Strauss, and a few selected ventures into the Italian repertoire. Her greatest claim to fame, however, was her excellence as a singer of lieder, or German art songs. She was married to Walter Legge, the artistic director of the record label EMI, who produced some of the greatest recordings in history, by Herbert von Karajan, Otto Klemperer, Walter Gieseking, and Maria Callas, to name just a few. Walter was also a strict taskmaster, and he kept at Elisabeth until every detail of her diction, phrasing, and nuance was perfect. Her recordings are superb, but they strike some people as a little cold.

That's not why no other agency would touch her, though. It's because during the war, Elisabeth had been rumored to be a member, or at least a supporter, of the Nazi Party and the mistress of a high-ranking Nazi official. I don't know if the rumors were true, but they stuck, and some countries remembered them longer than others. By 1948, she was singing at both Covent Garden and La Scala. America, however, was very tough on this particular issue. Schwarzkopf didn't appear in New York in recital until 1952, and even that was somewhat controversial. And she didn't sing at the Metropolitan Opera until 1964.

Ann probably thought that it couldn't hurt Elisabeth to have a Jewish publicist. The upshot was that Elisabeth became my first paying client in music.

For me, of course, it was a big break to work with such a wonderful singer. I didn't find the job as difficult as you might think. Despite the resistance Elisabeth met with in this country, people were not waving a Nazi flag over her all the time. She was such a wonderful artist that many people were ready to be forgiving.

And working with her gave me an in with the Colbert office. It even gave me my own desk there. I wasn't, technically speaking, an employee, but I had a place to hang my hat. Every morning, I would stop by Miss Chagall's office, pick up my mail, and then head over to the Colbert agency and work there the rest of the day.

One day when I was there, Ann came in, fresh from a trip to Europe.

"Herbert," she said, "I just signed the greatest soprano you ever heard in your entire life."

"Oh, really?" I said. "And who would that be?" After all, I had heard a lot of great sopranos.

"Her name is Joan Sutherland," Ann said.

Ann, of course, was quite right. Joan Sutherland, the Australian soprano, would go on to a thirty-year career selling out theaters to people clamoring to hear the great bel canto heroines—Donizetti's Lucia di Lammermoor, Bellini's Sonnambula, Rossini's Semiramide—filtered through her astonishing voice, set off with clear, ringing high notes.

Joan Sutherland became my second paying client.

Then Ann went to California and heard a performance of *Wozzeck*, Alban Berg's other great opera, and signed the young American mezzo-soprano who was singing the part of Marie. She had been gaining experience in the opera houses of Germany for a few years, and her name was Marilyn Horne. Marilyn, who would go on to become the most important American mezzo of her time, became my third paying client in music, for the princely fee of $75 a month.

So I launched my professional career as a paid classical music publicist with three of the greatest female singers of my generation. Not bad for a beginner.

chapter II

LUCIANO MAKES HIS ENTRANCE

How I Met and Marketed the Young Pavarotti

What's the biggest difficulty about working with Luciano Pavarotti?" someone once asked a major opera administrator.

She answered, "Herbert."

If you'd asked me in 1980, I might have said *she* was. But that comes later.

The administrator in question is Joan Ingpen. She was the person who really discovered Luciano. You better remember that, too; she certainly won't let you forget it. Joan is a tough lady with one of those buttery yet impregnable English accents, supported on the foundations of a steely alto voice. For about twenty years, she was one of the leading opera administrators in the world, charged with hiring artists—or not hiring them, as the case might be—for Covent Garden, the Paris Opéra, and, finally, the Metropolitan Opera. It was at the Met that she was, shall we say, a little difficult. She once had the temerity to tell me, Luciano Pavarotti's manager, that I knew nothing about music. And she didn't always seem to have a proper respect for Luciano, either.

"Which version of Mozart's *Idomeneo* are you going to stage at the Met with Luciano Pavarotti?" someone asked her in 1982, when Luciano was preparing to sing the title role of that opera at the Met for the first time. There are two versions of *Idomeneo*; after the opera's premiere in 1781, Mozart revised it for a performance in Vienna. One difference is that "Fuor del mar," Idomeneo's showpiece aria, is considerably simplified in the later version.

Joan answered sweetly, "We'll do whatever version Luciano manages to learn."

But if her regard for Luciano—and for his manager—was not at its highest point during her years in New York, Joan must have judged things differently back in 1963. In those days, of course, hardly anyone had ever heard of Luciano Pavarotti.

Ironically, Joan started out as what I later became: an artist's manager. Her firm was called Ingpen and Williams. Williams was her dog. Joan has always been something of a one-woman show. As a manager, she had some impressive clients: Hans Hotter, the greatest German bass-baritone of the postwar years, and, at the very start of her career, my future client Joan Sutherland. Even after Joan Ingpen switched horses, as it were, and began working at the Royal Opera House, Covent Garden, she kept an ear out for young talent. Kiri Te Kanawa, the beautiful (if boring) Maori diva, and the Welsh soprano Margaret Price were both fostered at Covent Garden on her watch. Both of them went on to sing with Luciano many times in the course of big careers.

Joan Ingpen came to Covent Garden in 1962, and in the spring of 1963 she found herself, in her perpetual quest for new talent, at a performance of the Dublin Grand Opera Society. Actually, it wasn't the society itself; the company had started presenting a spring season with young Italian singers, with financial assistance from the Italian government. Joan and her husband had a house in Ireland—she's part Irish—and so she used to attend performances there every so often. That spring, she saw Verdi's *Rigoletto* with a young tenor named Luciano Pavarotti. And Joan needed a tenor for *La Bohème*.

There were a lot of magnificent tenors around in the years Luciano was coming up. As I said, opera in those days was ruled by sopranos: it was the ladies the audiences flocked to see, and the ladies who sold the tickets. But there were plenty of notable tenors as well. There was Franco Corelli, with his matinee-idol appearance and rich, full sound—although he was a complete neurasthenic, racked by nerves, manifested in stage fright that led to full-scale tantrums before performances, while his wife screamed at him from the doorway. There was Carlo Bergonzi, who was nothing much to look at but had a beautiful voice. There was Richard Tucker, the American who once told a friend of mine, through his mouthful of bad teeth, "You know, it'sh a helluva reshponshibility to be the greatesht tenor in the world." There was Nicolai Gedda, a reserved Swede with a hell of a sound, whom critics loved but audiences could never really warm to, and the amazing Jon Vickers, whose powerful voice drowned out some of his less attractive attitudes (he once told a stage director that he didn't need a faggot to tell him how to kiss). Personality issues aside, this was pretty impressive company.

And there was Giuseppe di Stefano, a star Italian tenor with a shining ribbon of a voice, a preferred partner (and sometime lover) of Maria Callas, and one of Luciano's heroes. Di Stefano was scheduled to sing *La Bohème* at Covent Garden in the fall of 1963. Joan Ingpen's problem was that, lovely as his voice was, di Stefano was notorious for canceling performances, and she didn't have a backup. Before Joan even got to Covent Garden, her predecessor had given permission to André Turp, a French Canadian tenor who normally would have been available to step in if needed, to do other performances exactly during the period of the *La Bohèmes*.

At an American house this would be unheard-of. American

opera houses always have a cover singer waiting in the wings: they have to. No one wants to risk having to cancel a performance in San Francisco because the tenor gets sick and the nearest singer who knows the part is five hours away. This example is etched in every opera director's mind in the States, because it actually happened once at the San Francisco Opera on opening night. Carlo Cossutta was scheduled to sing Verdi's Otello, one of the most demanding roles in opera, not something you can fill with just any young singer who happens to be hanging around backstage. Cossutta got sick, and the company had to fly in Plácido Domingo from New York, and the performance started at 10:30 at night. Plácido loves that kind of eleventh-hour heroics. So would any singer, for that matter. But they could give a theater manager a heart attack.

In Europe, on the other hand, distances are so relatively small that if somebody gets sick the general manager gets on the phone and calls around until he finds somebody else who can fly in for the evening. The only thing to worry about in Europe is the weather. Once, when the Paris airport was fogged in and Luciano had to get to Vienna for a performance, he memorably demonstrated that Austria is just a taxi ride away from France. I'm sure the driver never forgot that fare.

But with a known canceler like di Stefano, Joan felt that it was asking for trouble not to have a standby on hand. After all, the airport in London fogs up with some regularity. And then she heard Luciano.

She said to her husband, who was at the opera with her, "I've found our tenor."

Whatever potential Joan had seen or heard, her husband had missed it. He said, "You can't possibly be seriously thinking of putting *that* onstage at Covent Garden."

Luciano was never what you'd call a stage animal, but at that point in his career, when he'd been singing for only a couple of years, he was pretty awful. It wasn't that he was fat, since he had yet to achieve the impressive girth he was to reach in later years, but onstage, he was, to put it tactfully, something of a lump. Even at the height of his career, he was no Method actor. A number of years later, when he was rehearsing *Ballo in Maschera* at the Metropolitan Opera, he was standing onstage for his big solo aria and he began fiddling with his costume or with something on the set in a very natural manner while the director, Elijah Moshinsky, was trying to figure out what to do with him.

"Yes!" Moshinsky said, probably finding it easier to encourage whatever Luciano was doing than to come up with a stage direction the tenor could understand. "Do that!"

Luciano got worried. He stopped, looked up, and said to Moshinsky in anxious tones, "But if I do that, will the audience know I'm acting?"

The audience certainly wouldn't have known he was acting in 1963. Nobody would have known he was acting. But Joan heard that voice. She said to her husband, "We'll bring him over early. We'll coach him. And yes, I will put him onstage at Covent Garden, if I have to."

For Luciano, it was a pretty quick start. It didn't seem quick to him, of course. To understand Luciano, you have to consider how many international superstars came out of Modena, Italy, where he was born. The only one who comes to mind is Mirella Freni, the now legendary soprano, who's the same age as Luciano. Mirella and Luciano supposedly had the same wet nurse when they were babies, and Mirella always says that you can see who got all the milk. At the height of Luciano's fame, you could see who got all the attention, too, which was not entirely to Madame Freni's taste. These days, everybody talks about Freni as if she were the Second Coming; they forget that, although she had a much faster start than Luciano, for years and years she could barely get her foot in the door at the Metropolitan Opera House. And no prima donna likes to be upstaged.

But Luciano and Mirella, and Enzo Ferrari, one other well-known Modenese, are the exceptions that prove the rule. Modena is not generally known as a cradle of celebrity. And, as Luciano's ex-wife, Adua, always says, "We're peasants." Luciano is a very simple guy from a very simple family. His father was a baker and his mother worked in a factory, and he was basically raised by his grandmother while his parents worked. In fact, he grew up surrounded by women, who spoiled him rotten.

Luciano didn't exactly manifest a poetic soul in his early years, either. He was a type that in the States would be known as a jock. He preferred soccer to solfège or, for that matter, to study. The singer in the family was his father, Fernando, who tended to be rather critical of his son's vocal excursions—even after his son had become one of the most recognizable superstars in the world. Fernando, you see, considered himself to be the great singer of the Pavarottis. It was only his crippling stage fright that kept him from making a big career of his own—or so, at least, runs the family legend. Even in old age, Fernando would readily explain to all comers that he himself was the real Pavarotti talent. Fernando later got to sing a few performances with his famous son—in, for example, the role of Parpignol, the toy seller in *La Bohème*, who has all of two lines to sing. I must confess that I wasn't convinced he was right about who had the talent in the family.

But when Luciano was growing up, Fernando did keep music in the house. He was addicted to recordings of the great singers: Beniamino Gigli, Aureliano Pertile, and other guardians of the Italian tradition. He also brought Luciano to hear Gigli in person when the tenor came to Modena to sing Donizetti's *Lucia di Lammermoor*. After the curtain descended, the applause was overwhelming, and Gigli sang virtually a whole second program of encores. In later years, Luciano was on the receiving end of countless backstage visits from starstruck young fans; but at the age of twelve, he was the one who came, awed, into the great tenor's dressing room after a rehearsal and got up his nerve to ask Gigli a question.

"Maestro, how long did you study?"

"I stopped studying three minutes ago," Gigli said. "I am always studying."

Luciano has told that anecdote ever since. When I think of some of the travails we had getting him to learn roles in the later years of his career, I can only wish that he had taken it to heart and studied half as much himself.

Luciano also learned early on that singing meant travel. When he was about twenty, he went with his father and the town chorus to compete in the Eisteddfod, an international music competition, in Llangollen, Wales. The chorus won first prize, and some people have claimed that that prize marked the start of Luciano's career. But don't tell Joan Ingpen that.

When Luciano left school, there was a family debate about whether he should be a teacher or a singer. The upshot was— both. Luciano started out as an assistant teacher in an elementary school while studying voice with a local pedagogue, Arrigo Pola. Fernando was in favor of teaching. Much as he loved opera, he wanted to see his son settled in a stable, lucrative career. Teaching wasn't really Luciano's thing, however. He started selling life insurance, of all things, on the side. Ever the fast talker, he was soon making more money from selling insurance than from teaching and left the classroom altogether. But ultimately he decided that all the talking he had to do as a salesman was hurting his voice. So he quit that job, too.

Meanwhile, he was learning even more clearly that singing meant travel. Arrigo Pola had moved to Japan to teach there, and Luciano started working with Ettore Campogalliani, a renowned teacher of many future opera stars, who happened to be teaching Mirella Freni as well. The only hitch was that he lived in Mantova, about forty miles from Modena. Luciano and Mirella used to make the commute together, along with Leone Magiera, who was Mirella's first husband and, much later, Luciano's regular coach, accompanist, conductor (officially), and whipping boy (unofficially).

At the same time, back in Modena, Luciano met a girl named Adua Veroni, his future wife. How they met depends on which of them you ask, and when you asked them, but according to

Adua, it was more or less love at first sight. Italian marital mores, however, are a little different from those in the States: in a Catholic country, you get one chance at marriage, and you better get it right. As a result, Luciano and Adua didn't rush into marriage. The arrangement was that they would get married after his first professional engagement. They ended up waiting for eight years. Four decades later, it would take them almost as long to end their marriage as it took them to get into it.

In 1961, at age twenty-five and after several years of study, Luciano was about ready to call it a day with the whole singing idea. He decided to enter one last competition—the Achille Peri competition in the town of Reggio Emilia—before throwing in the towel and going home to Modena to become a full-time teacher. And, in fact, he didn't win. I think he came in third. But third place was enough to claim part of the prize, since all the winners got to sing in a staged production of *La Bohème*. They also got some modest financial remuneration. I think it yielded Luciano all of $50, but at the time he was perfectly happy with that. (In fact, it was possibly the last time that Luciano was ever perfectly happy with his fee for a performance.) Rodolfo, the leader of the bohemian artists in their Parisian garret, became his signature role for the next three decades. And he and Adua were married a few months later.

He may have had a slow start, but things came very naturally to him after that beginning. It helped that Alessandro Ziliani, a tenor turned significant agent, was in the opera house at Reggio that night. Ziliani had actually come to hear another competition winner, the bass Dmitri Nabokov (son of the novelist Vladimir), but Luciano got his attention. A few months later, Ziliani set up an audition for Luciano with Tullio Serafin, the great conductor, which led to Luciano's debut in *Rigoletto*, in Palermo, in 1962.

Significantly, though, Luciano didn't go straight to the top in Italy. He started singing all over the place: in Amsterdam, Belgrade, and Belfast. In my opinion, this was very lucky for him. The Italians, like every other nationality in the world, tend to look down on their own. In America, everyone worships musicians from Europe; in Italy, similarly, everyone wants to hear the latest stars from the Met, or Paris, or Covent Garden. Had Luciano made his way only in Italy, the course of his career would have been quite different. Getting out of the country opened up other opportunities for him. Singing in Dublin, for example, led to Joan Ingpen's signing him up as a cover for Covent Garden.

Many cover artists never make it onstage, but it was still a good gamble for Luciano. He arrived in England eager, friendly, and almost completely devoid of either stage presence or a working knowledge of English. The language barrier worked both ways: back then, the name Luciano Pavarotti was quite a mouthful for most native English speakers. So Luciano was given the same nickname as the only other Luciano most English speakers had heard of: "Lucky."

It proved a fitting nickname. Di Stefano sang one and a half performances, then canceled in the middle of the opera, so that Luciano had to make his Covent Garden debut singing only the second half of a performance. Half a performance is better than none—certainly to the enthusiastic audience. Luciano had a big success right away. As fate would have it, di Stefano canceled not only the rest of the run but also his scheduled appearance on the TV show *Sunday Night at the Palladium*, England's equivalent of the *Ed Sullivan Show*. Luciano took over for him there, too, and for the first time—and certainly not the last—he appeared, via television, in thousands of homes.

His luck held. Because Joan Ingpen, as I said, used to be the manager of Joan Sutherland, who was by then already becoming a star of considerable importance. Joan Sutherland was a rather statuesque lady, and she was constantly on the lookout for tenors as tall as she was. It was a tough search. As any opera lover knows, Italian tenors do not generally count height among their outstanding attributes. One second-echelon tenor at that time was unfortunately named Dino Formichini: *formica* means "ant" in Italian, and Dino, bearing a name that can unfortunately be construed to mean "little ants," was just about as tall as one. He appeared opposite Joan in Bellini's *La Sonnambula* at the Metropolitan Opera, and Joan spent the whole evening running away from him so no one would notice the extreme difference in their heights.

Joan Ingpen called up Joan Sutherland and said, "Joan, I've got a tenor who's tall, and he's got a lovely voice."

Joan must have pricked up her ears. She and her husband, the conductor Richard Bonynge, were hiring singers for a thirteen-week tour of Australia. And Luciano, it just so happened, sang exactly the repertory at which Joan excelled. Bel canto opera—that is, Italian opera from the first part of the nineteenth century—takes a special kind of voice. To sing the long and often virtuosic vocal lines of Rossini, Bellini, and Donizetti, you need flexibility, beauty of sound, and high notes to burn. Luciano had all of that, in spades. Also to his advantage was the fact that he had to be one of the few singers around who was not only taller than Joan but also wider. Ricky Bonynge came and heard him do an audition at Covent Garden, and "Lucky" had another job.

As it turned out, Joan and Ricky had a chance to try him out before the tour even started. Joan was singing *Lucia di Lammermoor* with the Opera Guild of Greater Miami, and her tenor, Renato Cioni, got a last-minute offer to sing *Tosca* in Paris with Maria Callas because someone else had canceled. Even in her later years, Callas was not someone you turned down, and Cioni had no hesitation about dropping Miami from his schedule. This left the director of the Opera Guild, Arturo di Filippi, in something of a predicament. Tenors who can sing Edgardo, the male lead in *Lucia*, don't grow on trees, and he wanted someone of comparable stature—figuratively, anyway—to Joan. He embarked on a long and fruitless search, as the date of the premiere drew closer.

Ricky said, "I think you should try this new tenor we've found."

Di Filippi was naturally reluctant to gamble his production on a no-name tenor. But finally, because he couldn't find anybody else, he did. Thus, in 1965, Luciano made his American debut.

It just goes to show that opera is always a gamble. Renato Cioni goes off to the bright lights of Paris and leaves provincial Miami to an unknown. But look who ended up being the big star. Cioni wasn't bad, but have you ever heard of Renato Cioni? I rest my case.

Luciano was still as green as grass. He's often recounted the story of his airplane journey from Italy to Miami. He thought it must be a very expensive plane ticket, because the plane went to so many places: he had about ten stops before he got to Miami. (Later in his career, he would realize that private jets fly a more direct route.) When he arrived at the opera house—which was actually more like a high school gym—he was struck by all the Mercedeses and Cadillacs in the parking lot. "Whose cars are those?" he asked.

"Those cars belong to the members of the chorus," he was told.

So he was awestruck because the Florida Grand Opera could afford to pay its chorus so much money. Of course, it was a completely volunteer chorus: those cars belonged to doctors, lawyers, and other professionals who worked by day and sang in the chorus for the love of it, and for nothing. One of those chorus members was a woman named Judy Drucker, who made friends with Luciano and invited him to her house for parties. Judy later became an important classical music presenter in Miami, and she put Luciano on in concert dozens of times. Luciano used to quip that you always have to be nice to the girls in the chorus because you never know who might end up hiring you later.

The Miami engagement went very well for Luciano, and the Australia tour that followed was even more important for him. Luciano, at that time, was very amenable to anything, happy just to have engagements and willing to work hard. It was all part of gradually building up the kind of headlining career that I think he was hoping to have even then. And it was a good thing that he felt

like that in Australia, because the tour was a lot of hard work. Luciano sang *Lucia*, *Sonnambula*, Verdi's *La Traviata*, and Donizetti's
comedy *L'Elisir d'Amore*. Usually, opera singers need to rest their
voices for at least a day, and preferably two or more, between performances; on this tour, Luciano was once called on to sing two
dress rehearsals in a single day. He couldn't very well say anything
in protest because Joan Sutherland was working just as hard as he
was. Joan wasn't one of those divas who coast on their reputations.
She was extremely professional. She could sing a dress rehearsal in
the afternoon and a performance in the evening without blinking
an eye. It taught Luciano a real work ethic—at least at that point
in his career. You don't mess around with Joan Sutherland.

To be able to sing that much takes technique, and Luciano has
always maintained he learned a tremendous amount from Joan in
Australia. The most important thing was breath support. To understand how singers project their voices, think of a crying baby:
as anyone who's ever had one knows, a baby can cry for hours and
not get tired. That's because the sound is supported from the diaphragm. Joan had a rock-solid diaphragm, and Luciano couldn't
keep his hands off her. That is, he was constantly feeling her ab-
domen to figure out what she was doing. He came back from
Australia a much more solid singer—technically speaking. Come
to think of it, he was more solid in other ways, too. Luciano could
already pack away a lot of food, especially when he was on the
road.

He also became Joan and Ricky's preferred tenor—and their
relationship moved into the recording studio. Lucky's luck was
still holding. Joan wanted to commit a number of her signature
bel canto roles to vinyl, and Decca, her record label, logically
enough turned to a star bel canto specialist to sing opposite her:
the Spanish tenor Alfredo Kraus. Kraus was an elegant singer,
both musically and personally, who was famous for taking excellent care of his instrument and refusing to submit to the hectic
pace of the modern jet-set tenor—one reason he was able to keep
singing gorgeously well into his sixties. He was also famous in the

business for being extremely interested in money. He had his own recording company in Spain, and he wanted Decca to give him the Spanish and South American distribution rights on anything he recorded for them. Decca, of course, already had its own distribution contracts; but Kraus couldn't, or wouldn't, get that into his head. So he refused to record, for example, Donizetti's *Daughter of the Regiment* in 1967, and Decca, rather reluctantly, had to accept Joan and Ricky's tenor, who had already recorded with them the small tenor role in *Beatrice di Tenda*: Luciano Pavarotti.

In point of fact, Decca had already released a solo album of Luciano's. But not very enthusiastically.

At some point when Luciano was just starting out—it may have been the same *Rigoletto* Joan Ingpen heard in Dublin—the great record producer John Culshaw heard him sing. What Legge was to EMI, Culshaw was to Decca; and whatever great recordings Legge didn't produce, Culshaw did. His masterpiece was the first-ever recording of the four operas of Wagner's *Ring* cycle, a project that everybody thought was impossible and that took seven years to complete. Culshaw heard Luciano, and he heard a fantastic voice, and he took it upon himself to offer to record him. Then he contacted Moritz Rosengarten at Decca and said, "I've got a new tenor."

The chairman of Decca Ltd. was Sir Edward Lewis, an archetypal elegant English gentleman. Rosengarten, or "Uncle Mo," who dealt with the artists on the big recording projects, was Sir Edward's polar opposite: a hardheaded, direct, and very savvy Polish businessman. The two of them made an intriguingly mismatched pair. For all their differences in style, it's certain that neither of them got successful making records of hefty unknowns. So when Culshaw told Rosengarten about Luciano, Rosengarten hit the roof.

"We don't need another tenor," he's supposed to have said. "We've got di Stefano, Corelli, even Jimmy McCracken, and we can't keep them happy. And now you've promised this guy a record. How big?"

"We didn't discuss the size," Culshaw said.

"Well, we'll do an EP," Rosengarten said, "and that's it."

As opposed to the standard twelve-inch LP, or long-playing record, an EP, or extended-play record, was generally only seven inches. In Luciano's case, it was big enough to fit a couple of arias from *Tosca* and *Rigoletto* and the aria from *Bohème*. They didn't exactly give Luciano red-carpet treatment in the making of it, either. This was in 1964, and nobody knew from Luciano Pavarotti. They flew him in, snapped a picture to put on the cover, did the whole recording in a couple of takes, and told him they'd send some copies when they were done. Still, it was a debut album on a major label, and Luciano used to hand them out like business cards. There aren't many copies of it around these days, although Decca rereleased the tracks on a compilation album it put out for Luciano's fortieth anniversary on the stage.

Decca may initially have been somewhat reluctant about using the unknown young Italian with Miss Sutherland, but there was one Decca executive who knew right away what he might have in Luciano. That was Terry McEwen in New York. Terry was a character. He was a big fat man who loved opera. As the head of artists and repertoire of London Records—which is what Decca was called in the States—he was practically a one-man opera company. He knew his artists, and he knew how to promote them, and he knew how to sell records. The artists loved him, in part because he was extremely generous; who's not going to love a generous record promoter? He always hosted after-performance dinners, and parties, and promotions—all, of course, with Decca's money. There was more money in those days. The American market represented something like 60 percent of worldwide classical sales, as opposed to something like 20 percent today. Back then, artists who recorded were virtually compelled to come over to the States to touch base with their fans. Stars would come in to do record signings at Sam Goody or Korvettes, and the lines would stretch around the block.

Terry understood better than many people the importance of

publicity. And whenever he had a new singer come over to America from Europe, he used to give them two names of publicists. One was me, and one was Edgar Vincent. Edgar, whose family comes from Holland, is every inch the continental gentleman. His Old World style and refinement appealed to a number of artists, such as Birgit Nilsson and, later, Plácido Domingo, who remains a principal client. My style, by contrast, may not have appealed to everybody. It was more, shall we say, forthright.

Anyway, Terry first heard Luciano on the trial pressing for Decca, and he knew. He said, "This guy is going to be one of the dominant tenors of his generation." And he contacted Decca's office in London and said, "Sign him." Eventually, they did.

It was in the fall of 1967 that I met Luciano. His first trip to New York was as, wouldn't you know, a cover. The company of Milan's La Scala had come over to Canada to perform Bellini's *I Capuleti e i Montecchi*—The Capulets and the Montagues, or, in other words, *Romeo and Juliet*—at Expo '67, and Luciano was singing the role of Tebaldo (Tybalt), which isn't even a very big part. Because he was close by and Herbert von Karajan was conducting a performance of the Verdi Requiem at Carnegie Hall, von Karajan brought him down to cover for Carlo Bergonzi, who was singing the tenor part.

And Bergonzi . . . didn't cancel. Luciano had to wait another year for his New York debut.

Decca, however, took advantage of the time that he was in New York to start getting the publicity machine rolling. They took him to be photographed by Francesco Scavullo, the commercial fashion photographer. That was something Terry had cooked up with the art director of *Harper's Bazaar*. All of Decca's European stars would arrive in the States with these dreadful publicity photos, and through the *Harper's Bazaar* connection, Terry began having Scavullo photograph his artists. Scavullo, in fact, did some fabulous record covers for Decca: Birgit Nilsson, Marilyn Horne, Joan Sutherland. All Luciano needed was new publicity shots, and he was escorted over to Scavullo's studio on a rainy Saturday morning to get some. Even then, when he was relatively trim, they couldn't find a tie big enough to go around his neck.

But photos alone aren't enough. Terry also talked to Luciano about finding someone to do publicity work for him.

Luciano was still so young and fresh and eager that everybody loved him. He was the pleasantest person in the world. Terry said, "Luciano, you're a nice guy. So you need a real bastard to do your publicity."

At least, that's how I remember it. One thing is certain: he gave Luciano my number.

Luciano left New York the second that Karajan's baton came down to start the Requiem, with Carlo Bergonzi onstage. And that's when I met him for the first time: in the cab, going out to the airport.

I loved the guy. He was like an eager puppy. He was so excited about everything that was going to happen to him, and so willing to do what everyone told him, that you couldn't help but like him. And the voice, what I had heard of it, sent goose pimples up your arms. We hit it off right away. And I signed him up.

Actually, signed up is the wrong term. In all our years together, I never had a contract with Luciano Pavarotti. What good is a contract? Many people regard it as sacrosanct, but the fact is, you can always get out of a contract if you want to. I've done it many times myself—often, in later years, on Luciano's behalf. And before you put too much faith in that little piece of paper, let me tell you something: if you need a contract to spell out the confidence that you have in your artists—if your relationship with your artists is so lacking in trust—then you're already on thin ice.

But Luciano was a straight arrow; contract or no, he was a man of his word. As was I. And Adua, his wife, who looked after their financial affairs, ran a tight ship. Still, I was shocked to find, between the first and fifth of the month, every month, that there was a bank transfer from Italy into my account for $250, which is what I charged for publicity by then.

Usually, getting money out of an artist is like pulling teeth. Especially an Italian artist. Throughout my career, I had to wrestle with more artists to get my commission than I like to recount. It was, after all, my money; I had earned it. But no artist likes to part with money. Not even Luciano—although that wasn't to be an issue for many years to come.

All I knew was, here was my retainer, coming in without my asking for it, every month. It was enough to make me change my view of Italians altogether.

It was the beginning of a beautiful relationship.

RANDY MICKELSON
(musicologist and voice teacher/coach)

In 1965, Joan Sutherland was very excited that she had found a tall tenor. She said, "I'm sick of going to embrace my male lead and having him come up to my navel."

She had found this tall tenor, and she and Ricky Bonynge were going to take him on tour to Australia; but shortly before that, they were doing La Sonnambula *together at Covent Garden. I was there to help with the musical preparation.*

So we were there, all sitting around the lunch table, and there was a phone call. Ricky went to get it, and when he came back in he said, "That was the tall tenor. He's just had all his wisdom teeth out and he can't come for Sonnambula.*"*

There was a silence. Then Joan said, "He has every tooth in his head God gave him. He just hasn't learned the part. Call him back and tell him to come up here and we'll teach it to him."

Joan proved to be right. And Luciano agreed to come up.

So time passed, and preparations for Sonnambula *were in full swing. The first night was going to be a gala for the Queen, and everybody was nervous. Eventually, a call came in from the tall tenor. Now he was in Lyon. He had decided to drive up from Modena in his Maserati or Ferrari that his father had bought him. Never mind that crap about his com-*

ing from a poor family. They weren't rich, but they could afford to buy him a Ferrari—at least a secondhand one. But the axle had broken, and he didn't trust the French to fix it, so he was having a spare part brought up from Modena. This meant more delay.

Finally, in the bustle of the last rehearsal before the dress, in walked the tall tenor, a handsome guy with a smile you would mortgage your house for. And under his arm was a score of Sonnambula with the cellophane still on it, unopened.

Joan was bustling off to rehearsal. In those days, Covent Garden sent limos to pick you up, and they were all parked in front of the house. There was more than one, because Joan had wigs and costumes and all kinds of things like that.

"I am on my way to Covent Garden to rehearse," she said. And Ricky seconded that.

"But," the tall tenor said, "who's going to teach me the score?"

Joan's response was something along the lines of "What, are you kidding?"

The upshot was that they all went off to rehearsal and left me to teach Luciano the score. I began playing "Prendi: l'anel ti dono," I'm giving you this ring, and Luciano stopped.

"A chi lo do? Who do I give it to?"

"Well," I said, "you are the sposo, the husband, and she is the sposa, the wife . . ."

He was so nervous his brain was shutting off.

So we worked like crazy until the dress rehearsal. It was Covent Garden in the 1960s, which meant that there were about a hundred people onstage and the whole production was in two colors, shit brown and shit khaki. There was an organ grinder with a monkey, and the monkey had a very long chain and it was running all over the stage, and it began winding the chain around Joan's feet.

Joan went way down to the front of the stage, by the footlights, and, without looking behind her, extended one hand out so Luciano could put the ring on her finger.

But the tall tenor entered from the other side, ready to put the ring on the hand she wasn't extending.

It was the last straw for Joan. "I am a homely woman," she said, "and I am not a graceful woman, and I am going to sing before the Queen, and the tenor can't even enter from the right side, and I have this chain wrapped around my ankles, and I'm going to end up falling into the orchestra pit."

And she went storming off to her dressing room. It was very rare for Joan to have a meltdown like that.

"Go after her with a sweet drink," said Norman Ayrton. Norman was the director of the production and a great friend of Joan's. "Get a lot of sugar in her to calm her down."

Meanwhile, Norman went down to the basement to see what was there, and took me with him. I think we happened on the sets from Don Carlo. Whatever it was, we found a bench that we took upstairs for Joan to sit on. It was a rather elaborate Spanish Baroque bench for the little Swiss village where Sonnambula was set, but it was what we found. The idea was that Joan could sit on the bench and extend her hand over her head, so it wouldn't matter which side the tenor entered from.

So the performance arrived, and of course the tall tenor made his entrance onstage about fifty measures too early and came up behind Joan on her bench.

"Help me," he whispered, through clenched teeth.

"I can't help you," Joan whispered back. "I've got to sing La Sonnambula."

So he stood there behind her. And when it was finally time for him to sing, he sang so beautifully it brought tears to your eyes. Joan had her head leaned back against his tummy, and she had a dreamy look in her eyes. And she didn't come in. Her line there was just one or two words; it wasn't a major blunder. But it was unlike Joan not to come in.

Later, she said, "It was so gorgeous I was just sitting there with my head against his tummy listening, and I forgot to sing."

chapter III

❧

THE PUBLICITY MACHINE

*The ABCs of the Most Essential
Tool in the Business*

Marketing an artist is basically like marketing a bar of soap. It may not be so nice to put it that way, but think about it. You've got to know your market, you've got to know your product, and you've got to know how to put it across, to make people want to buy it.

You think that's too commercial? Well, that's ridiculous. We're running a business here. That's the bottom line: classical music is a business like any other. There's no such thing as too commercial. If you ask me, in fact, one of the biggest problems with classical music today is that it's not commercial enough. Nobody knows how to promote anything. In other words, nobody knows how to get people to want to hear this stuff.

You have to create a sense of excitement, of anticipation, around an event. When I started in the business, everybody wanted to read about opening night at the Metropolitan Opera.

It wasn't just the music critics who went: society reporters, gossip columnists, and all the big fashion people and their photographers were out in force. When I was starting out in publicity in New York and would do just about anything to make money, I used to sell opening night at the Metropolitan Opera. That is, I had a few clients who wanted to be photographed in their fancy dresses, and I would take it upon myself to make sure they were. One of them, a children's fashion designer named Suzanne Godard, used to do this every year. She would go over to Paris and come back with the most incredible creations and wear them on opening night, and we got her picture in the paper that way all the time.

And now? Who cares about opening night at the Met now? In 2002, for its opening night, the Metropolitan Opera gathered three of the world's leading divas: Mirella Freni, Renée Fleming, and Olga Borodina, each to sing one act of an opera with Plácido Domingo. Getting those four singers together is pretty hot stuff, but not even the publicity department seemed to care about it. I said to Joe Volpe, the Met's general director, "Why the hell didn't you put out a photo call and have pictures done of the three ladies together with Plácido? Those pictures would have gone around the world!"

He said something along the lines of "Oh, Herbert." Which is what a lot of them say over there when I come to them with my ideas.

The fact of the matter is, their public relations department is pretty pitiful. They don't promote anything. I remember when Renata Tebaldi, Elisabeth Schwarzkopf, Joan Sutherland, and Lisa della Casa appeared together at a Met gala in 1964. I represented three of those ladies, and we made sure to get a picture. It appeared in a lot of newspapers. Above the fold.

You have to remember that publicity is a tool. It's a tool for increasing the value of the artist. The idea is to get that name of yours around so that people are coming to the box office and buying tickets to your concerts, which, of course, has positive repercussions for you both artistically and financially. I mean, if you really get a kick out of having your picture in the paper, that's one thing; but if you get a fatter check as a result of it, that's something completely different—and much better. If it doesn't mean higher fees, if it doesn't mean more money in your pocket, then publicity is a waste of time.

But few people seem to understand that. It's not just the Met: a lot of artists don't want to grasp the importance of publicity, either. More precisely, they don't want to pay for it.

Take Birgit Nilsson, the great Wagnerian soprano. Birgit was from a farm in Sweden, and she looked it. And when she opened her mouth, you could just about hear her in Sweden: a huge, powerful, dramatic voice. In 1959, she made a sensational debut at the Metropolitan Opera in Wagner's *Tristan und Isolde*. Isolde is hands-down the toughest soprano part in the repertory; hardly anybody can sing the thing, let alone sing it well. But Birgit could. The next morning, the review was on the front page of the *New York Times*. It was that good. The trouble was, Birgit knew it.

Now, Madame Nilsson was not ignorant of the value of a dollar. One of her most famous quotes later in her career, after someone asked her why she was appearing in the American hinterland, was, "The money is just as green in Iowa as it is in New York."

After her sensational Met debut, she felt that her own value had increased considerably. She shopped around among the New York agents and settled on someone who was willing to book her a whole U.S. recital tour for the following year, for a fairly impressive amount of money per evening. Then she went home to Sweden—and everybody forgot about her.

What if they gave a concert and nobody came? That's just about what happened to Birgit on her supposedly triumphant recital tour. The houses sold miserably and presenters began to cancel, trying to minimize their losses.

Birgit, of course, was furious. She complained to Terry McEwen (for she, too, recorded with Decca) that Americans were terribly uncultured.

"Why should they come to your concert?" said Terry. "Who are you?"

"I sing," Birgit said.

"My Uncle Sid sings," said Terry. "They've never heard of you. I haven't read your name since it was on the front page of the *New York Times*. Big deal: it was the garbage wrapping of the following day. Being in the newspaper once is not important. You've got to be in the newspaper regularly, and on the radio, and on television."

And he took a bar of Lux soap off the table and tossed it at her.

"When one-tenth of the people who know what Lux soap is know who Birgit Nilsson is," he said, "then you can complain to me that people don't come to your concert."

The upshot was that Birgit got a publicist: Edgar Vincent. And while she may not have become as well known as Lux soap, she did become without question, and with Edgar's help, the leading Wagnerian soprano of her generation.

TERRY MCEWEN

I called Ed Vincent, and he came right over to the hotel. Of course he was interested in Birgit Nilsson; are you kidding? I thought he would be better than Herbert, because Herbert is a little rough around the edges. Also, Herbert wouldn't know how to tell a woman how to dress, whereas Edgar would.

In those days, of course, it was very different being a publicist because there were so many places to publicize. There were seven papers in New York alone. There were magazines. There were radio shows. And then there were all the television shows that were actually interested in booking classical musicians: the *Bell Telephone Hour*, the *Voice of Firestone*, and, of course, the *Ed Sullivan Show*. Television rapidly became my biggest strength as a publicist. I worked very hard on developing my contacts there as fast as I could.

The whole atmosphere of classical music was different. It was a very exciting time. They would do *Tosca* at the Metropolitan Opera, and you'd have five different Toscas in a single season, and each one of the five would be a singer whose name is still talked about today in hushed tones of awe: Maria Callas, Renata Tebaldi, Leonie Rysanek, Dorothy Kirsten, and—low woman on the totem pole—Régine Crespin. Sopranos now can't touch the hem of Régine Crespin's dress. In those days, we didn't quite realize how lucky we were to have them; but nonetheless, everybody went to hear all of them, to compare the different performances. I was at the opera almost every night. I would come home at 5:30 to have dinner with my wife and two children—it was my rule that I had dinner with them every night—and then at 7:30 I would be out the door on my way to the opera.

It wasn't only the Metropolitan Opera, either. We had fantastic opera performances in concert from the American Opera Society, which happened to be one of my clients. It was run by Allen Oxenburg, a dumpy little guy who was extremely knowledgeable about opera. There was very little you could tell him that he didn't already know. He went all over Europe, he spoke every one of the European languages, and he got all of the big singers to come over and the cream of New York society would turn out to hear them. And was it worth it. These were monumental occasions. In the audience, you'd just sit there, gasping, "My God Almighty, listen to that." He had all of the greatest singers in opera at that time: Joan, Elisabeth, Maria Callas, Eileen Farrell, Marilyn Horne, Giulietta Simionato, Christa Ludwig, Jon Vickers, Cesare Siepi. Leontyne Price made her New York debut with him. Montserrat Caballé, the Spanish soprano, made her American debut with him in Donizetti's *Lucrezia Borgia*; when she finished the opening aria, "Com'è bello," the house broke into an uproar. You never heard the kind of ascending scales that she did, and this incredible, unending breath that sort of floated off into the ether.

Unfortunately, Allen had to shut down. Ironically, it was Ca-ballé who did him in. Caballé was a sweet, jolly woman—more like a little girl, really—who was later able to rival Luciano in girth (and they sang together many times, to prove it). In the opera world, she was famous for two things: her floating *piano*, or soft notes, and her cancelations, both of which she produced re-liably, and with increasing frequency, throughout her career. Ca-ballé had promised Allen she'd do some benefit recitals to raise money, and he counted on her very much. Alas, she pulled a cou-ple of her tricks, and consequently he was virtually forced out of business.

This is the kind of atmosphere in which I was getting my pro-fessional experience. And after the performances, there were al-ways dinners or parties with the artists and the record executives. Sometimes Carol and I entertained at home. Once, quite early on, we gave a party for Pilar Lorengar, the Spanish soprano, who was one of my clients at the time. Since Carol and I hadn't en-tertained all that much yet, we didn't own enough wineglasses, and we decided to splurge: we went out and bought some really nice ones. What we didn't know was that Madame Lorengar's husband, a dentist, had a clever party trick he brought out after a drink or two: he liked to eat glass. He maintained that as long as he chewed it very fine, it wouldn't harm him, and he must have been right, because he is still with us. I'll never forget the ex-pression on my wife's face as one of our expensive new wine-glasses vanished, with horrendous crunching sounds, down Señor Lorengar's gullet.

Meanwhile, my business was growing fast. I had finally taken my own office, in that same Fifty-seventh Street building near Carnegie Hall, and before too long I had to hire more staff and move into a larger space upstairs. My reputation was rapidly growing, too. Most of the best things that were going on in clas-sical music were coming through me. I was an extremely valu-able person to have on your side, and a lot of the artists liked my style. (A lot of them didn't, too, but that was their problem.) Very heavy on television, very heavy on trying to think of different things for the artists to do outside the opera house: those were my hallmarks. Some might say I was also very aggressive. But how can you be anything but? A good public relations person is there at the behest of the artist. The artist himself may not spell out for you that he wants you to call his record label twenty times and the *New York Times* ditto, and so on; but, on the other hand, it's taken for granted that you're supposed to do all that. And I felt it was very important to do it correctly and do it comprehensively. I mean, there are 2,500 pianists out there; how else are you going to get attention for the one you represent?

I had terrific contacts in television. I was very good at television because I was always coming up with ideas for ways to program things. Of course, in those days the producers were interested in producing classical music to begin with, in prime time no less, which certainly made things easier. I would devise entire programs, like one we did called "One to Six": a solo, a duet, a trio, a quartet, a quintet, and finally the famous sextet from *Lucia*. There were all kinds of things like that. The executives soon came to rely on the fact that if I proposed something to them, they were going to get something really, really good. Barry Wood at the *Bell Telephone Hour* or Bob Precht at the *Ed Sullivan Show* would always call me. In effect, I think they gradually got the idea that if you were talking about the classical music business, no one knew it better than Herbert Breslin. Of course, this only helped raise my star among artists, as well. Everyone wanted me to get them on the *Ed Sullivan Show*.

Including Elisabeth Schwarzkopf, my first client. Schwarzkopf, as I said, was one of the great German lied singers. Her husband, Walter Legge, was an incredible stickler for detail; he aspired to some Germanic ideal of perfection, and Elisabeth was supposed to carry it out. Walter was a famous monster. He was really terribly hard on her.

German singers are a world unto themselves. For some reason, artists from the German-speaking world have never had as wide an appeal as those from some other countries. That's not to say there haven't been very great and popular artists from Germany, and Ann Colbert represented a lot of them: Elisabeth, and Dietrich Fischer-Dieskau, a baritone who's even more revered than Elisabeth as a recitalist and a singer of opera, and Hermann Prey, another fine baritone, who was fated to remain in Fischer-Dieskau's shadow for most of his career. Hermann got so frustrated about this that he wanted to leave the Colbert office for a while. Mrs. Colbert said to him, "Look, you can make a perfectly fine career on what he turns down. I get five hundred offers for him; he takes fifty. You want the other four hundred and fifty?" I don't know if Hermann was all that happy with this response, but he had a very respectable career.

Fischer-Dieskau acted as if he were above all that. He had an almost priestly attitude about singing and about being who he was. High class is not quite the term I'd use to describe him; I'd say he was more highfalutin. He gave the impression that his bodily emanations, shall we say, didn't smell. Plenty of aficionados seem to be perfectly willing to believe it. I publicized events like Fischer-Dieskau and Elisabeth doing a concert of Hugo Wolf lieder at Carnegie Hall, with Gerald Moore as the pianist. In the classical music world, that's about as gold plated as it gets. Working with prestigious events like that helped me build my reputation. But my God, a whole evening of Wolf: how boring.

This kind of repertory is part of the reason German singers have a relatively limited appeal. In fact, there's been a divide between German and Italian music in the classical world for hundreds of years. German music is regarded as the acme of high art—the most profound symphonies, the most poetic lieder. Italian music, by contrast, has often been dismissed as lowbrow popular entertainment. In the nineteenth century, the term for it was *macaroni*—Italian peasant fare, not haute cuisine. Guess which one the public still goes for. There's never been a German artist, however respected, for whom you could get $25,000 a concert. Elisabeth Schwarzkopf was an elite singer; she was never going to appeal to the masses. Ann Colbert was very savvy. She priced Elisabeth at a level she felt people would be willing to pay. She never charged too much.

The price a singer gets for a concert isn't necessarily an indication of an artist's quality, but still, it is usually taken as a reflection on the artist. Walter Legge always felt that Mrs. Colbert was not charging enough money for Elisabeth. And he was always after me to get her on the *Ed Sullivan Show*, which would bring her to a wider audience—a sign that she had arrived.

It would also be a sign that the allegations of her Nazi past had been forgotten, for which reason I thought that my getting her on was pretty questionable. In those days, there were certain entertainers who were persona non grata, and anyone with Elisabeth's background definitely qualified. I did finally manage to get the *Ed Sullivan* people to book her. But frankly, I think someone made a mistake.

The *Ed Sullivan Show* was an incredible hassle because you had to get to the studio at eight o'clock in the morning, and you were there until nine in the evening. First, you had to block out your scene onstage, and then repeat it, and then you rehearsed, and then the orchestra came and you rehearsed again. There was so much time wasted it was unbelievable. And all this on a Sunday.

On the Friday before Elisabeth's appearance, I was sitting in my office when I got a call from Bob Precht, who happened to be Ed's son-in-law.

"Oh, Herbert," he said, "I'm sorry to have to tell you this, but we have to tape. This week's show is so heavy that we have to postpone her appearance, and we have to tape her for next week's show. We'll need her at seven o'clock tomorrow night."

I said, "But, Bob, how can I do that? She's giving a concert in California tonight, and she isn't even coming in until tomorrow."

His response was, in effect, "Do or die."

There are times when working for an artist is comparable to having five heart attacks. This was one of them.

Now, Schwarzkopf was known as a great beauty, and indeed

she was—onstage. Offstage, she looked more like a *Putzfrau*, a cleaning woman. I remember after one performance a wealthy couple gave a big formal party at their home in her honor, and she let it be known that she had to go home and take her bath before she arrived. We all waited: one hour, two hours. No one dared to eat, of course, until the diva made her entrance. Everyone assumed that she had gone home to take off her stage makeup and get herself all dolled up for the party. Finally, at nearly two-thirty in the morning, the doorbell rang and the hostess practically yanked open the door. There was Elisabeth, fresh from her bath. She had taken off all her makeup, pulled her hair back into a dowdy bun, and thrown on a dirndl skirt. She looked as if she'd come to do the floors.

The hostess was speechless for a moment. "Elisabeth," she finally said. "How *quaint.*"

At four-thirty that Saturday afternoon, at Kennedy Airport, it was definitely this "quaint" incarnation of Madame Schwarzkopf that descended from the plane to greet her long-suffering publicist. She had been in the air since eight that morning. She was wearing a loden coat, and her hair was a mess.

"Elisabeth," I said, "you look terrific."

"Ach, ich bin so müde"—Oh, I'm so tired—were the first words out of her mouth.

"Well, you don't look *müde,*" I said. "You look wonderful."

"I can't wait to get to bed," she said.

"Well," I said, "maybe you'll feel better on the car ride into town."

She said, "No, I want to go to sleep immediately. No food, nothing. I'm going right to bed."

I thought, Oh boy, Herbert, you have your work cut out for you with this one.

So I said, "Well, Elisabeth, I have some news for you. Walter called, and Walter says he wants to be one hundred percent sure that your appearance on the show is absolutely fabulous. So what we have to do now is, we have to go to the studio and have them light your dress."

Am I a genius or what?

"Light my dress?" Elisabeth said.

I said, "Light your dress. Because he wants you to look great."

Elisabeth might have overruled me, but she wasn't about to countermand a dictate from Walter. We drove right to the Ed Sullivan Theater on Broadway. As we entered the building, the first thing we encountered was the blare of a loudspeaker: "Miss Schwarzkopf to the fifth-floor dressing room, please! We're expecting you down here in ten minutes!"

"*Was ist das?*" said Elisabeth.

We got her up to the dressing room and took out her dress, which looked like a *shmatte*—that's Yiddish for "rag"—and sent it off to be pressed, and Elisabeth sat down in front of the mirror and took off her hat. Everyone was eyeing her as if she had come to do the windows. Then Ernie Adler, the hairdresser, stepped up with a curling iron. It was, arguably, a foolish thing to do. You don't take a curling iron to Elisabeth Schwarzkopf's hair unless you want to have the hair in your hand.

"Vat you doing!?" Elisabeth snapped.

"Well," Ernie said, "I was just trying—"

"Are you stupid to do a thing like that!? Give me the brush!"

Ernie backed down quickly and Elisabeth took over, and did her hair, and did her makeup, and gradually re-created herself. By the time she got down to the studio, in her freshly pressed dress, she was looking like Marlene Dietrich.

"On the mark, Miss Schwarzkopf," they said immediately.

She said to me, "Where I go?"

"You go to your mark," I said, "and when they say, 'Sing,' you sing."

So Elisabeth went to her mark, and Ray Block, the orchestra leader, struck up the band, and I said, "Sing, Elisabeth, sing!" And Elisabeth sang, and they got their tape, and she went home and went to bed.

But after all that, they never aired her segment on the show. To be honest, I never asked why it didn't air. I knew the answer myself. Her past, once again, had come back to haunt her. And I had a great relationship with the people at the *Ed Sullivan Show*. I wasn't going to jeopardize that fighting a hopeless battle. Elisabeth never knew the difference anyway because by the time it was supposed to have aired she was back in Europe. So somewhere in the archives of the *Ed Sullivan Show* is a tape of Elisabeth Schwarzkopf doing some operetta aria or other. I forget which one.

After about ten years, I stopped working for Elisabeth because she left the Colbert office. She and Mrs. Colbert and Walter had some kind of a run-in. I'm sure it wasn't Mrs. Colbert's fault, because she was very correct. But Walter was really a big jerk.

My second client, Joan Sutherland, was not much more receptive to the publicity machine than Elisabeth was. When Joan started out, you wouldn't have picked her as a great future diva, either. She studied singing in Australia, with her mother, and there she won a competition that paid for her to come over to England. She studied for a year and then joined Covent Garden. She didn't exactly join it as a star; I think she got twenty pounds a week, which even in 1952 was not very much money. And for the next several years, she was a utilitarian soprano who would do virtually anything: little tiny roles like Clotilde, the handmaid in *Norma*, which is only a few lines, although it meant she got to bask in the reflected glory of the Norma, Maria Callas.

Meanwhile, Joan got married to Ricky Bonynge, and he worked with her very intensively, and they unlocked this incredible soprano voice that just kept going up the scale, and up, and up. Initially, Joan was convinced she didn't have high notes, so Ricky simply wouldn't let her look at the keyboard when he played her exercises and took her higher and higher, without her realizing that she was nailing powerful high Cs and Ds without blinking an eye. Gradually, people around her came to realize it, though, and Joan began to sing around Britain. In 1958, she flew to Vancouver to make her North American debut as Donna Anna in Mozart's *Don Giovanni*, and on her way home she stopped off at the Metropolitan Opera to sing for Sir Rudolf Bing, the legendary general director of the Met for twenty-two years.

Bing ran a famously tight ship. He didn't suffer fools lightly, or monkey business, or excessive fees (for a while, I think, his top fee stopped at $1,000 a night). When in 1958 Maria Callas delayed too long in committing to the contracts he had proposed to her, Bing fired her, knowing full well that he would be remembered for that one act as much as for anything else he did at the Met (and he was). Bing, incidentally, was not a big fan of Luciano's, either, once Luciano appeared on the scene. "I must say that seeing that stupid, ugly face everywhere I go is getting on my nerves," he said. By then, of course, he had retired from the Met, and Luciano's fame was already secure.

For her audition for Bing, Joan sang "Caro nome," a showpiece aria from Verdi's *Rigoletto*. Unfortunately, she sang it in English. There's been a lot of debate over the years about singing opera in its original language as opposed to one that the audience can understand. Generally, the operatic elite views it as preferable to sing opera in the language in which it was written—even when that means teaching a whole Anglophone cast to sing in Czech—and opera in English tends to be tarnished with an aura of provincialism. In any case, Mr. Bing was not impressed. It's possible that Joan's diction was partly to blame. While Joan could sing the notes better than anybody else around, her pronunciation was opaque at the best of times—even when she was singing in her own language. She herself often told the story about a recital that she closed with a set of English folk songs. Afterward, a fan came backstage to tell her how much she'd liked those songs. "But, Miss Sutherland," she added, "why didn't you sing them in English?"

Whether it was her singing in English, her diction, or something else, Bing didn't jump to hire her. In essence, he said something along the lines of "Don't call us, we'll call you." In actual fact, it wasn't that long until Joan appeared at the Met, but she made her New York debut with the ever-reliable American Opera Society, singing with yet another client of mine, Marilyn Horne, in Bellini's *Beatrice di Tenda*.

Even before her New York debut, however, Joan had her

breakthrough at Covent Garden, and her career took off. Covent Garden had at that time a very creative general director named David Webster, and David saw something in this house soprano and decided to revive *Lucia di Lammermoor* for her in 1959. They prepared Joan extremely well, sending her to Italy to be coached in the role, working with her at the house—which is something, unfortunately, that most opera houses these days no longer do. They engaged Franco Zeffirelli to direct and Tullio Serafin to conduct—the crème de la crème. Joan had a tremendous success. And because of the way the press worked in those days, every-body read about it. An event like that was considered breaking news. That's changed, certainly in the States. How many music reviews do you see on page 1 of the *New York Times* today? In any case, Joan went on a triumphal tour of *Lucia*s: Paris in 1960, La Scala in 1961, and, later that year, her Met debut. Mr. Bing, evidently, could resist her in person, but no sane general manager could resist the kind of hype Joan was getting by 1961.

The rest is history. Joan became a huge star, not only musically but also at the box office. She sold out every performance she ever did at the Metropolitan Opera, even things like *Esclarmonde* by Massenet, which is not exactly a greatest-hit opera, to put it mildly: no one's ever heard of the thing. But when Joan sang it, there wasn't a ticket to be had. Her voice was simply a phenom-enal instrument. It knocked you out of your chair. Until Joan, the only person I'd heard sing the mad scene from *Lucia* was Lily Pons, who basically chirped away at it, not always on the right pitches. Joan came along and bopped out this incredible mad scene that bowled you over, and at the end she hit you with a stunning high E-flat. It was a totally different ball game.

I remember waiting for Joan to disembark from the *Queen Mary*, arriving for her first summer tour of the United States in 1962. One reason I remember is that it was there I met Hans Boon, who worked in those days for Terry McEwen at London Records and had come (as had I) to greet the star. Hans is a walk-ing encyclopedia of opera repertory and references. For years, I used to tease him by asking when he was going to leave London Records and come work for me, and in 1979 he did. But on that day in 1962, little knowing that we'd be seeing each other almost constantly for the next forty years, we simply shook hands and waited together at the foot of the gangplank with the Rolls-Royce ready to bring the singer to her hotel, as off the ship, before Joan, came about seventeen pieces of mauve-colored luggage, plus one battered tan case containing her music. That's not even counting the costume boxes that were shipped over from Covent Garden. Joan was not to the manner born, but she picked up those habits very quickly.

HANS BOON

When I was at London Records, Herbert would be on the phone to us ten times a day, snarling, "What are you doing about this one? What are you doing about that one?" which is what he does to everybody. He was just making sure that you'd remembered to place an ad, for example, in the program for the performance. All the record companies used to do that in those days. If Carlo Bergonzi walked into the Met to sing one night and there was no ad in the program for his records, Terry McEwen would hear about it the next day. And if Herbert was taking care of the artist and he saw the program without an ad, he'd be after you in the opera house that night, wanting you to, in essence, put the ad in the program for that night, even though it was five minutes to eight.

I was on the receiving end of this for seventeen years. Then I went to work for him.

Joan proved to be one of my toughest clients. The problem was that she basically didn't want publicity. She hated giving interviews, and when she did give an interview, she didn't have much to say. Everything she had to say, she said when she sang. It was a mistake to turn to her for great insight, say, into the world of classical music. Let's face it: she didn't know that much. I think Ricky had a better understanding of what PR could do for somebody. He was pretty smart, and she was pretty dopey.

As a result, I had to come up with all kinds of creative ways to get Joan before the public. I had Arnold Scaasi design a whole wardrobe for her, and then I had Eugenia Sheppard, who was a big fashion editor for the *New York Herald Tribune*, come in and photograph her, and they wrote it up. I had her sing on all the television programs: the *Bell Telephone Hour*, the *Voice of Firestone*, the *Dinah Shore Show*. Joan appeared on that with Ella Fitzgerald, and the three of them—Dinah, Ella, and Joan—sang "Three Little Maids" from Gilbert and Sullivan's *The Mikado*. Can you imagine those three powerhouse ladies in that piece of fluff? Don't even talk to me about so-called crossover today. In those days, people knew how to do it right.

Of course, I also got Joan on the *Ed Sullivan Show*. Every time Joan had a premiere at the Metropolitan, she would be on *Ed Sullivan* the following Sunday like clockwork. She was on it eight times. Joan didn't mind doing the television work quite as much because, in general, all she had to do was sing. There are some people who might find it less taxing to have a simple conversation with an interviewer than to hit a high E-flat at the end of the mad scene, but Joan wasn't one of them.

Not all her appearances were completely painless, however. One Sunday morning when I went to pick up the diva bright and early at the Hotel Navarro on Central Park South to take her over to the Ed Sullivan Theater, I found her in a foul mood. She hadn't slept a wink, she informed me, because there was a Spanish dance troupe quartered above her. By the time we got into the studio and she was confronted with the inevitable blaring shriek from the PA system—"Miss Sutherland to the dressing room, please! Miss Sutherland!"—the climate was definitely oppressive.

Together, we entered the elevator to go up to the dressing room. The *Ed Sullivan Show*, of course, had all kinds of acts—

elephants, clowns, you name it—and as we got into the elevator, a monkey jumped on Joan's shoulder.

Joan went rigid.

"See, Joan," I said, "everybody loves you."

You have to keep a sense of humor about these things. But despite that inauspicious beginning, the program went off without a hitch. Joan was machinelike in her professionalism. No matter how tired she was, she always turned in a top-quality performance.

Another idea I had for Joan was an eight-part television series called *Who's Afraid of Opera?* I sat down with Nathan Kroll, a television producer and an old friend of mine, and we tried to figure out how to reduce an opera to twenty-six minutes. We took our inspiration from the children's program *Kukla, Fran and Ollie*, and did it with puppets. The idea was that Joan would come out on the set dressed as Lucia, and one of the puppets would say, "Joan, why are you so unhappy?" She would answer, "Well, I'm unhappy because my brother wants me to marry someone whom I really don't love, and if I have to go through with it I just may kill him." Then she would sing. We did Rossini's *Barber of Seville* and a few others; Offenbach's *La Périchole* came out especially well. The programs were broadcast on PBS in the early 1970s and then went all over the world.

An eight-part television series is a pretty amazing thing to get for a classical artist. It wasn't just the prestige: it was also great money. I got a contract for $100,000, which was equivalent back then to something like $1 million today. I was so pleased with myself that I decided to tell Joan in person. She was recording Offenbach's *Tales of Hoffmann* in Geneva with Plácido Domingo, and I ran over to see her. She wasn't expecting me, and she couldn't hide a shudder when she saw me. "What are *you* doing here?" she said, as if I were some unpleasant apparition come to trouble her—which is, quite frankly, how she saw me most of the time. It was a pretty sobering reception for someone who had come to bring her $100,000. In this business, you learn not to expect gratitude. Just your commission. Well, not only your commission. For that contract, I think they paid me a little extra.

The irony is that now many of those television shows that I got Joan have been rereleased on video, and they're wonderful souvenirs of the soprano in her prime. And after all these years, and all that resistance, Joan is quite happy to have them.

RICHARD BONYNGE

Joan had a sort of love-hate relationship with Herbert. Because Herbert was always chasing and chasing—you know what he's like. He would say, "Oh, I can make you so much money."

Joan said, "I've got enough money; I don't need any more."

I think Herbert could never quite make Joan out, because she's not on the American wavelength. Well, it's not strictly American. What I mean is that she's not on a publicity kick, and she couldn't care less whether she's in the newspaper or not. She doesn't need adulation; she's a very private person. She used to say, "I use Herbert to keep the press off of me."

Occasionally she would tell him off good and proper. He'd want her to do too many things, and she just didn't want to, and she'd explode. But it was all water off a duck's back to Herbert. He'd come bouncing back, and he never took offense. Ever. He was really quite wonderful that way.

My third client, as I said, was the mezzo-soprano Marilyn Horne. Jackie, as everybody calls her, was bound and determined to make a huge career. The problem is that mezzo-sopranos are somewhat circumscribed in their possibilities. If you're singing in Verdi's *Aida*, the star of the show is the soprano who sings Aida. The mezzo-soprano role, Amneris, may be an amazingly difficult part to sing, but she's not the prima donna; it's Aida who gets the limelight. Jackie tried to circumvent this problem by finding operas with mezzos in the title role, like Rossini's *Tancredi*, but operas like that aren't really vehicles to take you to the pinnacle of stardom, either. Jackie did very well for herself and had a wonderful, long career, but she always wanted more. "I want the Pavarotti treatment!" she would exclaim to me later on, after Luciano had begun his meteoric rise. Alas, that treatment is seldom accorded to mezzos.

In 1970, Jackie made her Metropolitan Opera debut in Bellini's *Norma*, with Joan Sutherland. Adalgisa, the young initiate to the druid priestess, had become something of a calling card for Jackie: by then, she and Joan had been singing Norma and Adalgisa together for long enough that somebody dubbed them the "Druid Duo." The Metropolitan Opera was putting on a new production to show them off, and the *New York Times Magazine* decided to do a story on Marilyn Horne. On top of that, they even decided to put her on the cover, which, from a publicity point of view, is pretty hot stuff. However, they didn't call on her alone. They decided to photograph both members of the "Druid Duo" together for the cover and then have the story on Jackie inside. And that was how it ran.

To say that Jackie was furious is putting it mildly. "What the hell are they putting *her* on the cover for?" she railed. "It's my story!" But that is a mere paraphrase of the language with which Jackie actually regaled me. Jackie has a mouth that can present you with every curse word you ever heard, and she used all of them about that magazine cover. To some people, sharing the *New York Times* cover might not seem like grounds for a major upset, but from Jackie's point of view, she deserved the cover herself.

Of course, she may also have been a little upset with me for something I had said at the dress rehearsal about how I thought she should sing louder to make herself heard in the Met's big auditorium. You never know what's going to set these people off.

So those were my first three clients. Pretty soon, of course, I had a lot more. I represented Régine Crespin, and Cornell MacNeil, and Renata Tebaldi, and Nicolai Gedda. I represented Rudolf Firkusny, the legendary Czech émigré pianist. I even represented Marcel Marceau for a while. After all those loud sopranos, it was nice to have someone who knew how to shut up.

MARILYN HORNE

I signed with Herbert around 1961. I think it was for something like $100 a month. I don't know if that was the going rate then, but it was all I could afford. Ask Herbert; he'll remember how much I paid him.

[It was $75. She would never have paid $100.]

Herbert is a great idea man. He comes up with all kinds of things for you to do. One of the best ideas that he came up with, shortly before we parted company, was a project of Rossini operas that I did at Carnegie Hall. We did Tancredi, La Donna del Lago, *and* Semiramide, *and they were highly successful. Completely sold out.*

I did a lot of appearances on the Tonight Show, *and* Merv Griffin, *and* Mike Douglas; *those were all shows that would have classical artists on. That was a way of really getting to a broader public. That all came from Herbert. I know he arranged the* Ed Sullivan *program on which Joan and I sang* Norma. *It was the only time I was ever on the* Ed Sullivan Show, *because it stopped soon after that. That was just after my Met debut. I know he arranged that. I don't think it would have been a tough arrangement, because we were the toast of the town for a while.*

Herbert got a lot more feisty as the years went on. He seemed a lot shyer in the early years. We were together for twenty-two years, though, and over the years we got to the point where we could have a really good fight. We would stand on the corner of Fifty-seventh Street and Seventh Avenue, yelling at each other, having a nice, good old fight.

Usually it was about what he thought I should be singing. "Why do you have to sing those dreary Mahler *Kindertotenlieder, a song cycle about dead children?" he'd say. For me, it was the love of the music, the poetry, you know. But he didn't think that was career-making stuff.*

You could say that all of this work was a kind of preparation for my career with Luciano Pavarotti.

Except that I didn't need any preparation for Luciano Pavarotti. Luciano was a dream client. He had a natural gift for promotion: he was completely attuned to promoting himself, and to the benefits of doing it, right away. He loved interviews. He had a pretty good idea of what he wanted to say and how he wanted to present himself. With that knowledge, an artist is already way, way ahead. The fact is that very few people have any idea how to present themselves. Often, when you're talking to someone—even a great artist—the person has very little idea of what he wants to say. He doesn't even have very much *to* say. Take Nicolai Gedda, that cool Swedish tenor whom I mentioned before. Nicolai was a wonderful singer. He could sing in any language—French, German, Italian, Russian—he was always extremely well prepared, he was adored by the critics, and he made hundreds of recordings. But it was very hard to get him to do interviews, and when he did do them, they didn't exactly set the world on fire. Luciano was the exact opposite. Here was a guy with a great face, a wonderful smile, and a wonderful sense of humor. He charmed everybody. That combination of qualities doesn't grow on trees.

He had a knack for coming up with a snappy answer. There's a much-told story about Luciano doing a televised interview with the journalist Pia Lindstrom, Ingrid Bergman's daughter, half sister to Isabella Rossellini, with looks befitting her pedigree. Pia said to Luciano, "They say your vocal cords were kissed by God."

"I think He kissed you all over," Luciano responded.

Actually, I think it was Herbert von Karajan who first said that Luciano's vocal cords were kissed by God. But Luciano would hardly have given Karajan the same kind of answer. He had a certain spicy humor, but he observed the proprieties. At least, he did with the big guys.

The lesser known had to fend for themselves. I remember one interview he did in Florida for a local radio station. The host was Judy Drucker. It was still several years before she began her career as a concert presenter, but she and Luciano were already good friends. Luciano loved to flirt with her. That in itself was hardly enough to pick her out of the crowd, however; he loved to flirt with everybody. He would come out with a "Hello, beautiful"—the word *beautiful* has four syllables when Luciano says it—and they all went weak in the knees, to judge from the big, sappy smiles that he generally got in response.

Luciano told Judy he would be happy to do an interview with her and told her to come over to his hotel suite. When she got there, he told her to come into his bedroom.

"Now," he said, "you lie down next to me on the bed, like *this*, and we put the tape recorder on my stomach, like *this*, and I put my arm around you, like *this*, and then we do the interview."

Maybe Judy was inexperienced, or maybe she didn't know what else to do, or maybe there was something else going on. But she did what he said, and they did the interview like that. They remained good friends for the next forty years. And, she insists, nothing more.

In recent years, he's been known to ask her, "*Cara*, did we ever do it together?"

"Listen," she says, "if you have to ask me, it couldn't have been that good, so obviously we didn't."

I started working with Luciano in 1967, and in 1968 he made his debut at the Metropolitan Opera. I didn't begin by getting his name all over the map. It's not a good idea to overhype a young artist who's just starting out. I'd rather let people find out how good he is than trumpet everywhere that I discovered him myself. I've never liked to "discover" people—not in that sense. My feeling has always been that it's better to go in like a lamb and come out like a lion than to go in like a lion and come out with your tail between your legs. Too much early hype can backfire. Remember the tenor Roberto Alagna? Before his Metropolitan Opera debut in 1996, every bus shelter in New York had a huge poster of his face. He was supposed to be the Second Coming. It turned out he wasn't even the fourth coming. Today, admittedly, he's got a career, but it's nothing like the career he was supposed to have ahead of him in 1996. He doesn't even sell out at the Met.

My approach with Luciano turned out to be fortuitous. True, all the ingredients at the Met were right for a big triumph. It was his good-luck opera, *La Bohème*, with his townswoman Mirella Freni. But Luciano got sick. He was coming in from San Francisco, where he'd made a great debut the year before, and while he was there he picked up the Hong Kong flu. "Should I sing or not?" he wondered. It wasn't the first time he was to deliberate that question, although later in his career he usually came up with a rather different answer. As it was, he canceled the first performance and waited a week before giving it a try. He sang one performance, still sick, made it through part of the second one, and, as di Stefano had done when Luciano got his big break in London five years before, canceled after one and a half performances and fled back to Italy to recover.

Although it wasn't the most remarkable of debuts, I think people got an idea of what they had. The Met, at least, reengaged Luciano. He was signed up for Alfredo in *La Traviata* and another *Bohème* in the 1970–71 season. In the year he didn't sing in New York, he appeared in some other major houses: San Francisco, Rome, La Scala. When he got back to the Met, he was asked to step in as Edgardo in *Lucia*, as well as sing the roles he originally contracted for. In those days, Luciano was happy to do that kind of thing on short notice.

Then came 1972. In that year, the Metropolitan Opera mounted a new production of Donizetti's *Daughter of the Regiment*, with Joan Sutherland in the title role and Luciano as Tonio. Tonio is one of those country-bumpkin characters that are such an integral part of opera buffa, or Italian comic opera. Their role, generally speaking, is to fall madly in love with the heroine, whom they usually manage, against the odds, to win in the end, either by luck or by a shrewd application of common sense. Luciano always did well in these bumpkin parts, probably because there's a healthy dose of the peasant in his own makeup.

Tonio, however, has another obstacle. In his big number, "Pour mon âme," the tenor has to sing no fewer than nine high

Cs. High Cs are a very special kind of note. Not every tenor has them, and even those who do use them with a healthy measure of caution. A high C is a climax, an acme, the cherry on the sundae; no composer who knows voices writes too many of them. Donizetti was composing a showpiece—and pushing the envelope. High Cs, as we know them today, were still a fairly new phenomenon in 1840, when the opera was written. Singers sang them in falsetto until 1831, when Gilbert Duprez sang a full-voice high C for the first time. It didn't win universal approval. Rossini thought it sounded like "the squawk of a capon whose throat was being cut." In the voices of a lot of tenors, it still does. Many of them, faced with a high C, will transpose the music down a half step or so, bringing it more within reach. Luciano himself wasn't above doing that as his career went on.

In 1972, however, Luciano still had high Cs to burn. He was also experienced in the role: he had already sung it at Covent Garden and recorded it with Joan. By this time, he had developed a pretty substantial girth. He was, to put it mildly, a big, big man. He was wearing an outfit that made him look like a toy soldier. He bounced around the stage. And he made the role completely his own. He took that silly role and sang like a god, and popped out all these high notes, and dominated the evening. He had the audience eating out of his hand. There were screams when he finished. It was a defining night of his career. That performance marked the beginning of the Luciano Pavarotti everybody knows today. From there, he went into orbit.

As I spent my days thinking about ways to further all these singers' careers, I was also thinking about my own. Business was going beautifully. But somehow, I wasn't completely satisfied. There was a certain frustration in publicizing careers over which I had no control. Why stop at marketing soap when you think you can help make the soap itself even better? If I booked artists' performances myself, I thought, I could be even more effective in helping to develop their careers. I could earn more, too. In short, I wanted to manage.

In fact, I had already started making my first tentative steps into management a few years before.

One day in 1963, I put on my stereo a recording that had come into my office from somebody I knew at Epic Records, a subsidiary of the Columbia label. It was a performance of *Iberia*, by Isaac Albéniz, played by a Spanish pianist I'd never heard of. She was terrific.

I said, "Jesus, if this lady can play the piano in real life like she plays on this recording, she must be incredible. Who is this woman?"

Piano is another one of my great passions. That's why my friend at Epic had sent me this recording to begin with. I can hear right away if the performance is good or not. And I knew that this woman I was listening to was really, really good.

Her name was Alicia de Larrocha.

Alicia is a tiny little woman, less than five feet tall, with tiny but incredibly strong hands. She wasn't completely unknown, at least not in the piano world. Artur Rubinstein had known her since she made her recital debut; she was four years old at the time. She had studied with the Catalan pianist Frank Marshall, who was a student of the great Spanish pianist and composer Enrique Granados. She had made her American debut in the 1954–55 season: she appeared with the Los Angeles Philharmonic, and she gave a concert at Town Hall in New York. She got very good reviews. And she had made a few recordings for a Spanish label called Hispavox. It was one of these, rereleased by Epic, that I'd heard.

But for some reason nothing much was happening in her career. Managers seemed to be avoiding her. The general wisdom was that it was difficult for a woman pianist to have a major career. In those days, female keyboard stars were few and far between. There were some well-known ones, but they were seldom accepted on an equal footing with the men. Alicia was forty years old. She was not particularly glamorous, and she was rather shy. When she walked out on the stage, she walked slightly askew, so she wouldn't have to look at the audience. People didn't think she was, shall we say, star material. But by God, she could play the piano.

I did some research to find out how I could get hold of her, and I learned that she was living in Barcelona with her husband and two children, running the conservatory where she'd studied and practicing a lot.

I sat down and wrote her a letter. I said, "Dear Madame de Larrocha. My name is Herbert Breslin. I am a publicist for classical artists, and I think you are terrific, and I would like to bring you over to the States."

She didn't answer.

So I wrote her again. And again. And again. One thing about me is, if I want something, I'm not shy.

Alicia still didn't answer my letters. She thought I was some kind of crank.

There was only one thing to do. I went to Spain. She couldn't possibly ignore me, I reasoned, if I showed up in person.

Of course, I was right: she didn't ignore me. She couldn't, since there I was on her doorstep. She let me in, and I met her and her husband, who was himself a pianist, and they decided I wasn't a monster. Others in New York might have told them differently, but they trusted their own impressions. The Spanish are extremely reserved; our meeting didn't have the kind of warmth I might have encountered from an Italian family. We were all still feeling our way. Nonetheless, we got along quite well. And I persuaded Alicia that I was going to bring her to New York.

I was a publicist, not a manager. Publicists are supposed to get the press to pay attention to bookings that have already been made; they aren't supposed to go out and get the bookings themselves. But Alicia didn't have any bookings for me to publicize. If I wanted to work with her, I would have to take on a slightly different role. I was ready for the challenge. I was already convinced I was a better manager than anyone in the business. I just didn't have the experience to back it up.

I called up everybody I could think of. I called up Ronald Wilford, the omnipotent manager at Columbia Artists Management International, an agency known to all and sundry as CAMI. Ron was a friend of mine. He was also a manager, and I wasn't. I said, "Ron, this woman is terrific. Let's try to get something for her." Ron was happy to share Alicia with me. Officially, he was her manager; I was her representative.

Then I got hold of Carlos Moseley, the manager of the New York Philharmonic. Carlos, it turned out, had already heard Alicia's recordings and been as impressed as I was. It was not difficult to persuade him to book her for her debut with the Philharmonic.

But I didn't want Alicia to come all the way over just for one performance. Although books and movies may lead you to believe differently, one performance, even if it's a smashing success, seldom counts for much. It can certainly get the artist's name out there, but that name will be forgotten again equally quickly unless you keep it in the public eye. Birgit Nilsson, as we've seen, had learned that.

I thought Alicia should give a New York recital, as well. I contacted a friend of mine named Norman Singer. Norman ran a recital series at Hunter College in New York that used to present all the leading artists. A lot of those artists were people I represented, so Norman and I had become very tight.

"Norman," I said, "this woman is terrific."

Norman thought that was just fine.

"You're always putting on the same old people all the time," I said. "Why don't you put on somebody new? I'm telling you, she's terrific."

"I'll think about it," Norman said.

Left to himself, he might have let things go at that. But you can't leave these people to themselves. That's not how this business works. So I kept battering at him about it.

One night I was at Hunter for some recital or other and I was talking to Norman at intermission, when Howard Klein, who was a critic for the *New York Times* in those days, came up to us. I knew that Howard had written favorable reviews of Alicia's recordings.

"Howard," I said, making sure that Norman was listening, "what do you think of Alicia de Larrocha?"

"Oh, she's great," Howard said warmly.

"You see?" I said to Norman. "This comes from a completely unbiased source. A *Times* critic."

"Oh, all right, all right, all right," said Norman. "I'll engage her, on your say-so. But I can't pay her much. I'll give her a thousand dollars."

"I don't care what you pay her," I said. "Just put her on."

So Norman did. I think he just wanted to get me off his back.

Alicia came to New York in 1965 for her Philharmonic debut and her Hunter College recital ten days later. Her Philharmonic debut came off very well. It was an auspicious beginning. But you couldn't call it a howling success. The reason was that she played Mozart's Concerto no. 23 in A Major, and you don't wow people with a Mozart concerto unless you're already world famous. It's very nice and very respectable, but it doesn't create the same effect as, say, the Tchaikovsky First, with all its fireworks and drama.

Things were a little different at the Hunter College recital. That was quite an event from the outset. Everybody who was anybody in the piano world had turned out to hear what this little lady could do. In the audience that night was a veritable gallery of the greatest pianists of the day: Rubinstein, Rudy Firkusny, Gina Bachauer, Claudio Arrau. Harold Schonberg, the chief music critic of the *Times*, who had given a warm review to Alicia's Town Hall recital ten years before, brought binoculars so he could get a better view of the way her fingers moved around the keyboard. Indeed, it was a truly fantastic sight. Schonberg evidently thought so, too, because his review the following Monday ran under the headline "The Extraordinary Pianism of Alicia de Larrocha."

Being a good press agent, I had hundreds of copies of that review printed up large and sent to everybody I could think of. And I tried to figure out the next step. I thought Alicia had to follow up this success with something even bigger. I decided to put her on at Carnegie Hall.

Presenting concerts is a wonderful way to lose your shirt. Renting out Carnegie Hall is no small risk. You're talking about a couple thousand dollars just for the hall, even in those days, and that's not even counting the personnel costs: backstage, box office, coat room. You have to advertise in the papers, which is another huge chunk of cash—it's even worse today because ad rates in the *New York Times* have gotten so high. And you have to sell 2,800 tickets to fill the place. Very few artists are able to sell out Carnegie Hall.

I think I paid Alicia all of $500 to start with. I said to her, "Look, if I make money, you'll make money."

And I promoted it. If I'm going to take the risk of actually presenting something myself, with my own money, I promote the hell out of it. Television, the radio, the newspapers—you name it. By this point, I had a staff working for me, so I could put several people on the job—and on the phone. "What about the talk shows? Did you call the *Times*? What about *Ed Sullivan*?" I didn't let up for a minute. I was thinking of those 2,800 seats. And I don't believe in losing money. I believe in making money. This belief turned out to be a good one to have, because I never lost money presenting an artist.

Well, almost never. I have to admit that Alicia didn't sell out Carnegie Hall that first time I put her on. But I kept at it. I was convinced the only way to sell her out was to keep bringing her back until she caught on. So I put her on at Carnegie Hall again. I was right, too. She did catch on. Eventually, Carnegie Hall started presenting her itself.

And once she caught on, Alicia never looked back. She came to the United States every year. She appeared more than ninety times with the New York Philharmonic, and with just about every other major orchestra, all over the world, in every piece you can imagine, from Mozart to the Catalan composer Federico Mompou. Her repertoire was incredible. And in the Spanish stuff—*Iberia*, Granados's *Goyescas*, things of that sort—she was simply incomparable. After all those years she spent at home practicing, she was extremely well prepared. She committed a lot of that repertoire to recordings, first with Decca, later with BMG. Those were all contracts I helped to get her. Ron Wilford and I continued to "share" Alicia; my official title remained "personal representative." Whatever you called me, I built up a pretty impressive career for her. I thought of all kinds of things for her to do. I had her come to the Mostly Mozart Festival, another client of mine. I had the idea that she should do a recital at Hunter College with another Spanish artist, Victoria de los Angeles. In the end, some people said I overexposed her. Which just goes to show that when you're successful, people will say all kinds of things.

Alicia was widely recognized as one of the greatest pianists—male or female—of her generation. She retired when she was eighty, in 2003. Our relationship lasted for forty years. Most of my relationships with artists have been very long-lasting. Except, of course, for the ones that weren't.

Alicia de Larrocha

Once, in Barcelona, when a letter came from New York, my husband and I were very suspicious because the letter said "public relations" and there was a picture of a trumpet on it.

My husband's first reaction was, "Who is this nut who wants to steal our money? Those Americans—always thinking about money— money—money!"

So, we threw away the letter. And that happened three times.

Finally, somebody told us that that trumpet fellow was really honest. So I decided to come to the United States, and that "trumpet fellow" be-

*came my angel of good luck and, even more important, a very dear and
special friend.*

---

*So now, Herb, I'm giving you with all my heart full of love,
these good-luck trumpets, which I hope will bring you all the
happiness you deserve.*

This letter hangs framed over my desk, together with two
copies of the trumpet from my letterhead, which Alicia had cast
in solid gold.

Alicia's success helped confirm some of the theories I was developing about managing artists. It seemed like a logical extension
of what I was already doing as a publicist. When you're publicizing an artist, you have to have a strategy. You have to think about
the big picture. It doesn't help, for example, to get a feature in the
Sunday *New York Times* for an artist who's just making his first
concert appearances in New York. Even if you could get the
newspaper to print it, people would read it and then forget about
it. You want that article to appear at a time when the artist is performing in New York and Boston, and has some California dates
in a few months, and has a recording coming out. That way, the
name keeps bobbing up in the public eye and people start to remember it.

It's the same thing with managing: you have to think of the
bigger picture. Where should this artist be aiming to go? What
kind of audience can he appeal to? Where are his strengths now?
What area do we need to work on? But that kind of thinking is
all too rare among managers. Today, especially, there are very few
managers who create careers. Most of them seem just to be interested in taking whatever booking comes along. The point
seems to be getting as many concerts as you can for your artists,
like a cop writing traffic tickets to fill a quota. Never mind trying to make a plan for the next five years.

I came to the conclusion that if you want to get anywhere, you
have to manage the artist as well as publicize him. It's the only

way that you can really work on developing an artist. You have to be able to manage and publicize and do everything at the same time. Because you have certain objectives. You have to have a plan. Where do we want to go? What's the next thing we can achieve?

Ultimately, this philosophy came to mean the difference between Luciano Pavarotti's career and everybody else's.

One idea that interested me was booking recitals. Recitals aren't every singer's cup of tea. At the time Luciano came along, they were in something of a decline. They tended to be given either by lieder singers or by aging opera singers who weren't quite up to the demands of an opera role but who in a recital could transpose the song literature down as low as they wanted without raising any eyebrows. And recitals tended to be rather staid, formal affairs. But I didn't see why they had to be that way. I was very interested in an article I read by Henry Pleasants, a respected music writer, in the 1960s on what could be done to reanimate the song recital. I thought that showcasing a young artist, in a mixture of opera arias and songs (rather than the traditional song-only format), might be a way. And it seemed to me that, done properly, a recital could be a wonderful tool for helping an artist win a wider public.

Recitals, you see, are quite intimate. On the recital stage, you can't hide behind your costume, your character, the other singers, the conductor. It's just you onstage in front of the public, and you have to sing the whole evening. This is one reason a lot of opera singers aren't too fond of doing recitals. But if they work, then the public connects with you—not the role you're singing, but *you*, the performer.

At that time, I had two young tenors on my client roster; I did publicity for both. I approached both of them about the idea of singing recitals. One was Luciano. The other was a young Spanish tenor named Plácido Domingo.

Luciano and Plácido seemed fated to be linked from the beginning. Not that they were at all the same kind of tenor. Luciano was a lyric tenor who specialized in bel canto roles and shining high Cs. Plácido was a more dramatic tenor who leaned toward verismo opera and heavier roles, and top notes have never been his forte, as he himself will readily admit. Once, Johnny Carson had Plácido on the *Tonight Show*. "Are you nervous on a day when you know you have high Cs to sing in the evening?" Carson asked.

"Oh, no," said Plácido. "I've never had a high C."

As different as they were, however, Luciano and Plácido had a lot in common. When they started out, they were the two most promising young tenors of their generation. They both made their debuts at the Metropolitan Opera the same year, 1968. They were both extremely ambitious. They both had that intangible dynamic that characterizes artists who are going to be a big success, which is something you don't find very frequently.

And from the very beginning, they were both pretty savvy about publicity. Whatever one had, the other wanted. They used to open up the newspaper in the morning, and if one saw that the other had gotten an article, he'd call me up and bawl me out.

To me, these two young tenors were the ideal candidates for testing my ideas about song recitals. I sounded out Plácido about the idea. He wasn't especially interested. Plácido was very involved with opera, learning new roles and doing as many of them as he could. And Plácido never listened to me.

Luciano was quite the opposite. He was amenable to anything, and he knew a good idea when he heard it. In those days, if I'd said, "Luciano, we're doing a concert on the moon," he would have said, "Fine, let's go. Just make sure it's sold out."

So on the heels of his success in *Daughter of the Regiment*, I set up three recitals for Luciano.

I thought I might try booking other things for him, as well. I was spending so much time working on Luciano's career, and I had so many ideas for it, that I thought I should take the next step, beyond simply acting as his publicist.

I said, "I would like to manage you."

He was fine with that, too. As I said, Luciano knew a good idea when he heard it.

I had to end my working relationship with Plácido. Two tenors was one tenor too many. To this day, his wife, Marta, regards me as something of a traitor. At least, she looks daggers at me if ever she has the misfortune to encounter me backstage.

And so I began to manage the career of Luciano Pavarotti.

chapter IV

HOW TO MANAGE A TENOR:
AN INTRODUCTION

Launching the Greatest Career
of a Generation

In 1972, I went to Modena for the first time. By then, Luciano and I were like family.

I had had friendly relationships with my clients before. Joan and Ricky and I, for example, would sometimes go out to dinner when they were in town. I once took Joan to see *A Funny Thing Happened on the Way to the Forum*, on Broadway—Burt Shevelove, who wrote the book for it, had produced Joan on the *Bell Telephone Hour*—and we sat there laughing our heads off. But still, there was a certain reserve.

There was no reserve with Luciano. We were on the phone ten, twelve, a hundred times a day. When he was in town, I ran over to his apartment—first in the Hotel Navarro, later in the Hampshire House—at least once a day, to discuss something or other. There was always something to talk about. We had infinite amounts to say. Not only were we both working intensely on his blossoming career, we were also laying the groundwork of a good, strong friendship. My whole office was at his disposal.

Not that he ever actually came to my office. In fact, in thirty-six years, Luciano Pavarotti never once set foot there. We went to him.

And I went to him at home in Modena many times. But as close as I was to Luciano, and although we'd worked together for five years, my first immersion in Italian culture felt very, very unfamiliar. Luciano was the most generous of hosts. He brought out sausages from the cellar, and cases of Lambrusco, the young sparkling wine, fizzy as a delicate soda pop; that's his favorite beverage. (It is, he'll happily tell even grizzled oenophiles, the best wine in the world.) But partly because Luciano is so generous, his table—and, indeed, his home—is always crowded with people. There was a cluster of immediate family and extended family and people who came along who might or might not have been family. With my still limited command of Italian, it was hard to keep track of them.

His wife, Adua, of course, I knew and already felt close to. She had her hands full. Not only did she still manage all of the couple's financial affairs, but she had their three small daughters, Lorenza, Cristina, and Giuliana, with whom she was left on her own a lot of the time.

Then there was Fernando, Luciano's father, still looking somewhat skeptically at his son's success, and full of advice and observations about singing—and about tenors who knew how to do it better than Luciano. And there was Adele, Luciano's querulous mother, who went through life complaining about her ailments. Adele's great claim to fame was that she never once attended a performance by her famous son; the nervousness that seeing him onstage would cause her would be too much, she said, for her weak heart. (That weak heart managed to pump her through eighty-six years in this vale of tears, but it seemed to require an inordinate number of ministrations from those around her along the way.)

And there were countless others. I tried to keep them all

straight. There was Gabriella, Luciano's sister, fondly known as Lela, and Lucca, her son, wheelchair-bound from birth. There was Franco Casarini, whom everybody calls Panoccia, Luciano's oldest and closest friend from boyhood, who was to remain his sidekick and card-playing partner throughout their lives. There were other friends and relations. Adua had something like eight sisters, and there was always an aunt or two around. It's no wonder Luciano had big tables in all his homes. He needed them.

Enjoyable as it was, I felt uncharacteristically ill at ease. It would take me a while to get my bearings among these people. And the feeling of strangeness only intensified when it came time to go to sleep. Air-conditioning still doesn't enjoy the popularity in Italy that it does in this country, and thirty years ago it was virtually unknown. It was summer, and I was boiling. I opened the windows as wide as they would go. To Modena's insect life, this was a sign of veritable Pavarotti-like hospitality. A cloud of mosquitoes streamed in and circled my defenseless body, whining past my ears before settling to take a bite out of yet another portion of my anatomy.

Sleep was impossible. At least there was a phone by my bed. Part of my discomfort may have derived from a few hours of enforced separation from this essential instrument of my daily life. I decided to call home. Unfortunately, I had neglected to commit to memory the requisite dialing codes. I resorted to a process of trial and error. Patience, unfortunately, is not one of my virtues, especially when I'm short of sleep. I wanted to get the damn phone to work. I started dialing numbers almost at random.

Suddenly, my own phone rang, shrilling loudly in the midnight silence.

"Herbert," said Luciano's sleepy voice, "what are you doing? That is an intercom by your bed. It is connected to all the other bedrooms. You are waking up everyone in the house!"

I was mortified. It seemed like the worst possible entrée to a family I didn't know. But perhaps it broke the ice. They were all very nice about it the next morning. As the day wore on, I became subject to a certain amount of ribbing. I gave as good as I got. "Why don't you people have screens in this country?" I said. "I'm going to have to buy you a set."

I may not have known it then, but Luciano's immediate family was ultimately to become almost as close to me as my own. I have tremendous affection for Luciano and Adua and the three girls. I didn't have to buy those screens, though. Ever accommodating, Luciano simply moved to a new house, where I never had another mosquito problem.

Of course, I was at the receiving end of plenty of late-night Pavarotti phone calls myself. One night in New York, Carol and I were yanked from a deep sleep by the sound of the ringing phone. Groping my way out of bed, I was sure someone had died, as you always are when the phone rings in the early hours of the morning.

But no one had died. It was Luciano.

"Herbertino," he said, "can you give me the number of Kurt Herbert Adler in San Francisco? I have misplaced it."

"Christ, Luciano, do you know what time it is?!" I said. "It's three o'clock in the morning!"

"Oh, no, it's all right," said Luciano reassuringly. "It's perfectly all right. It's only midnight in San Francisco. He will still be awake."

Sometimes it can be difficult to know whether Luciano is teasing you or not.

From the beginning, Luciano wasn't like any other artist I had worked for. For one thing, there was that voice. The sound of his voice always floored me. I would get goose pimples. Let me be clear: when you're working for artists, it doesn't really matter what you, as a listener, think of what they're doing. After a few years of hearing them sing, or play, or whatever it is they do, over and over, you may not be quite as captivated by their artistry as you were at the beginning. There's nothing wrong with this, and it doesn't mean they're bad artists; it's only natural. So I didn't have to get goose pimples when I heard Luciano sing. They weren't, shall we say, part of the job description. But I did, every time. It was just so damn beautiful.

Luciano's attitude was also different from that of other artists. His savvy about public relations had already demonstrated that he had a particular kind of dynamism that was rare. He was alert, he was active, he was amenable. Whatever you asked him to do, he did it and he did it brilliantly, and he had an idea of why you were asking him. He didn't question. These qualities were all part of the intangible package that indicated to me he had the potential to become a very, very big star. And that gave me the incentive to work harder myself.

I think my approach appealed to Luciano. When I met him, he hadn't really had anybody working for him. His first agent in Italy, Alessandro Ziliani, would get him engagements and take a commission; fine. But the idea of having somebody give you ideas or come up with ways to propel you forward is not in the Italian vocabulary. When Luciano first got to New York, having an agent work for him was probably the last thing he thought he needed. But after we started talking, he quickly recognized the advantages I was offering. It wasn't just a question of getting him his next engagement in Athens or Paris or San Francisco; it meant devising a comprehensive plan of attack. Luciano liked what I was doing for him. He liked me. He liked my style, he liked my freshness, and maybe he even liked my rudeness. And I loved the guy. Everybody loved the guy.

So what was my plan for Luciano? Figure out our objectives, keep him in the public eye, and make sure that each step we take is a step forward. Everything that we did had to have some sort of strategic meaning. Unless, of course, there was nothing else on the calendar and they were offering him a lot of money.

Another part of my strategy: get him out of the opera house. The Metropolitan Opera was a death trap.

On the face of it, that sounds absurd. Opera singers, after all, are trained to sing in opera houses. And the Metropolitan Opera has the reputation of being one of the leading houses—if not *the* leading house—in the world. Singers work their whole careers to sing there. Why would you want to leave?

Well, I didn't want him to leave altogether. Luciano, of course, would continue to appear at the Met until the very end of his career. But I thought it was important for him to develop other options.

Opera houses, for one thing, tie you down. When you sign on to do a production, you commit to several weeks of rehearsals. During that time, you're not earning very much money. (One option, of course, is to skip the rehearsals, but that wasn't an option Luciano would take until later in his career.) You're also limited financially in an opera house. You can't go any higher than the house's top fee. Well, most of the time you can't.

The three major opera houses in America are the Metropolitan Opera, the San Francisco Opera, and the Chicago Lyric Opera. The Met, until 1972, was ruled by Mr. Bing. Mr. Bing would never go over his top fee, but there were a few ways to bend the rules. If your artist was going to spend, say, eight weeks in New York, you could negotiate a contract that meant he was getting paid for the equivalent of a performance and a half a week, or twelve performances. Sometimes, people negotiated contracts for even more performances. That doesn't necessarily mean they sang them all. In 1972, however, Bing retired, and the Met entered a shaky period, artistically and financially. There was a new policy that the house was to have an open, democratic, populist face—partly because there wasn't enough money to do anything more elaborate. These financial constraints, naturally enough, put an end to all hanky-panky with the number of performances in a singer's contract.

In Chicago, until 1980, you had Carol Fox, who cofounded the Lyric Opera in 1954. Carol was a bitch on wheels. If Luciano showed up late, for instance, she'd get on the phone and say something sharp to me in her rude little way. "Well, Carol," I'd say, "you've gotta take it or leave it." All these people had to contend with me when they were dealing with Luciano. Carol, however, was a very savvy opera administrator. Chicago used to have wonderful lineups. All the big international singers would go there to try out their roles before they came to New York; she had a lot of major American debuts. Carol also had a top fee, but she wouldn't tell you what it was. If you approached her the right way, there was usually some leeway there—sometimes as much as a couple of thousand dollars per performance.

San Francisco was different, at least for Luciano, because San Francisco was like home. Kurt Herbert Adler, the Viennese patriarch of the house, held sway for more than twenty-five years. Kurt loved Luciano. He was Viennese, so sometimes he screamed at him—or screamed at me, in lieu of him—but nonetheless, he would do anything for him. He offered Luciano parts Luciano wanted to try out for the first time, and he had the coaches there to teach them to him. And Luciano had a whole circle of friends there. He was always happy to go to San Francisco. And Kurt was happy to pay him.

So those were the big American opera houses. But when you think about it, three opera houses isn't much to hang a career on. If you get too dependent on any one theater and then somebody decides not to engage you one season, you're out of luck. It's important for an artist to develop other resources.

It's also important to remember that if you're singing in New York, Chicago, and San Francisco, you're not singing in thousands of other cities and towns across the country. The U.S.A. is a big place. To really succeed, it seemed to me, you needed a presence everywhere, all over the country. Luciano concurred 100 percent. He was always eager to come to his public. Every single audience member was important.

I often had occasion to remember this after a performance, when fans lined up backstage to see him. Luciano would greet each one individually, exchange a few words, sign their programs, offer one of his incomparable smiles to their flashbulbs. As I said before, patience is not one of my strong points, and this colloquy rapidly grew tedious.

"Luciano, come on," I'd say, shifting from foot to foot. "This is ridiculous. It's twelve-thirty in the morning! Let's go home!"

"*Calmati*," Pavarotti would reply. "Calm down. We are not going to leave until I have seen the last person." And we didn't.

One major factor in Luciano's independence from the opera

house—and one way he got his name around the country—was his record contract with Decca. Luciano has been an exclusive artist with Decca virtually from the beginning (apart from one very nice recording he made with Mirella Freni for EMI, Mascagni's light little opera *L'Amico Fritz*). That record company was a very powerful thing for Luciano to have in his corner, and not only because it earned him the privilege of dozens of postperformance dinners courtesy of Terry McEwen. In those days, back when classical record companies actually sold records, the labels put a lot of muscle—and a lot of money—into supporting their artists. As I said, record signings were a major event. Luciano once did a record signing at Sam Goody's that lasted more than seven hours. We didn't get out of there until after midnight.

So Decca was actively helping to push Luciano, all the time. After his success in *Daughter of the Regiment*, people started calling him "King of the High Cs." Decca jumped on it and issued a compilation album—excerpts of things Luciano had already recorded—with that title. It sold like gangbusters. He later made a television special with the same name. Plácido Domingo, who didn't have an exclusive recording contract with anybody, didn't have that kind of power behind him, and I think his career suffered for it, although he certainly made a lot of recordings.

But Luciano, as he got better and better known, decided he wasn't happy with the way Decca was treating him. Basically, he wanted more money. If an artist says he's not happy with something or other about his business affairs, don't be fooled: it's always about money. He wants more of it. Luciano insisted that I make an appointment for the two of us to fly over to Zurich to talk to Moritz Rosengarten.

By now, Rosengarten had overcome his initial reluctance concerning Luciano. Artists who sell a lot of records have a way of becoming very popular with record-label brass very quickly. More than that, though, Rosengarten genuinely liked Luciano. He used to send him gold Rolex watches and things like that.

That was all very nice, but it wasn't what was on Luciano's

mind. He was thinking about advances and royalties. One thing singers don't like about record contracts is that your initial payment is an advance against the money your records are going to make in the future. In other words, when the money from sales starts coming in, you have to earn back your advance before you can get any more money. Luciano didn't want an advance; he wanted a payment. But, of course, he wanted royalties, too. He wanted to get paid for making the recording, and in addition he wanted to start getting royalties as soon as the record hit the market.

So off to Zurich we went, and we were ushered into Rosengarten's swank office.

"How do you do, Mr. Pavalotti?" Rosengarten said.

"Pavarotti," Luciano corrected him, his Italian diction at its most precise.

"Yes, Mr. Pavalotti," Rosengarten said, unperturbed. "How very nice to see you. Please sit down."

"Pava-ROT-ti," Luciano said again.

"You wanted to see me, Mr. Pavalotti," said Mr. Rosengarten, settling into a chair. "What was it you wanted to talk about?"

Rosengarten was not naïve. He knew exactly what Luciano wanted to talk about. He had been dealing with artists for years.

Luciano, less experienced than he and goaded by the mispronunciation of his name, began to explain what he wanted to talk about. In a matter of seconds, he was launched into a full-blown diatribe of truly operatic proportions. He touched on his royalties, his advances, his promotions, his repertoire. Rosengarten certainly had things to say in response. He tried to say them. But he hadn't learned from Joan Sutherland how to support his voice. His attempts at interjection were drowned out in a flood of impassioned, Italian-accented verbiage.

He finally stood up and lifted a heavy glass ashtray from his desk. That got Luciano's attention, and he paused.

"Mr. Pavalotti," Rosengarten said, "this is an ashtray. When I am holding it, it is my turn to speak. Then, when I give it to you and you are holding it, you will speak. That way, everyone can be heard."

Luciano looked at him in astonishment. Then he laughed. The tension was broken. There was no great cause for tension to begin with. Mr. Rosengarten was no fool. He was only too glad to come up with a contract that would please Luciano, who, after all, was a major player for Decca. Luciano remained an exclusive Decca artist for the rest of his career. Decca had no reason to quarrel with him.

I'm not sure how many other singers had deals like that, but I wouldn't think too many. Not many have the clout. I've heard that Giulietta Simionato, a wonderful Italian mezzo of the 1950s, wouldn't sign a contract that involved royalties. She always wanted to be paid fully up front. I can understand her thinking. The whole royalty business is very strange. Most royalty payments are probably inaccurate, anyway. You can't keep track of them, because the record company just gives you a printout with the number of records sold. Whether what they say there is accurate or not is open to question.

The other major factor in establishing Luciano's independence from the opera house was recitals. Those were my babies.

Opera, as I said, has the financial disadvantage that you're restricted by the rehearsal period, and limited to the house's top fee. With recitals, you don't have that problem. For a recital, you can ask for as much as they'll pay you. As Luciano and I were later to prove time and time again.

To tell the truth, though, Luciano didn't care about the money at the beginning. In the early years, he never asked me how much he was going to get paid for a recital. He only had one condition: it had to be sold out. That kind of thinking shows an extraordinary degree of intelligence. If you want great publicity and huge success, there's no better way than having your concerts sell out. It's a gold-plated calling card.

For one of his early recitals, however, a presenter—an Italian singer, no less—stiffed Luciano. She booked him for a recital in

Providence, Rhode Island; he came, he sang, and she never paid him. Of course, at that point in Luciano's career, we're only talking about $4,000. Then again, at that point in his career, $4,000 mattered more than it would matter later. Luciano was furious.

"We must suit her," he said.

Luciano often threatened to "suit" somebody or other. He never got the word quite right, but he seemed to have the concept of legal action down cold. He didn't actually "suit" anybody, to the best of my recollection, but he was crazy about the idea.

He never let me forget about that concert. He brought it up all the time. When I got tired of hearing about it, I would point out, "Well, you know, that presenter was one of your Italian friends." That would shut him up in a hurry.

After that, he modified his conditions a little bit. He had three rules for every concert. The event had to be sold out, he had to get his fee, and nobody could lose any money. That proved to be a very good formula. It made everybody happy. Nobody lost any money on Luciano. Least of all Luciano himself.

The other advantage of a recital is that you can go anywhere. All you need is a stage, a piano, and your evening clothes. You can appear in small towns and large, and Luciano did.

But there are downsides, too. In an opera, you may have only two or three big numbers in an evening; in recital, you have to sing for more than an hour. This means preparing a large amount of music—never Luciano's strong suit. There's no prompter sitting by the footlights to help you when you forget the words. And you have to be ready to face the audience, only a few feet away.

"Could you cope with that?" I said to Luciano.

Luciano thought he could.

Which is how, on February 1, 1973, we found ourselves at William Jewell College, a little Baptist college in Liberty, Missouri, waiting in the wings of an 800-seat theater that was, of course, sold out.

I wanted to put Luciano on at Carnegie Hall. But Carnegie

Hall is not a good place to launch experiments. So I booked three recitals for him, a kind of mini-tour. I thought starting small was a good idea. William Jewell College had a wonderful little auditorium, and a philanthropist had left it a fund of money that enabled it to attract an array of important artists. From there, we would go on to Dallas and end up at Carnegie Hall. By then, he would be nicely warmed up and a little more accustomed to the process.

It was a good thing I did that. Because Luciano, of course, got a cold just before we left.

Working with opera singers is a recipe for nervous collapse. The more carefully you make your plans, the more likely it is that they'll get sick when the big night rolls around. "Oh, my God," I said, "what are we going to do?"

Sara Tucker, Richard Tucker's wife, was a great help. Being married to a leading tenor—the man who, as I said, regarded himself as the greatest tenor in the world—she was well used to dealing with the breed. She would ring Luciano's doorbell and come up with that all-powerful curative, chicken soup. Italian and Jewish wisdom intersect on a few key issues, and the restorative power of soup is one of them. Luciano chugged away at it, and coughed, and blew his nose. Being in the presence of a singer with a cold is impressive. The training that enables them to make their voices heard in huge spaces also amplifies their coughs, sneezes, and nose blows to epic proportions.

Cold or no cold, we decided to give it a try, boarded the plane, and flew out to Kansas City. Liberty is just outside Kansas City, but Liberty didn't have the kind of accommodations that would suit even a rising opera singer. Luciano wasn't yet as demanding as he would later become, but he did require a certain level of care. He was favorably impressed with the Presidential Suite at Kansas City's Muhlenbach Hotel. We kept the chicken soup coming. And the night of the performance found Luciano, suited up and ready to go, about to take the stage with his accompanist, Eugene Kohn.

I've been given credit for pushing a handkerchief into his hand at this key point. Despite what people say about me, however, I cannot tell a lie: it wasn't me. The handkerchief was Luciano's idea. Since he had a cold, it was a logical prop that evening. Of course, it also solved the recitalist's age-old problem of what to do with his hands when he sings. For Luciano, especially at the beginning, the handkerchief helped. Not only could he use it for regular handkerchief functions, wiping his nose or his brow; he could wave it at the crowd, use it for emphasis in a song, or use it as a hiding place for throat lozenges. All kinds of things went onstage in that handkerchief as the years passed. It became his trademark and remained, throughout his career, a versatile prop.

Song recitals are tough even for veteran singers. Often, you see singers backed into the curve of the grand piano as if seeking shelter, standing stiffly, hands locked together, with the glazed expression of a deer in headlights. We avoided that problem by turning the piano. We did this in such a way that Luciano could see the pianist very easily, and also see the words. While Luciano excelled at committing notes to memory, he seemed, throughout his career, to have trouble keeping the proper words attached to them. We didn't want to risk a memory slip at his very first recital, especially with some of the things we'd come up with for him to sing, like three songs by Ottorino Respighi, an early-twentieth-century composer who wasn't necessarily someone you'd associate with Luciano.

But that night, he sang the words beautifully. Adrenaline, and the heat of the footlights, helped drive away the cold for the duration of the performance, and Luciano's first U.S. recital was a resounding success. We didn't have a lot of press there that night. I tried to keep the whole thing as low-key as possible and save the press for Carnegie Hall. Still, that recital was a kind of epochal event. In fact, in years to come, an American recital debut at William Jewell College became a rite of passage for young tenors. Francisco Araiza, Ben Heppner, Marcelo Álvarez, and Juan Diego Flórez all followed suit.

The recital in Dallas also went extremely well. But most important, of course, was the Carnegie Hall recital on February 18. I wanted to make sure Luciano was very, very prepared, so I rented out the hall one afternoon before the recital and had him run through the whole thing, full voice. There were all of six people in the audience. Foremost among them were Joan Sutherland and Ricky Bonynge, and Luciano was really singing for them. He sang his heart out and came down to us in the auditorium afterward, glowing and a little breathless from the exertion.

"Joan, we fat people know how it is," he said, wiping his brow. Joan gave him a cool stare in her best diva manner.

"Luciano," she said, "*we* are not fat. *You* are fat. *I* am big."

For that first Carnegie recital, I wanted to process the ticket requests from my own office. It seemed the best way for me to gauge where we stood at that point in his career. Plus, the Carnegie Hall box office charged something like a hundred dollars a day to provide ticket services, and that seemed like an expense we could cut out until the day of the concert, when it was absolutely necessary for last-minute returns and things like that.

Of course, I was also promoting the event like crazy. I took out a big ad in the Sunday *New York Times* announcing that Pavarotti would be appearing in recital.

On Monday, I arrived at the office and had trouble opening the door. There seemed to be some kind of obstruction. What it was, it turned out, was a pile of envelopes containing checks and ticket orders. They were stacked up inside the mail slot, three feet deep. That was the first real indication I had that something was going on here that was not happening with anybody else. No one else was drawing that kind of public.

The demand was so tremendous that we had to seat people on the stage. By the time Luciano came out, the atmosphere in that hall was electric. And Luciano was ready. His cold was gone; he had his handkerchief; he had his big smile; he looked terrific. He made his entrance to a tremendous ovation, and things just kept building from there. The practice in Missouri and Texas had paid off. He was in top form. It was a pretty nice program, and he was comfortable with it, and the applause went on for what seemed like hours. And the reviews were every bit as ecstatic as the audience had been. Luciano was simply irresistible. There were a number of moments when you could say that Pavarotti, the star, was born; that first Carnegie Hall recital was one of them.

Recitals became a big part of Luciano's career. But they were only a part. We never had just one thing going on. We always tried to have five, six, seven events coming up. One thing followed another, and all of them, of course, were very well publicized. We worked hard on keeping Luciano in the public eye. We were never shy about going out to find that public. Some big-name singers, for instance, tried to get out of doing the Metropolitan Opera's annual national tour, when the company used to go on the road to present opera in smaller cities around the country. It was a big hassle, and it wasn't as prestigious as appearing at the Met itself. Luciano, however, was willing to go on those tours. He understood the importance of reaching out to his public. And they loved him for it.

Nonetheless, the Metropolitan Opera remained a fly in the ointment. Despite Luciano's many triumphs at that house, he never felt he was their preferred tenor. He often felt slighted in favor of Plácido Domingo.

Mr. Bing, as I said, didn't have much use for Luciano. The situation didn't improve after his departure. By the late seventies, a power troika had emerged with Anthony Bliss as general director, James Levine as music director, and John Dexter, the stage director, in charge of productions. Jimmy and John had great artistic goals for the theater. John was a director who excelled at minimal, modern productions. He was brilliant with pieces like Poulenc's *Dialogues of the Carmelites*, a wonderful opera from 1957. The Met still has its Dexter production of that opera, and it remains one of the best things they do. But John was less adept at the classic operas by Verdi and Puccini. You don't necessarily want a minimalist, abstract *Aida*. And Luciano, of course, was not the best person in the world to carry out John's ideas. Acting was never Luciano's strong point. He wasn't a singer who was going to plumb the psychological depths of a character, even if he'd known how to go about it. So he and John didn't really connect.

Back then, it was the same story with Jimmy. Jimmy wanted to explore a wide repertory of different kinds of opera. Jimmy has never made a secret of his ambivalence about bel canto opera, which was Luciano's big strength at the time. His interests lay with pieces like Berg's *Lulu*, which is atonal, very difficult, and not anything Luciano would ever get near with a ten-foot pole. The perfect tenor to explore Jimmy's interests with him was Plácido Domingo. Say what you will about Plácido, he's always had a tremendously wide-ranging repertoire, and he learns fast. So Jimmy and Plácido became very thick. Luciano felt he was excluded from the inner circle.

It was driven home to him when the Met discussed with me a new production of Verdi's *Rigoletto* in 1977. The Duke, the opera's leading tenor role, was to become one of Luciano's strongest characters. The role of the libertine, carefree, heartless womanizer, with its famous aria "La donna è mobile," fit him like a glove, in more ways than one. The Met offered Luciano the new production's opening night. And then, lo and behold, they withdrew the offer. Opening night went to Plácido.

Of course, we were furious. But what can you do? As a manager, you have very few options in dealing with the Met. You can scream and yell, but all you're going to do that way is antagonize them, and then they won't have your artist back. In those days, I was always waiting for an axe to fall in our dealings with the Met. They didn't treat Luciano very honorably.

And yet we had to suck it up because they kept giving him work. While Luciano might not have been the administration's favorite tenor, they couldn't deny that he was certainly the public's. In 1977, the company began a big campaign to get their performances televised on PBS, part of their new policy of trying to attract a wider audience. *Live from the Met* lasted only a few years, partly because of the expense and partly because, frankly, there's nobody around in opera today whom a wider television audience is really all that interested in hearing and seeing. Several months ago, I was at a dinner party with some people from the Met, and one of them began bemoaning the fact that the Met couldn't get on television anymore.

I said, "Well, what the hell are you presenting that anyone wants to watch?"

She said, "Oh, HER-bert."

As I said, people at the Met are always saying "Oh, Herbert." At least, that's what they say to my face. Behind my back, I'm sure it's a lot worse.

Anyway, in 1977, no one yet knew that opera on television wasn't going to be a great new popular venture. One reason they didn't know was that their first broadcast was such a huge success. And no wonder. It was *La Bohème*, with Luciano Pavarotti as Rodolfo and Renata Scotto, the Met's reigning diva at the time, as Mimì.

Luciano, of course, was very excited, and very nervous, about doing this live performance. Make no mistake: no matter how many times he's sung, Luciano is always nervous before a performance. So is any artist worth his salt, for that matter.

To reassure himself that all would go well, he warmed up thoroughly in his dressing room, singing his aria "Che gelida manina" all the way through. It was stunningly beautiful, climaxing with a glorious high C.

"Go get 'em, Luciano," I said.

Somewhat cheered, Luciano made his entrance. Of course, he had no reason to be nervous. Rodolfo is, as I said, one of his signature roles. The bohemians clowning around in the garret; their departure for the café, leaving Rodolfo alone to finish writing his article; the entrance of Mimì, the little seamstress come to beg a light from her upstairs neighbors: all went beautifully. Mimì lost her house key; the two searched for it on the floor; and Rodolfo's hand happened to stray across Mimì's in the dark. "What a cold little hand," he sings. It was Luciano's first big moment, and he was singing gorgeously as he explained to Mimì what he did and who he was. Now that she had entered the room, he continued, all his dreams had vanished, but only because now—rising to the high C—"I'm filled with hope!"

Crack went Luciano's voice.

Actually, you're never supposed to say your singer cracked. You say he had catarrh. Whatever it was, it didn't sound very good. Luciano was very upset. But part of being a performer is getting over your mistakes and going on. Luciano continued for the rest of the evening and turned in a fine performance.

Perhaps nobody had told him that there was a scheduled interview feature at intermission. The network had decided to interview Renata Scotto. As I said, she was the Met's reigning diva at the time, so it made sense to have her on the air to talk a little bit about herself. It made sense to Scotto, that is. I don't think it made sense to Luciano.

Scotto may have made some kind of comment about colleagues and their attitudes. And Luciano may have construed an insult in that. Or maybe not. In any case, he paid the soprano a visit in her dressing room at the end of the night. "*Tu sei una bella ruffiana*," he told her: You're a fine ruffian. But in Italian, the connotation is much worse.

Perhaps he was annoyed by something she'd said. Or perhaps he simply thought she was trying to get too much attention for herself. *He* wouldn't have been a rascal, of course, if he had been the only artist interviewed for the intermission feature. Of course not.

Whatever it was, he never forgot it. I don't know if that was the start of it, but it certainly wasn't the end of the bad blood between the two.

Be that as it may, the broadcast was a tremendous success. It attracted the biggest television audience ever for an opera. Luciano's star continued to rise. A few days after that broadcast, a Hungarian soprano whom Decca was pushing like crazy, Sylvia

Sass, made her Met debut as Tosca, with José Carreras as her Cavaradossi. Ever the good colleagues—when it suited them—both Luciano and Plácido came out to hear her. Plácido happened to enter the auditorium first. As he came down the aisle, the audience, catching sight of him, broke into a round of applause. Plácido happily acknowledged it and took his seat—a prime seat, on the aisle, in the center of the orchestra section. Luciano was to be seated right behind him. And, perhaps not entirely coincidentally, Luciano came into the auditorium about thirty seconds after Plácido did. The audience was already primed for applause, and Luciano, of course, is easier to spot than Plácido. But more to the point, absolutely everyone had seen Luciano live on television just a few nights before. The theater exploded with a thunderous ovation. It must have been hard for Plácido to swallow. Over and over in their careers, circumstances made a rivalry between those two tenors hard to avoid.

Luciano was always first. First to give recitals, first to broadcast live from the Met. A year later, he became the first artist to give a solo recital, with piano, from the Met stage. That was also broadcast live on television, and it was also a big success.

But then, everything was a big success for Luciano in those days.

chapter V

LIFE WITH LUCIANO

The Tenor's Lighter—and Heavier—Side

W hat is Luciano Pavarotti like in private?" people often ask me.

"Well," I say, "Luciano doesn't make a great difference between his public and private personae. He's pretty much the same wherever he is. What you see is what you get."

"Ohhhh," people say. They think I'm being evasive.

The thing is, I'm not. It's true that there's very little division between Luciano's public and private selves. Picture the tenor as you know him from the stage or your television set: a big, outgoing presence. Now picture taking that presence and inviting it into your home for dinner. Believe me, it's a lot to contain in your living room.

Although I had been the recipient of Luciano's ready, generous hospitality, the prospect of reciprocating it was something else again. Luciano's house is basically set up to accommodate guests.

The central piece of furniture in all his residences—his New York apartment at the Hampshire House, his home in Modena, his summer house in Pesaro, his apartment in Monte Carlo—is a big table, right in the middle of the room. And anyone who crosses Luciano's threshold is inevitably greeted with the same question: "Do you want something to eat?" This is true even when the visitor is the doctor, summoned for a house call because of one of Luciano's innumerable maladies. Before the examination even begins, the doctor is practically ordered to sit down and have a plate of pasta. Luciano, of course, joins him; you wouldn't want a visitor to eat alone. Later, Luciano is very insulted when the doctor sends him a bill for his services. After all, the doctor was fed in his home, as a guest. Now you're beginning to understand the Italian mentality.

An important part of the equation is that, in his own home, Luciano knows the ropes. In fact, you could even say Luciano *makes* the ropes. He's a lot less comfortable when he's not the one calling the shots. And as a guest, it's very difficult to call the shots. Luciano, of course, doesn't let that stop him, especially not with regard to his favorite subject. That subject would be food.

I don't know where Luciano's concern with food came from or exactly when it began. But I do know that concern is far too mild a term for Luciano's consuming passion. Luciano thinks about food all the time. It's not just that he likes to eat: he loves to smell food, to touch food, to prepare food, to think about food, to talk about food. When he comes into a room, he begins sniffing like a dog, and his first question is, "What smells so good?"

"*I* smell so good, Luciano," I used to say.

It didn't stop him for a minute. He would already be past me and into the kitchen, lifting the lids on all the pots and inhaling the fragrant steam from whatever was cooking. There was always something cooking. To invite Luciano Pavarotti over without cooking something would be unthinkable.

In fact, he often orders up the menu himself. When Joe Volpe,

the general director of the Metropolitan Opera, invited Luciano
to dinner one night a few years ago, Luciano began calling Joe's
wife every day, several days in advance. He wanted to know what
she was going to serve. On the day itself, he called again to announce that he would be arriving early to help her cook. She had
to regretfully decline. It wasn't that she didn't want to cook with
Luciano; she just didn't think he would be able to fit into the
small galley kitchen of their New York apartment.

Long before I ever had him to my house, my dealings with Luciano involved food. Luciano had a set routine whenever he arrived in New York. He would take the car service in from the
airport and have them bring him straight to Grace's Marketplace
on Manhattan's Upper East Side. He would roam the aisles ener-
getically and come out laden with several shopping bags to add to
his pile of luggage. Then, and only then, would he go on to his
apartment and unpack.

Luciano's culinary tastes are very specific. There are certain
things he likes and certain ways to cook things. Arborio rice, for
example, the stubby-grained Italian rice that's used for making
risotto. Luciano's preferred arborio rice used to come from
Grace's Marketplace. For years, whenever I or anyone from the
office went over to Italy to see him, we had to bring arborio rice.
To many people, bringing arborio rice to Italy might seem a little redundant—after all, Grace's Marketplace imports the stuff
from Italy in the first place—but not to Luciano. His other demand, inevitably, was garlic. "Don't they have garlic in Italy, Luciano?" we asked. Not the same kind of garlic they have in the
States, apparently, and don't forget the garlic powder, either.
Once, a whole container of the stuff came open in my suitcase
when I was going to Modena. When I arrived, everything stank
of garlic. I told Luciano that I was going to charge him $1,000 for
a new Hermès bag (and I did, too). He just laughed.

Once Luciano called our office from Italy to ask Hans to run
over to his apartment and find a certain box of pasta that he had
in the cupboard. Hans was fully prepared for Luciano to demand

that he send the pasta over to Italy, too, probably by express mail. Fortunately, he just wanted to know the brand. He probably told everyone in Italy that it was far superior to whatever they were eating. Luciano always knows best.

He knows best about wine, too. As I said, the best wine in Italy, according to him, is Lambrusco. Lambrusco is indeed a delicious beverage, light, sparkling, and delicate. Luciano is fond of sending cases of it to people as tokens of his appreciation, and he's not above taking some along with him when he's on the road. The problem is that Lambrusco doesn't age or travel well. If you don't know how to ship it properly, you send the stuff a hundred yards and it falls flat and sour. I can't imagine how many recipients of Luciano's generosity have opened their wine bottles and sniffed in perplexity at the vinegary grape juice inside.

Given Luciano's choosiness, you can imagine that having him over to your house is a daunting proposition. And you would be right. So it was with some trepidation that we prepared to have him out to our country house in the Hamptons for the first time. We decided to have a barbecue, which was something we did for Alicia de Larrocha every year: we thought it might appear fun and ethnic to a European. I'm not sure how many barbecues Luciano had attended in his life, but he seemed to be a willing participant. In fact, he stopped the car on the way out when he saw a roadside farm stand selling corn on the cob. He bought a few ears, shucked one, and began eating it raw. He seemed to like it just fine that way. Still, the trepidation was evidently mutual.

For that first visit, Luciano used a car service to get out to our place. This wasn't unusual; Alicia came out that way, too. Luciano's car was perhaps a touch larger than Alicia's, but then Luciano is a touch larger than Alicia.

Our house is quite small, with a little driveway to one side, no more than fifteen paces from the door. From within, Carol and I watched as the enormous black limo pulled into the driveway. It sat there for a few minutes. Nothing happened. Then the car went into reverse, backed up a little bit, and turned to steer a course directly across our small front lawn. It stopped right at the front porch, so that Luciano could get out and walk directly into the house. Those fifteen paces, evidently, were a little daunting.

Or maybe it was just that he didn't want to have too far to carry all the food he'd brought. Pasta, olive oil, cheese, you name it: he had brought enough to feed an army. "Luciano," I said, "did you think we weren't going to feed you?" Luciano can be an overwhelmingly generous person, but in this case I think his motives were less sharing than self-serving. Literally.

All his fears vanished, however, when he got into the backyard and saw the barbecue. We had been right not to worry. Carol's barbecue chicken sent Luciano into a state of bliss. He insisted that she write the recipe down for him. She was happy to oblige.

That chicken tasted so good to Luciano that the memory stayed with him for a long, long time. For years after that, every time he saw Carol he would demand that she write down her recipe for barbecue chicken. She must have written that thing down forty-five times. I don't know what he did with it. I'm quite sure he never tried to make it himself.

On another visit he made to the Hamptons, a different kind of preparation was required. From Luciano's point of view, he was showing that he trusted me enough to put himself in my hands. From my point of view, my tenor was making yet another demand. Luciano announced that he wanted to come out and go horseback riding.

Horses are another great passion of Luciano's. Even passion is almost too tame a word to convey the intensity of Luciano's interests. Horses have played a huge role in his life. This weighty sybarite, who is happy to sleep until noon in the normal course of events, would rouse us at six in the morning to go examine a stud horse if there was one conveniently located in the area where he was on tour. "Conveniently located" might mean anything up to a two-hour drive. Once we got there, we'd sit, often in the rain, while Luciano surveyed the prospect with delight. In years to come, he would build up an entire stable of his own.

But all this was still in the future when Luciano expressed his wish to go riding in the Hamptons. It was the country; there were horses; he would ride. All that his manager had to do was find a horse that could carry Pavarotti. Like many of Luciano's plans, it sounded simple enough, from his perspective. And almost impossible, from mine.

Fortunately, Carol and my daughter, Andrea, were taking riding lessons that summer, and Carol asked the owner of the stable if it might be possible to arrange a mount—a very large mount—for Mr. Pavarotti. Since he couldn't very well swing into the saddle from the ground, Luciano would also require a mounting block. The stable owner said that he thought it could be managed.

On the appointed day, Luciano arrived for his visit, and we brought him over to the stable and got him installed on the mounting block as the horse was brought out. It was a very large animal indeed, not quite coal black but dark enough. A trainer, almost vibrating in his excitement at encountering Luciano Pavarotti in the flesh, led the horse into place, and Luciano raised his leg to get into the saddle. The horse took one look over his shoulder at what was about to get on him and stepped aside.

"Steady, Lucy," said the trainer.

The horse was led back into position, and Luciano made a second attempt. Once again, the horse moved away, with, if anything, greater alacrity.

"Easy, Lucy," said the trainer.

The process was repeated several times, but with no more success. Horses will, in fact, take the measure of their rider before he gets on, and "Lucy" had decided that he was not about to bear the burden to which the trainer proposed to subject him.

After several minutes, Luciano said, "But I see that this is a male horse. Why are you calling him Lucy?"

"Oh," said the trainer, "that's his nickname. It's short for Lucifer."

"Lucifer?!" Luciano exploded. "My God, you want me to ride a horse named for the Devil? Herbert, are you trying to kill me?"

That was the end of our riding excursion. Luciano's superstitions are not to be taken lightly. They've brought whole opera houses to a standstill, and they weren't going to be suspended for a mere horse. We went home and soothed our tenor's ruffled nerves with a liberal application of barbecue chicken.

One issue that often came up when I entertained Luciano was that he was suspicious about my generosity. He loved to twit me about my supposed stinginess. In fact, I don't think of myself as especially stingy. I remember one Christmas when I presented Luciano with a Pavarotti-sized bottle of his favorite cologne, Imperial from Guerlain. It was really enormous. Even Luciano was impressed with that one. Nonetheless, he loved to stereotype me as tightfisted. He saw himself, of course, as the soul of generosity and an excellent host. He tried to find ways to remind me that I was less talented in that regard than he—or ways to test me to see how far he could push me before I squawked.

So it was that one year, about twenty years ago, we both happened to be in Paris at the same time. I had fulfilled one of my lifelong dreams by buying an apartment there. My first apartment in Paris wasn't big—in fact, it was a small studio—but it overlooked the gardens of Notre Dame, and it made me very happy. It evoked *La Bohème*, down to the many flights of stairs that were its only means of access. I had waxed enthusiastic to Luciano about my new home, and one day I invited him over to see it, making clear, of course, that it was quite a climb to get there.

I expected him to bridle at the mention of the stairs, but to my great surprise, Luciano said he would be happy to come. He did, however, have one condition. He wanted to plan the menu.

"Of course," I said, ever the willing host to my client.

Luciano presented me with a menu that was elegant in its simplicity. In fact, it would require almost no kitchen preparation time at all. His requirements were few, and the shopping list was straightforward and easy to follow. He wanted a kilo of beluga caviar, three bottles of Roederer Cristal champagne, the most expensive smoked salmon from Petrossian, and Stolichnaya vodka.

To buy all this, of course, would cost several thousand dollars. Luciano obviously thought that I would balk at the expense, after which he would be able to taunt me for my lack of generosity. I wouldn't give him the satisfaction. I accepted his list without a murmur and said that I was looking forward to having him.

On the appointed day, Luciano made his way slowly up the stairs and eventually arrived at my apartment, huffing and puffing and wiping his brow. Despite a few complaints about the climb, he was in good spirits. He loved to play this kind of game. His mood only improved as he surveyed the table where I had laid out everything elegantly, exactly according to his specifications. With a smile, he sat down and requested a spoon for the caviar.

I offered him one, but he rejected it peremptorily. It emerged that what Luciano wanted was not a demitasse spoon or even a teaspoon. It had to be a tablespoon.

With this implement, he dug into the mound of caviar and ingested a generous mouthful, which he washed down with a few mouthfuls of Cristal champagne. Smiling broadly as we talked, even glancing around to admire the view from time to time, he continued to pack it away.

"You're eating too much of this stuff," I eventually suggested, as the caviar continued to disappear at a steady rate.

"What are you afraid of?" said the tenor sweetly.

"You'll make yourself sick," I said.

"Don't be silly," Luciano replied. "What's the matter? Can't you afford it?"

"I can afford it just fine," I said.

We spent a pleasant afternoon together, talking over one thing and another, as Luciano ate more than a pound of caviar. Finally the visit drew to a close. He needed, he informed me, to go home and rest. He had me pack up the rest of his provisions to take with him—presumably in case he should feel like a snack on the way home.

That night, I was the recipient of yet another late-night phone call from Luciano. He was desperately sick to his stomach.

"I will never eat caviar again," he swore, amid groans and various imprecations.

He kept that vow for several years. He finally broke down on the Air France Concorde, where the stewardess served him a jar of caviar with the drinks. He managed to get that down with no ill effects, possibly because it was considerably less than a kilo of the stuff.

We never discussed that menu again. Nor did he complain about my generosity for a very long time—except to mention, more than a few times, that I had tried to kill him.

It's true, though, that it's hard to be generous to someone like Luciano. It's extremely difficult to get him a gift: what can you buy for someone whose tastes are extremely specific and who, when he sees something he likes, immediately buys several of it? I tried my best. One Christmas I got him a crystal sculpture of a horse, a big horse's head, from Baccarat. I guess he liked that all right. But the only time that I know I really scored a success was with something I bought him on a whim: a Hermès scarf. He liked it so much that he went out and bought himself a whole stack of them the next time he was at the airport. Hermès scarves have remained Luciano's favorite accessory. He seldom appears anywhere, at home or in public, without one or two draped over him. They're bright, decorative, and concealing. They also cost about $700 a pop. Today, Hermès is happy to custom-make Luciano's extra-length neckties for him, as well. He's done a tremendous amount to promote their products.

As he became well known and well heeled, Luciano had more and more of his clothes custom-made. He always had full suits of evening clothes available in several different sizes to accommodate his ups and downs. I always say that in the course of his career Luciano has to have gained and lost more than 5,000 pounds. It's hard to quantify precisely, because no one knows for sure how much he weighs. Whenever anyone is gauche enough to ask, Luciano has a ready answer. "Oh," he'll say, "I went on a diet last night. So today I weigh ten pounds less than I did last night." He never reveals an actual number. Sometimes, however, he buys his shirts a size or two larger in the neck, so he can run his finger around the collar and show people how much weight he's lost.

His diets were another thing that made it difficult to entertain him. He was usually on one, and you never knew what he was allowed to eat. Luciano is as extreme about dieting as he is about everything else. He will latch onto one thing he's supposed to eat, like steamed chicken and vegetables, and eat only that every day, twice a day, until he eventually loses interest. He certainly devoted at least as much energy and thought to his diets, when he was on them, as to his regular meals when he was not. Luciano is an expert on everything, and losing weight is no exception. It doesn't shake his belief one iota that none of his famous diets seems to be particularly effective.

One day he was lying in his dressing room at the Met with his upper body exposed—which is not a pretty sight—when Sissi Strauss came in. Sissi is the Met's liaison for foreign artists; she's the person they turn to when they need an apartment, a doctor, or simply a friend in a strange city. Sissi is Viennese, with a little lilting accent, and that means, among other things, that she's very well put together, a stylish woman with flair. You'd certainly never call her heavy. She stood averting her eyes from the swaying belly flowing over the edge of the chaise longue.

"Luciano," Sissi said, "how are you?"

"I'm not good," Luciano said. "I've put on ten pounds and I can't get it off."

"Oh, I know how you feel," said Sissi. "My husband and I have both gone on Slim-Fast."

"Oh, no," Luciano said. "No. Slim-Fast is no good. If you want to lose weight, you should be on my diet. I'll write it down for you."

And the king of the high Cs—and the high scales—eased himself ponderously upright on his chaise, rather like a beached whale, and pointed a finger at Sissi's trim form.

"If you were on my diet," he told her sternly, "you wouldn't look like that."

chapter VI

YES, LUCIANO

The Blockbuster That Wasn't

By 1981, nobody was more famous than Luciano. Nobody in the opera world, at least.

He was giving outdoor concerts to tens of thousands of people in San Francisco and elsewhere. He'd had the covers of both *Time* and *Newsweek*. A *People* magazine poll was about to show he was the second most popular male singer in America, right behind Kenny Rogers. He'd set his first record as the highest-paid concert singer in a venue, when he got £15,000 for an appearance at the Manchester Palace Theater. Little did we know that £15,000 was only the beginning.

He had served as the grand marshal of the Columbus Day Parade in New York, clop-clopping along on a massive police horse named Maverick, tightly flanked by two mounted policemen so Maverick wouldn't take it into his head to bolt. Directly behind him were Ed Koch, the mayor of New York; Mario Cuomo, the governor; and Jimmy Carter, the former president of the United States. They all followed Luciano, stepping over the horse manure left—quite literally, and rather liberally—in his wake.

"Do you know me?" he'd asked America, by way of an American Express television commercial, and America had responded with a vengeance. If they didn't know him before that commercial, they knew him now. It paid only about $25,000, but it was worth it. That one commercial brought him to the attention of more people than everything he had done leading up to it. Some people criticized him for doing the commercial. They said it was selling out. Those people weren't musicians, though. Musicians were too busy banging down my door begging me to get them the American Express commercial, too.

I did manage to get it for one of my publicity clients, Itzhak Perlman. He was delighted, until I sent him a bill for my commission on his fee. Itzhak maintained that that kind of thing should have been covered by the monthly retainer he paid me rather than charged as an additional fee. I maintain that I earned that money fair and square. Every other artist I represented would have been happy to pay me that commission for the American Express ad. At least, they would have been happy to pay me before the fact. No artist is very happy when it comes to actually giving out money.

So Luciano was famous. Up to a point. But in the United States, there's only one place to go if you want to truly reach the pinnacle of fame. Hollywood. And that's where we were headed.

In the glory days of opera, singers used to make movies all the time. Big opera stars, in fact, were making movies even before the movies had sound. There are silent film versions of *Carmen* and *Manon Lescaut*, to name just two, and Enrico Caruso was immortalized mouthing the words of "Vesti la giubba," the famous aria from *Pagliacci*, in the 1919 feature film *My Cousin*. Once talking pictures came in, the floodgates were open to any singer brave enough or attractive enough to take the plunge: Grace Moore, Lily Pons, Lawrence Tibbett. Tenors often made the leap in spite

of their awkward physiques. Beniamino Gigli made several feature films, baby fat and all. Lauritz Melchior, the great Danish
Wagnerian whose stature was as bearlike as his voice, played
friendly, avuncular roles in a handful of movies. Jussi Björling, the
hard-drinking Swede with the light and melting voice, was also
approached for a leading Hollywood role, but he turned it down,
so the studio went with its second choice, Mario Lanza, for the
film *The Great Caruso*. Lanza, of course, was a huge star; although
he only once actually sang a role on an opera stage, he had a phe-
nomenal career in movies. Metro-Goldwyn-Mayer hoped to create a second Lanza with Luciano Pavarotti and relaunch the grand
tradition of studio musicals in the bargain.

Yes, Giorgio began when a young producer came up with the
idea of a Pavarotti film and got the ear of David Begelman, the
head of MGM. Begelman had overseen the making of a few successful movies you may have heard of: *The Way We Were*, *Close
Encounters of the Third Kind*, things like that. Those, however,
were made by Columbia Pictures, where David was once president. He left that job after he was caught embezzling money from
the studio and forging checks. In Hollywood, there are consequences for that kind of thing. The actor who blew the whistle
on him couldn't get a film for four years. Begelman, on the other
hand, got off with a hefty fine and, soon enough, a new job as
president and CEO of MGM. (There was a whole book, *Indecent
Exposure*, written about the incident.) Begelman ended up leaving MGM after a couple of years and starting up two of his own
production companies, the last one of which ended up in federal
court in the mid-1990s, at which point Begelman blew his brains
out. Given his dramatic history, it should come as no surprise that
he loved opera. He was very excited about making a film with
Luciano Pavarotti.

Yes, Giorgio had all the ingredients it needed to be a blockbuster. MGM lavished on it the best of everything. We had an
$18 million budget, which was big money in 1981: Steven Spiel-
berg made *E.T.* the same year for $10.5 million. We had three

months of shooting in glamorous locations: Italy, Boston, San Francisco, the vineyards of the Napa Valley, the Metropolitan Opera. We had an Academy Award–winning director, Franklin Schaffner, whose credits extended from *Patton* to *Planet of the Apes*. We had, as scriptwriter, Norman Steinberg, who was one of the writers on *Blazing Saddles*. We had a special song for Luciano written by John Williams. We had Eddie Albert, playing me. We had the greatest tenor in the world, Luciano Pavarotti. I made sure to get a credit as executive producer on that film, which is the kind of thing you can do if you manage the star. In addition to looking out for your artist, you have to look out for yourself. An executive producer credit on a major motion picture is something that can be very useful to your career. I was sure I was on my way to becoming a big-time Hollywood player.

Unfortunately, the film bombed.

Yes, Giorgio is about a famous singer named Giorgio Fini—Norman Steinberg's nod to Fini's, Luciano's favorite restaurant in Modena—who loses his voice right before a big open-air concert in Boston and is "cured" by an attractive doctor named Pamela Taylor. (The "cure" for Giorgio's psychosomatic malady is a shot of vitamin B-12 in the ass, another detail from life: all of Luciano's secretaries were adept at giving him his B-12 shot.) Giorgio decides he likes Pamela and hounds her to follow him to California, presenting her with airplane tickets, which she refuses, only to change her mind and drive out from Boston instead, thereby breaking the first real-life rule of anybody interested in having a fling with an opera singer: always accept the free plane tickets. (In real life, of course, it's highly unlikely that you would be offered any.)

Giorgio and Pamela embark on a fling, starting in the gorgeous villa at Strawberry Hill, near San Francisco, with the help of a pair of shockingly stereotyped Asian domestics, who are called upon to bring them food at regular intervals throughout the evening in every room in the house, leaving it somewhat open to question whether Giorgio's idea of an orgy is of a culinary or a sexual nature. As their time in California continues, Giorgio orders Pamela not to fall in love with him—though it doesn't seem very likely, on the face of it, that she would—and then they take off in a hot-air balloon for Francis Ford Coppola's vineyard, here standing in as the home of Giorgio's childhood friends, who create awkwardness by asking about Giorgio's wife. Coppola was happy to have his vineyard used. He loves opera. He once even directed an opera himself, Gottfried von Einem's *The Visit of the Old Lady*. OK, it's not exactly a household name, but you have to start somewhere. It might have been even more helpful to us if he had directed *Yes, Giorgio*.

Meanwhile, Pamela has become a fixture in the space of only a few days, and Giorgio's manager—that would be me, as played by Eddie Albert—enlists her help in trying to lure Giorgio back to the Metropolitan Opera, where he's sworn he'll never sing again after a traumatic onstage incident some years back. After Pamela manages to sway him, she overhears Giorgio on the phone to his wife and erupts in a jealous outburst. "I love you!" she shouts, eliciting from Giorgio the response that she will spoil everything. In the climactic final scene, Giorgio triumphs at the Met in *Turandot*, to the point of encoring "Nessun dorma"—a definite departure from the reality of the notoriously encore-free Met—and Pamela gets up and leaves the theater, walking across Lincoln Center Plaza in tears, knowing that their fling is over and she must go on.

I've always maintained that the biggest problem with *Yes, Giorgio* was that the studio marketed it wrong. They should have said, "Come see and hear the greatest tenor in the world." After all, the movie has more than half an hour of footage of Pavarotti singing, in his prime. People flocked to experience that in real life. Instead, the studio tried to bill the movie as a romantic comedy. And the public, it seemed, wasn't willing to buy the idea that Pavarotti could be a romantic hero. They just said, "How could that pretty young woman fall for that big fat guy?"

Which is very ironic. In real life, women were falling for that big fat guy all the time. But audiences didn't want to see it. I really think that was the issue. I don't think the fact that this supposedly sparkling romantic comedy revolved around a doomed and openly adulterous affair could possibly have been the problem.

In retrospect, we should have known there were going to be problems from the number of actresses who turned down the leading role. By the time we showed up for filming, the studio had gone through a whole roster of stars. Candice Bergen had been asked; Sally Field's name had come up; Goldie Hawn reportedly turned the part down. Blythe Danner was supposed to play it but had to withdraw because of a death in her family. Sigourney Weaver was in hot contention, but for some reason that didn't work out. So the role had fallen to Kate Jackson, perhaps the least charismatic of Charlie's Angels.

I don't know exactly what happened to Kate, either. But the story around the studio was that Kate ended up talking to Cher about the project. And Cher gave her a piece of advice.

"Never," said Cher, "never *ever* do a movie where you can't get your arms around your romantic lead."

Kate must have thought that made sense. In any case, after she and Luciano had done their screen tests together, she dropped out of the picture. The studio had to scramble to find a warm body to replace her, one who could fit into the costumes that had already been designed. They ended up with a nice B actress named Kathryn Harrold. She was an attractive woman, nice figure, had made a few movies before. Somebody on the set referred to her as a "comedy assassin," but let's face it, Luciano wasn't exactly playing up the comedy, either.

Meanwhile, in real life, Luciano was having no problem with women at all. Quite the contrary. In fact, there had been a significant change in Luciano's life.

Let me back up a couple of years.

An opera singer's life isn't all Hollywood parties and fancy dinners. In fact, life on the road is pretty boring. You spend a lot of time in hotel rooms in strange cities, killing time until the next rehearsal. Luciano not only didn't like this: he couldn't tolerate it. He was raised in a busy household, his own homes are always full of people, and he is not someone who has a lot of resources to deal with solitude. Even in the early days, someone from our office—usually me—had to travel with him on his recital tours. You'd get checked into the hotel, and get into your room, and before you'd even unzipped your bag, the phone would ring. "Come."

So you'd go running down the hall and find him sitting there, with no particular demand other than that he wanted company. He wanted to play cards. He wanted to do his crossword puzzle and have someone there to ask about the answers. Since the puzzles were in Italian, it was hard for us to help him much, but then he could twit us for our lack of language skills. Luciano always liked having something to criticize.

But my staff and I couldn't stay with him every minute, even if it sometimes seemed like we did. And Adua was in Italy most of the time, raising their daughters. So it was inevitable that eventually Luciano would acquire a—well, a secretary.

Luciano had had various people helping out with his day-to-day chores for a long time. Since the early 1970s, he'd been getting vast quantities of fan mail, and he had no idea what to do with it. He'd put it in a hotel laundry bag and give it to one of his friends to answer for him, together with a stack of signed photos. He had quite a few friends who were willing to do this for him—not that he gave them much of a choice. "Here," he'd say as he was departing, leaving them literally holding the bag.

Clearly, this was only a stopgap solution. So Luciano began experimenting with help on a more regular basis. For several years, he had a secretary named Annamaria Verde. She was a chubby Italian girl, and there was no hanky-panky there. Annamaria was less a secretary than a mamma. She cooked for him and looked after him and answered his mail and kept track of his appointments and kept him company, and later, after she got married, she and her husband offered him a place to go when he was in New York and wanted companionship.

But Luciano needed even more time than Annamaria could give him. In fact, he needed care twenty-five hours a day, eight days a week. And he wouldn't mind if the caregiver was easy on the eyes, either. A number of women passed through his life during this period. There was Giovanna Lomazzi, a wealthy woman who lived in Rome, but she never really served as a secretary. There was Julia Prola, who *was* hired as a secretary and who expected to keep a secretary's hours. She wanted to be out of there every day at five o'clock. That wasn't exactly what Luciano had in mind.

Then Luciano made one of his first forays into pedagogy, a set of master classes at the Juilliard School in New York. It proved fateful in more ways than one.

A master class involves a number of young musicians getting up and performing, one by one, for a professional and then hearing what the professional has to say. To the public, master classes are billed as a great chance for young singers to benefit from veterans' wisdom and insight. To musicians, they're often seen as a way for those veterans to showcase themselves at the expense of the hapless students. Not infrequently, the "wisdom and insight" the young musicians receive seems less uplifting than downright vicious. Elisabeth Schwarzkopf was particularly famous for sending students offstage in tears, probably because her idea of constructive criticism involved making the kinds of comments she herself had routinely gotten from her husband throughout her career.

Luciano wasn't vicious, of course. But he wasn't a teacher, either. And his master classes were not like anybody else's. For one thing, I got them broadcast on television. They drew a huge viewership because everybody wanted to see Pavarotti. Most of all, the viewers hoped that he would sing a little bit to show the students how the music was supposed to go. It was a good thing that they wanted that, because that was about as far as Luciano's teaching skills went. Luciano has never been a great musician, in the sense in which musicians understand the term. Nobody argues that he makes beautiful music, and has a beautiful voice, and phrases the music he sings so gorgeously that your heart stops. But when it comes to things like sight-reading, or counting time so he knows when to come in, or any of the other technical things that make up the craft of musicianship, Luciano is a little bit challenged. It doesn't help that he can't read music.

Of course, all the musicianship skills in the world aren't going to help anybody sing as well as Luciano does. What Luciano sings on is pure instinct. He just knows how it's supposed to go. So it's hard for him to explain to somebody else what he's doing. He might say, "Use your diaphragm." But how do you use a diaphragm? That, he couldn't really tell you.

It was precisely because he knew he wasn't a great musician that Luciano was extremely nervous about the master classes. He felt people were going to expect him to give profound advice to the young singers, and he wouldn't know what to say. It's true that his comments were a little perfunctory. He was especially challenged when a young mezzo-soprano came out and sang an aria from Mozart's *Le Nozze di Figaro*. Her name was Susanne Mentzer, and she went on to have a significant career at the Met and elsewhere in roles exactly like the one she was singing here, Cherubino, the young pageboy. (Mezzo-sopranos are fated to spend a lot of their careers playing young boys, with varying degrees of plausibility.) But she was a challenge for Luciano. For one thing, she was excellent; there was not very much to correct. For another, Mozart is pretty much outside Luciano's repertory. There isn't even a lead tenor role in *Nozze*.

So Luciano stuck to the basics. "The words are, *Non so più cosa son, cosa faccio*," he said. "So you must sing them very clearly. *Non so più, cosa son, cosa faccio.*"

He showed her what he meant a couple of times. And then he thanked her very much. I'm not sure how much benefit Susanne derived from these pearls of wisdom. But the audience was delighted.

It must be said that Luciano was very serious about trying to give something back to the profession, and to young singers. He wanted to help them the way he had been helped himself, with a vocal competition that would give the winners a chance to perform in an opera onstage. The master classes at Juilliard may not have been so wonderful for insiders, but they were a big hit with the public, and they only intensified his desire to do something for the next generation. In 1981, the Pavarotti International Voice Competition was born. Luciano always thought big. His competition wasn't a little local thing: auditions were held around the globe. Of course, someone had to set all of those auditions up, but that kind of thing didn't bother Luciano. The Pavarotti competition, which ended up being held every few years, cost millions of dollars and a lot of manpower. Even the winners' circle was larger than life. One year there were more than fifty first-prize winners. All the finalists won that year, in fact, except for an overweight soprano named Alessandra Marc. Alessandra ended up being one who actually went on to have a career, although her weight held her back—even in the Pavarotti competition. Luciano, that paragon of physical fitness, wasn't crazy about the way she looked.

But that competition, important as it was, wasn't the main thing that came out of those master classes. The main thing was another student who sang for Luciano. Her name was Madelyn Renée.

I can't definitely say that sparks flew when Madelyn came out onstage. And I'm not sure exactly what the chronology was between them. I mean, I don't remember if they had already met, if they first clicked when he saw her at the master class, or if it all happened a little later. After all, I was only Luciano's manager, not his pimp.

But I do remember that, some months after the master class, Madelyn turned up at a dinner after a performance of *Elisir d'Amore*. It was one of Terry McEwen's dinners, with all the usual suspects: Annamaria Verde; Dr. Umberto Boeri, a good friend of Luciano's in New York; Mario Sereni, who had sung that night as well; Hans and me; and a number of other people who fell into the blanket category of Pavarotti groupies. Nobody asked too many questions about what Madelyn was doing there. It was not unusual for Luciano to show up in the company of an attractive woman or two. And Madelyn was extremely attractive, not only in the physical sense. She was very funny. She was good company. She had pizzazz. She ordered escargots, and in true Pavarotti fashion they were passed around so that everybody could try one. By the time the plate reached the foot of the table, they were gone.

I think that by then Madelyn may already have been Luciano's secretary.

At first, Madelyn's "job description"—the part of it that was available for public consumption—involved answering Luciano's fan mail in New York. After she graduated from Juilliard, Luciano came up with a new role for her. She would travel with him, answer his mail, pack, keep track of his pills, play cards, and do other things mutually understood by both of them that didn't need even nominal contractual attention. In return, he would act as her voice teacher, pay her a salary—not huge, believe me—and give her invaluable firsthand experience of a successful singer's life on the international stage.

Were they in love? Sure they were, after their own fashion. Luciano had never had anybody like Madelyn in his life. She was a great-looking girl, and she dressed like a million dollars. And she was an American girl. She was independent, and she stood up to him. He liked that. He liked the way it made him feel to go places with her on his arm. He liked it when she bossed him around a little bit. He probably liked her voice, although I won't say that Madelyn was the greatest singer in the world. But Luciano liked teaching her and having her listen to what he said.

And of course she was crazy about him. He was hard to resist. To be selected out of the crowd by somebody that magnetic and powerful is pretty intoxicating. And she was getting things out of it, too. She got his advice. She got to share his lavish lifestyle. She got his connections. She wasn't in it for nothing. She was a smart cookie.

There was nothing clandestine about their relationship. They appeared at social occasions together; they traveled together.

Well, they didn't *always* travel together. Luciano would only fly first class, but he didn't get rich by throwing his money around. He had a very healthy respect for the value of a dollar, or a lira, or whatever your currency of preference happened to be. So we would book his secretary a seat in coach. That's not as demeaning as it sounds, because we always managed to get her bumped up to sit in first class with him, once they were at the airport. Luciano just didn't have to pay for it.

The only time Madelyn didn't travel with him was when he went home to Italy. Then, she discreetly melted away for a few weeks. Of course, Adua knew Madelyn, since Madelyn was around whenever Adua came to join Luciano on his travels. Adua knew that her husband needed someone to help with his work. She knew he needed companionship. She was away from Luciano so much that she may even have been naïve enough to think that there was nothing else going on. Those articles in the gossip magazines about his glamorous protégée? All lies, he would assure her, looking deep into her eyes.

"A loving wife will believe anything her husband tells her," she later said.

What was she going to say? "I knew he was cheating on me, and I put up with it"?

So by the time we got to Hollywood to make *Yes, Giorgio*, Madelyn was very much a part of the picture. In fact, Luciano had her put on the payroll as his dialogue coach. And believe me, she earned her salary. The whole process of making a movie was very unfamiliar to Luciano. It's hard to make a movie in a language that's not your own. It's hard to make a Hollywood movie, period: they don't pay you the big bucks for nothing. You have to get up at the crack of dawn—especially hard for a tenor who likes to sleep until noon—and go get makeup put on you for a couple of hours. You have to hang around the set and do retake after retake. And after a whole day of shooting, you have to go back to your hotel and learn your lines for the next day. Madelyn really had to stay on top of him for that part of it.

Luciano likes to be in control. So do I. Neither of us was in control in Hollywood. In that world, I had very little clout. I had a number of changes I wanted to make to the story, but I couldn't get anyone to listen to them. Let's face it, classical music is pretty small potatoes to the big Hollywood guns. I was a little out of my depth.

Not that I wasn't having a great time. I was learning a lot, too. Those agents in Hollywood made me look like a pussycat. Our agent, John Gaines, was the original limo man. He had all the accoutrements, all the perks—and in Hollywood, there are many, many perks—and the biggest mouth you could hope to find. Of course, he couldn't manage to pronounce Luciano's name correctly. "Pavar-OH-ti," he called him. "How's Pavar-OH-ti?" He couldn't have cared less if he pronounced it right or not, and he was right not to care, because what really mattered was getting the picture made. Hollywood agents are not shrinking violets. They're rather monstrous people. But when you're dealing with that kind of money and fame and ego, you have to be. And you can get away with it. I kept my eyes and ears open.

Luciano's way of trying to maintain control was to go into defensive mode. He was very afraid of being made to look stupid. He wasn't going to let anybody make a fool of him. For one thing, he was very self-conscious about his weight. He had reason to be. In our first interviews about the movie, the studio heads let Luciano know that he was going to have to lose some. On camera, everyone looks heavier than they are, and if there's one thing Luciano didn't need, it was to look heavier. Luciano was amenable. He vowed he would go on a diet and lose fifty pounds. He must have gone on the wrong diet. When he showed up to start filming, he'd gained fifty pounds. The studio wasn't too thrilled about that.

Luciano wasn't thrilled, either. He had ways of compensating. Whenever he saw a photographer on the set, he would grab Kathryn Harrold and pull her in front of him to help conceal his bulk. The leading ladies of the opera world were used to Luciano mauling them, but a Hollywood actress tends not to be very enthusiastic about that kind of behavior. A certain amount of tension started to build up between them.

But more to the point, Luciano didn't want to look silly. He wouldn't do anything that could make people laugh at him. Since he was cast as the lead in a comedy, this became quite a problem. It was ironic, too. In real life, Luciano has a fantastic sense of humor. Even on television, he was great at tossing off one-liners with that big, easy smile. But for the movie, he clammed up. The scene that most people cite as the film's all-time low is a food fight between him and Kathryn Harrold. She's trying to convince him to go back to the Met, while the two of them are in the kitchen preparing dinner for the assembled company, and they end up dumping pasta and cheese all over each other. Very few people would think of trying to play a food fight seriously, but Luciano did.

NORMAN STEINBERG

When I was working on the screenplay, I went down to hear him sing in San Diego, and he sang "I Left My Heart in San Francisco" at a reception. And he did a real Tony Bennett version, with a lot of mike shtick and everything. Coming from him, it was hilarious.

So I wrote a scene into the film for him to do it, as a hoot. But when it came to shooting the scene in San Francisco, at the Crystal Room of the Sheraton Hotel, he wouldn't do it on camera. He wouldn't make a joke of it. He said, "I will not be the buffo."

And so the scene became ludicrous. A guy singing an operatic version of "I Left My Heart in San Francisco" is stupid.

It was when he wasn't actually being filmed that Luciano was best at playing the role of the movie star. At parties, for example. The social part of the Hollywood experience was fabulous for both of us. The city embraced him. There was a party at Chasen's, the famous Hollywood eatery, and at David Begelman's home in Beverly Hills. All the stars and starlets turned out to meet Luciano, which is no small feat, because it takes a lot to get people to come out in Hollywood. The gossip columns kept running pieces about him and his new Hollywood cronies: Frank Sinatra, Walter Matthau, Jacqueline Bisset, Charlton Heston.

He also knew how to play the movie star on the set. The scene we filmed in Boston was a case in point. There were two outdoor concerts in *Yes, Giorgio*, one in Boston and one in San Francisco, and those concerts were real. That is, thousands of people turned out to hear them, and we had an orchestra, and we had conductors—Emerson Buckley in Boston, and Kurt Herbert Adler in San Francisco. Each of them was quite an event. In Boston, we had a turnout of more than 50,000 people. Everything was ready to go. And then the tenor couldn't sing. No, not in the screenplay—in real life. Luciano had decided to inject a touch of realism to the proceedings.

The problem was his hotel bill. Luciano generally assumes that someone else will be paying for everything. He also travels with a sizable entourage of friends, family, and whoever the hell else, and his entourage for this momentous occasion in his life was particularly grand. He had run up a bill of something like $25,000. The studio balked, and Luciano balked right back. If the bill wasn't paid, he said, he wouldn't sing.

There were tens of thousands of people out on the lawn. There were about eleven cameras set up, and boats with more cameras, and helicopters flying around with even more cameras. There was a whole symphony orchestra. And nothing was happening.

Finally, Franklin Schaffner said, "Fine. I'm going to go out onstage and announce to those hundred thousand people that Mr. Pavarotti will not be singing until everyone on this lawn ponies up a dollar to help cover his expenses."

In the end, the studio backed down and paid the bill. When you think about how much money they put into that movie, it was a drop in the bucket. Their investment was remarkable, considering that the public wasn't exactly clamoring for a new movie about opera. *Yes, Giorgio* was one of the last old-school big-budget movie musicals, and nobody ever quite understood why it was made. The studio tried to get everything right. They created an actual production of *Turandot*, with sets and everything, and hired Lotfi Mansouri, the opera director, as their consultant. They tried to get Joan Sutherland to sing the title role, but she declined; so they got Leona Mitchell, a perfectly respectable soprano, instead. They filmed at all these locations. They spared no expense.

You can't always tell, when you're in the middle of things, how they're going to turn out. Even when we were looking at the final version, it seemed like *Yes, Giorgio* could conceivably be a success. All right, the movie was a dog, but there are many, many dumber movies that have made a lot of money. It all depends on how you publicize it. But I couldn't really tell a Hollywood studio how to publicize their movie. They have whole offices and huge staffs working on it. There just wasn't any way for me to do it.

Some people absolutely loved *Yes, Giorgio*. Very few of these people happened to be reviewers. "One of the most unintentionally hilarious films I've ever seen," said Gene Siskel, giving it a resounding thumbs down. "Franklin J. Schaffner has directed as if no one let him in on the scam," observed *Time*. "A 110-minute cluster of embarrassing clichés," said the Toronto *Star*. "Ridiculously corny," noted the New York *Daily News*. Before we made the movie, Luciano was talking about possibly making five more. After the reviews came in, of course, it was all my fault for pushing him to do this terrible project.

He would never see that it was an achievement that the film was made at all. Lots of films that are going to be made never actually are. Plácido was supposed to make an updated version of *The Merry Widow* with Julie Andrews after *Yes, Giorgio* was released, and nothing ever came of that. But Luciano had a Hollywood feature. There was a there there. Which is already fifty times better than anybody else in the opera business has accomplished lately.

KATHRYN HARROLD

I was hoping certain things would happen when we made the film that didn't happen. There was a kind of sleepwalking quality to the whole project. I think it was a combination of every single person involved, including the director. I think people started to sense that it wasn't going to be what they wanted.

For me it was very hard to do the kind of work I wanted to, because Luciano and I had totally different styles. I would have liked in a perfect world to have had more of a connection between us, so that the acting would have been more moment-to-moment, more alive. But that wasn't what was going to happen here.

Madelyn came to me before one scene, where we had to kiss, and said Luciano was nervous about that. I thought it was funny that she would even come to me. He was a good kisser. He didn't seem nervous to me.

When someone comes running up to me holding a picture of Yes, Giorgio *with tears in their eyes, I know it's an opera fan. It does happen. It's shocking. They must have their cars filled with pictures of everyone.*

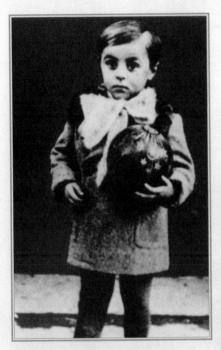

The age of innocence (which didn't last long):
Luciano and me, aged about four and six.
Fortunately, my parents didn't go in for bows,
as Luciano's evidently did.

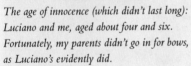

Collection of Herbert Breslin; courtesy Photofest

For better, for worse: Carol and I on our wedding day, January 28, 1954, and Luciano and Adua in London in 1973, after some twelve years of marriage. Luciano's necktie definitely qualifies as one of the "worse" parts. Collection of Herbert Breslin

My first clients: Joan Sutherland, Renata Tebaldi, Elisabeth Schwarzkopf, and Lisa della Casa, photographed before a Metropolitan Opera gala in 1964. From the very beginning, I worked only with the best. Elliott Erwitt/Magnum

After I heard the recordings of the pianist Alicia de Larrocha, I tracked her down at home in Spain to persuade her to let me bring her to the States. To judge from this picture, she was probably drawn to my boyish good looks (circa 1968). Collection of Herbert Breslin

Joan Sutherland and Marilyn Horne, who got along just fine, both offstage and on, as the "Druid Duo" in Bellini's Norma. *But that doesn't mean that Horne—Jackie, to her friends—necessarily wanted to share the cover of the* New York Times Magazine *with her before her Metropolitan Opera debut in 1970.*
Metropolitan Opera Archives

Joan and the tall tenor, pre-beard.
Collection of Herbert Breslin

My friend Terry McEwen, of London Records, was the man who told Luciano, "You're a nice guy, so you need a bastard to manage you." Evidently, he later tried to butter me up by giving me a flower (New York, 1971).

Collection of Herbert Breslin

Terry McEwen and London's burgeoning star show off a new recording (that La Bohème *with Mirella Freni and Herbert von Karajan remains an all-time classic).*

Louis Mélançon/Metropolitan Opera Archives

Hans Boon was still working for London Records when he met Luciano. Fortunately, by the time he came to work with me, many years later, he had lost the sideburns.

Even at the moment of Luciano's biggest early triumph—Daughter of the Regiment at the Met in 1972—Joan still saw herself as something of a leader in their relationship.

Ricky Bonynge was the savvy one in that couple. As late as 1978, before his first duo concert with Joan, Luciano knew when to keep his mouth shut and let Joan and Ricky call the shots—at least, in front of the camera. Courtesy Photofest

For Joan, a dress rehearsal was a dress rehearsal. For Luciano, it meant it was time to bone up on his part. I Puritani *at the Met, 1976.* Metropolitan Opera Archives

Although their actual feud didn't take place for another couple of years, a keen observer could already detect outward signs of tension between Luciano and Renata Scotto when they did the first Live from the Met *broadcast of* La Bohème *in 1977.* Metropolitan Opera Archives

You should never look a giftola horse in the mouth—but it's okay to examine its pedigree. Here, Luciano examines the lineage of Noble, a mare who came as an extra perk for a concert. If he looks a little dubious, he was. He wanted a thoroughbred horse, but Noble was only a saddlebred, so he gave her back. Tony Leonard

This moment in Yes, Giorgio *may have been the best expression of what everyone on the set was really thinking by the time we got to this point in filming. In real life, Luciano was much too respectful of food to waste any by throwing it around, especially at a pretty woman like Kathryn Harrold.* Courtesy Photofest

Being superstars together: Luciano with some of the show-biz friends he hobnobbed with while he was in Hollywood. Sinatra and he even sang together at a benefit concert at Radio City Music Hall. Rod Steiger was sporting the beard for his role as a rabbi in The Chosen. Collection of Herbert Breslin

For Luciano, the most significant thing about the televised master classes broadcast as Pavarotti at Juilliard *in 1978 was meeting the young soprano Madelyn Renée, who quickly became his secretary.* Courtesy Photofest

Madelyn and I also made a pretty handsome couple. Allen Malschick

Luciano sometimes called Madelyn up onstage to perform a number or two during his recitals. His fans weren't always thrilled about this practice. Allen Malschick

Some of the gang kid around during a rehearsal: from left to right, Merle Hubbard, Madelyn, unidentified, Hans, and Judy Drucker. It appears that Merle is regaling the group with excerpts from his diary. Susanne Faulkner Stevens, courtesy Lincoln Center

Luciano and his manager.

Allen Malschick

Backstage before a concert, Luciano conceals himself behind his omnipresent props of the mid-1980s: a jumbo-sized Hermès scarf, me, and Giovanna Cavaliere.

Collection of Herbert Breslin

The two Judys: Judy Drucker, chorus-girl-turned-concert-presenter, shows off her star act, while Judy Kovacs (seated) emerges from her Tamara phase as Luciano's new secretary. Judy's friend Bob Burpee is happy to be a part of it all. My expression reflects some of the tension of working behind the scenes with Pavarotti. Allen Malschick

If only he had rehearsed half as much off-camera: Luciano and Sir Georg Solti prepare for the infamous Otello.   Terry Lott

Luciano wore an Otello costume only once, for a single act of the opera at a Met gala—and in an impromptu appearance beforehand chasing his secretary down Sixty-fifth Street.

When you get two Italians together, I don't want to get in the middle of it: Luciano and Joe Volpe engage in a friendly conversation during the Met's 1993 tour in Japan.

Henry Grossman

The powers behind the throne: me and the mad Hungarian, Tibor Rudas.

Collection of Herbert Breslin

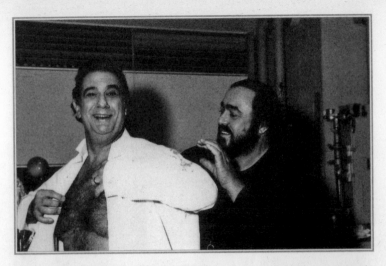

*Rivalry? What rivalry? Plácido Domingo and Luciano were all smiles once they began
cashing in on the Three Tenors phenomenon. Here, Plácido shows off his physique,
much to Luciano's amusement.*   Collection of Herbert Breslin

*In a bit of wish fulfillment, Luciano lets the other two tenors know how he'd prefer
them to behave during their upcoming concert.*   Courtesy Photofest

The Three Tenors and James Levine do their bit to uphold the integrity and seriousness of classical music. The champagne corks must have been flying to get Luciano's beard that black. Thomas Reitz, courtesy Photofest

Adua, keeping up a good front to the end, and me, looking oddly hangdog.

Collection of Herbert Breslin

Luciano and Nicoletta.

Olivier Wilkins

When Luciano decided to try Daughter of the Regiment *for his sixtieth birthday in 1996, everyone was a little nervous—including, it appears, Luciano's fellow singers.*
Metropolitan Opera Archives

The paterfamilias: Carol and I with two of our four grandchildren, Alexander and Isabelle Jaffe, in 2002. Collection of Herbert Breslin

A weighty conclusion: dress rehearsal for Tosca in Berlin, June 2003.
Bernd Uhlig

chapter VII

THE VIEW FROM THE (BIG) TOP

Conquering New Arenas—
and Old Colleagues

S o how do you keep a Hollywood star—even a failed Hollywood star—interested in the classical music world? How do
you keep finding new challenges for someone who's already broken all the boundaries of what you're supposed to be able to do
in the business? That was my job. Believe me, it wasn't easy.

The focus of my work with Luciano was starting to shift a little. It wasn't only about coming up with new projects anymore;
it was also about sifting through the many, many outside projects
people were always offering us, trying to figure out which of
them might interest us. And it wasn't just trying to figure out a
good next move; it was about trying to figure out what Luciano
wanted. Which was getting harder to do. Particularly because his
desires could change at the drop of a hat.

We'd talk to an eager television producer, stars in his eyes, convinced he had the greatest idea for a Pavarotti special ever to

come across the screen. Luciano would be charming and gracious and encouraging. As soon as the door had closed behind him, he would turn to me.

"Who was that man?" he would say, with a slight but unmistakable air of disdain.

It would be left to me to break the news to the producer that Luciano's conditions had changed or, often, that he wouldn't do the project at all.

Television was changing, too. Most of the shows that I made my career getting my artists on in the 1960s were already gone. There was no more *Ed Sullivan Show*. ABC did make a feeble attempt at launching a new, Ed Sullivan–style variety show at one point, and we got Joan Sutherland on the first one, but it didn't go anywhere, probably because the emcee was Howard Cosell, who was about as charismatic as a dead fish. ABC also did a television special on Luciano, showing him in candid moments with a few close friends: strolling with Richard Thomas, playing tennis with John McEnroe, and, of course, singing. I'm not sure whether those friendships have survived the test of time, and the television special probably didn't, but it did just fine when they broadcast it, and was very good exposure.

But one special is a drop in the bucket, and in the absence of regular variety shows like the *Voice of Firestone*, I had to keep finding new ways to get Luciano on television. I tried to come up with ideas for concerts that PBS would pick up: New Year's at the New York Philharmonic, for example. Or trio concerts: one with Luciano alone, one with Luciano and Joan, and one with Luciano, Joan, and Marilyn Horne. Those did very well, both at the box office and in the ratings.

They went well onstage, at least. Offstage, things with his costars weren't going all that well. Luciano's fame was changing his relationships with the opera world, too. People might say they were growing impatient with Luciano's increasingly cavalier treatment of the world around him. But the main thing is, they were jealous.

His special bond with Joan and Ricky, for example, had frayed.
Of course, Joan and Luciano recorded together like gangbusters
throughout the 1970s. But their dynamic had gradually altered.
When they started, Joan was the big star, generously taking the
tall tenor under her wing. Now, Luciano was the big star. And I
don't think he felt that Joan and Ricky gave him the proper respect.

He was probably right. As far as Ricky was concerned, Luciano was still something of a student. He had never developed
what you could call a facility for learning his music. And when he
did learn it, he could be a little casual about things like sticking to
the notes the composer wrote. Ricky is no Herbert von Karajan,
but he's a perfectly competent conductor, and he would call Luciano on things like that. Of course, Luciano didn't like it.

"Who does he think he is," he would say, "this no-good conductor?"

Ricky and Joan didn't particularly approve of what Luciano
was doing musically, either. They always felt he was a great bel
canto singer, and they didn't feel he should move from that repertoire into things like *Aida* and *Tosca* and everything else he was
singing. They didn't think much of his forays into bigger and bigger concerts. And they were probably not thrilled that, in spite of
all of his shortcomings, Luciano was turning into a superstar even
bigger than Joan had ever dreamed of being. I think they found
that a little hard to swallow.

As early as 1974, Luciano had begun to tug on his leash. Joan
and Luciano were scheduled to record Donizetti's *Maria Stuarda*
in Bologna; Luciano was going to record *La Favorita*, also by
Donizetti, with Fiorenza Cossotto. The Teatro Comunale in
Bologna is one of the best theaters in Italy. Not only is it beautiful, but it has fantastic acoustics. For Luciano, however, the most
compelling point in its favor was that Bologna is only about half
an hour's drive from Modena. In any case, Decca was quite happy
to record there, even though it involved a considerable expendi-
ture of effort and money to drag all their equipment down there.

So the recording date was set, and Joan showed up raring to go. She had had a big success with *Maria Stuarda* in San Francisco a couple of years earlier, and she was thrilled to have a chance to get it onto record for posterity.

The only problem was that Luciano hadn't learned his part.

This time, nobody had to teach it to him. For Pavarotti, Decca was willing to put off the recording. They simply recorded *La Favorita*. A year later, they dragged all their equipment back down to Bologna and finally got *Maria Stuarda*, too. By then, Luciano had managed to learn the role well enough to get through it. The recording came out all right. But it didn't turn out to be one of Joan's best, perhaps because the role was a little rusty by then, and I think she felt that Luciano had messed up her chance.

Luciano, meanwhile, was learning all kinds of lessons about how flexible record companies and opera houses can be, if they want you enough.

The San Francisco Opera was another case in point. Their accommodation of Luciano's wishes led, albeit indirectly, to a new low in Luciano's relationship with Renata Scotto.

Luciano, as I said, felt quite at home in San Francisco and regularly tried out all his new roles there. To open the 1979 season, Kurt Herbert Adler contracted Luciano and Scotto to appear in *Anna Bolena*. Donizetti wrote three operas based on English queens—Mary Stuart, Anne Boleyn, and Elizabeth I, the female lead in *Roberto Devereux* (and a character in *Maria Stuarda*)—and this trilogy is considered a pinnacle of the bel canto repertoire.

But by then, Luciano was casting his eye farther afield. For one thing, his high C was no longer as easy and reliable as it had been a decade earlier; voices tend to darken and get a little heavier as they age, and Luciano's was no exception—which meant that the high-wire acts of the bel canto roles were getting harder. For another, the real meat of the tenor repertory—the roles that made the great Italian tenors of the twentieth century, Caruso and Gigli and di Stefano and Mario del Monaco and Franco Corelli—lies not in bel canto but rather in the heavier, more dramatic operas of Verdi, Puccini, or Amilcare Ponchielli. Ponchielli was a re-spected composer and Puccini's teacher, but today he's basically remembered for one opera: the spectacular, melodious, melo-dramatic-to-the-point-of-kitsch *La Gioconda*. That opera is the source of "Cielo e mar," one of Luciano's best arias. Luciano de-cided he wanted to sing the whole thing.

Kurt Adler was happy to comply. As I said, he adored Luciano and would do just about anything for him—although not, as a rule, before complaining mightily to Luciano's long-suffering manager. And for once, Luciano had given plenty of notice: he made his wishes known at least a year before the premiere. So Mr. Adler called up Scotto and informed her of the change in reper-tory.

In 1979, Scotto was at the top of the heap. She was supposed to be the reigning Italian diva of the day. I'd managed her for a while earlier in her career and I couldn't get her through the door of the Metropolitan Opera, but then Jimmy Levine came along and took her under his wing and she became the queen of the company. She appeared in virtually every major Italian opera the Met did and in a lot of other theaters, as well. She was big news.

Big as Scotto was, however, there was one thing she wasn't big enough for, and that was the role of Gioconda. Gioconda is a sweet little ballad singer who roams the streets of Venice, singing for pennies and nurturing an unrequited passion for the disguised prince Enzo Grimaldi. This would seem an ideal role for the diminutive Scotto, who is something like five feet tall on a good day. Ponchielli, however, endowed his ballad singer with a pretty impressive set of pipes. If you encountered a real ballad singer on the street who produced Gioconda's volume, you wouldn't throw pennies: either you'd throw a $100 bill or you'd run in the oppo-site direction. The part is considered the province of dramatic sopranos—big, passionate voices. It was simply out of Scotto's range.

Adler knew this perfectly well when he asked Scotto if she would mind learning Gioconda instead of Anna Bolena. He didn't really think she would do it. The company had already gotten hold of Grace Bumbry, a former mezzo-soprano who had negotiated a change upward into the soprano repertory, and told her the part was hers.

Scotto also knew that Gioconda wasn't exactly for her. She considered Adler's offer for six weeks. She tested the part in her voice. Then she went to her manager and said, "I can do it. As long as nobody expects me to do it in the style of the big Verdi sopranos."

The public, of course, did expect it. But Adler couldn't say anything. He already had her under contract. Singers may disregard contracts or not at will, but if a theater director does, he's asking for big trouble.

Scotto showed up for rehearsals a day late because she got tied up recording *Traviata* with Alfredo Kraus on EMI. It didn't matter, though, because Luciano didn't show up for another two weeks. He had better things to do than hang around the rehearsal studio—even when he was rehearsing. After he arrived, the whole cast was summoned to Luciano's suite in the Huntington Hotel, and continued—after a fashion—to do their work there. At least, they continued up to the middle of act 2, at which point Luciano closed his score, got up, and left the room. That was as far as he'd gotten.

"What the hell is he coming here for if he doesn't know the goddamn opera?!" Adler raged at me.

"Well, teach it to him!" I said.

Adler basically had no choice, so he taught it to him. Or rather, Otto Guth taught it to him. Luciano had a few coaches scattered around the world who were responsible for his getting onstage at all. Preeminent among these were Gildo Di Nunzio at the Met and Otto Guth in San Francisco. Otto was one big reason Luciano liked to try out new roles in San Francisco. Luciano felt comfortable with Otto.

This, of course, was not calculated to endear Luciano to his fellow singers. It was no more endearing when the press turned up and had eyes only for Luciano. Opening night was going to be televised, and *TV Guide* came to photograph the two leading singers for its cover. As far as Scotto was concerned, that was one leading singer too many. She, after all, had the title role. Luciano probably agreed that two leads was too many. This kind of thing did very little to create a harmonious working atmosphere. Maybe it was a good thing that the *TV Guide* cover never ran.

Meanwhile, there was a certain anti-Scotto faction forming among members of the public. There's only one direction you can go from the top, and that's down. Some fans were getting a little tired of Madame Scotto, particularly given the vocal inconsistencies that were starting to creep into her singing. And some took exception to a couple of interviews she had given in Europe not long before. In one, she claimed that she communed regularly with the spirit of the legendary Maria Malibran, widely viewed as the greatest female singer who ever lived (a claim that is impossible to prove, since Malibran died after a fall from a horse in 1836, well before the age of recording). Scotto was probably speaking figuratively, but to some people in the opera world this is not unlike alleging that you alone are in possession of the word of God.

In Milan, an interviewer asked Scotto about another legend, Maria Callas. For a soprano, questions about Callas are inevitable, and Scotto was probably sick of hearing them.

"Callas was the past," Scotto said. "I am the present. I am now."

Of course, the Callas fans took that as a statement of incredible hubris. For one thing, many opera lovers simply don't accept that Callas *is* the past. EMI, her record label, has practically convinced the public that Callas is still alive, more than twenty-five years after her death. Whether she's alive or dead, her fans are ready to defend her to the hilt.

Some of this growing animosity found expression in an anonymous letter Scotto received shortly before the premiere, ostensibly wishing her good luck on her first *Gioconda*.

"My dear Madame Scotto," it said, or words to that effect. "I am so looking forward to hearing you in San Francisco. I was so glad to hear you in Milan: your tones are indeed better than Callas's, your top notes so blooming, your bottom notes so rich and resonant." (Scotto, at the time, was beginning to have trouble with shrillness of timbre; rich and resonant were not applicable adjectives, particularly to her lower register.) "But I do hope that Maria Malibran, when you spoke to her, was not perhaps teasing you and is not now rolling in her grave, twirling from the force of her laughter."

Basically, the underlying message was, "You have no business going anywhere near this part." And it was signed "Enzo Grimaldi." Which was the name of Luciano's character.

Now, Luciano is capable of many things, but this was completely outside his compass. I'm not even sure Luciano knows who Maria Malibran was. If Scotto had claimed in an interview to be communing with Enrico Caruso, it would have pissed him off but he would have found a different way to express his annoyance. This letter smacked of the knowledge and biting wit peculiar to a certain kind of hard-core opera lover: the standees at the Met, or the infamous *loggionisti* in Milan. But the letter enraged Scotto, and since she was already furious with Luciano she made a convenient target. She decided to believe that he had written it.

If you've seen Walt Disney's *Fantasia*, you know at least a little bit of *La Gioconda*, an excerpt of the ballet *Dance of the Hours*, which Disney illustrates with tutued hippopotami chased by a snapping crocodile. Between the girth of one of the singers and the animosity that was crackling in the air between the two leads by opening night, the hippo and crocodile imagery had more than a little application to this production. Scotto had worked herself into such a state that she kept threatening to cancel altogether. Luciano was not impressed with Scotto's affectations. He was very sensitive to prima donna behavior—in other singers. For some reason he never seemed to notice that he often behaved the same way.

Sometimes that kind of energy can help bring a little spark to a performance. Opening night was pretty electric. In the audience, the anti-Scotto contingent was out in force. Gioconda's big aria, "Suicidio," doesn't come until act 4, and Renata gave it all she had. Not, evidently, to everyone's satisfaction. *"Povero Ponchielli!"*—poor Ponchielli—came a shout from the audience. Actually, it could have been a cumulative comment on the evening. To my ear, Luciano had sung very well, but he had a few problems in the big ensemble in the third act. Some of that section is almost a cappella—that is, without orchestral accompaniment—and in that kind of passage, he had a tendency to get lost. It didn't help that, to ensure that the telecast would end on time, numerous cuts had been made in the music, which ended up confusing everybody. But you could certainly hear exciting singing that night, no doubt about it.

After the performance, the diva was seething in her dressing room. Luciano had taken a solo bow, an honor she felt should be reserved only for the singer in the title role. Her opinion of him was sealed. "Plácido Domingo, the greatest tenor in the world, would never do that," she fumed. "I will feel much better when I am back in New York and no longer in the middle of all these *gente di merda*"—shitty people.

At this sensitive moment, a distinguished and clueless well-wisher came to the diva's dressing room to extend his warm congratulations. To lend authority to his presence, he mentioned that he was a friend of Luciano Pavarotti.

It was too much for Scotto. "A friend of Luciano Pavarotti," she said, practically pushing the man out of her dressing room. "If you want Luciano Pavarotti, go and find Luciano Pavarotti. This is not a good friend. This is a bad friend."

Unfortunately for her, there was a film crew in the house making a documentary about opening night at the San Francisco Opera, and they got the whole thing on camera, much to the edification and amusement of the viewing public who saw it a few months later.

Scotto's relationship with Luciano was pretty much a write-off after that. The next time they sang together was in Chicago, a couple of years later, in Verdi's *Un Ballo in Maschera*. Sing together is perhaps a misleading term: what they really did was stand on the stage of the Chicago Lyric and sing at the same time. They didn't look at each other or interact. As a representation of a love duet, it left something to be desired. But they were pros. They knew how to sustain a mood. They managed to keep up that total lack of interaction for the whole run of eight or nine performances.

Scotto continued for a long time to act as if Luciano simply wasn't there. She made her point most noticeably in her autobiography, when she completely omitted any mention of Luciano's name, even in the discography and index. Considering the number of performances they had sung together, that was quite a feat. They finally made up, though. In fact, they had a big, sloppy reunion, as if they were dear old friends. For Luciano's fortieth anniversary on the stage, in 2001, Renata even came out and joined in the singing. It's practically a rule of thumb about opera feuds that nothing is so terrible it can't, or won't, eventually be reconciled. That's one reason I don't take it too seriously when artists blow up at me.

But the singer Luciano had the most trouble with was Plácido.

Singers are very competitive people. Rivalry is just a part of their makeup. Their thinking goes that if Madame X is getting attention, there's less attention left over for me. And opera singers can't stand not being the center of attention.

So whether or not there's any reason for there to be a rivalry, singers will practically go out of their way to imagine competition. I remember Birgit Nilsson standing in the wings of the Metropolitan Opera one night when Montserrat Caballé was singing. Somebody spotted her and said, "What are you doing here?"

"I'm here to hear Madame Aballé," Birgit said.

"Madame Aballé? You mean Madame Caballé."

"No," Birgit said sweetly, "Madame Aballé. She has lost her C."

That's a very typical kind of a story about opera singers. Birgit had no reason to feel threatened by Montserrat. They tended to sing completely different roles. But Birgit may have felt that Montserrat was becoming a bigger star than she was. It's very difficult to say. The only thing there's no doubt about is that Birgit *did* have a high C. Anyone who ever heard it is not likely to forget that.

So rivalry is inevitable, and rivalry between Luciano and Plácido was doubly inevitable because, as I said, they were the two biggest tenors around and they came up at around the same time. But I think Plácido felt it especially keenly.

It had to have been frustrating for Plácido. He was always number two. And Plácido worked like hell. He was tremendously ambitious, and he had all ten fingers stuck in ten different pies. He tried to learn the most roles, sing in the most languages, be in the most places. He put in all this work, and then Luciano got the lion's share of the attention. Plácido's attitude was, "I've earned it. I deserve it. More than he does."

But feeling he deserved it may have been part of the problem. On some level, Plácido is very self-consciously aware of being a terrific musician and a good-looking guy, and that may have come across a little bit. His attitude was not unlike that of Roberto Alagna, the tenor I mentioned before who set out, many years later, to follow in Luciano's and Plácido's footsteps. If you go up to Roberto after a concert and say, "Roberto, you were wonderful," he's likely to answer, "I know."

Plácido might not be so open about it, but he's basically the same way. After he sings, his feeling is, "I worked so hard and I was so good; why didn't the audience leap to its feet?"

Luciano was a little bit different. He certainly wasn't vain about his looks, and if you compliment him on his voice, he will probably say something disparaging. But in his prime, he approached every performance with one determination. With Luciano, it wasn't, "Why didn't they get to their feet?" It was, "I will bring them to their feet." And he knew how to do it. He knew how to reach people and get them so excited they would jump up and scream when he was done. That was one of the big, big secrets of his success.

Another, of course, was the voice. In his dreams, Plácido never had a voice like that.

Plácido also looked down on all of Luciano's nonoperatic activities—at least until he saw how well our strategy was working. After that, he changed directions and began following suit, but he was always tagging along behind. I always said, "If you want to know what Plácido will do next, just look at what Luciano was doing two years ago."

But Plácido didn't have anybody strategizing for him the way I was for Luciano. Sure, he had people working for him—people like Edgar Vincent, who filled the same combined manager-publicist role that I did for Luciano—but they didn't have the same function in terms of coming up with new projects for him and that sort of thing. Plácido would try to do those things himself.

Judy Drucker told me that once she was sitting on the beach in Miami and her cell phone rang.

"Judy? This is Plácido."

"Come on," Judy said, "who is this?"

"It's me, Plácido!"

"No, come on," she said, "who is this really?"

He finally convinced her it was really him. And then he revealed the reason for his call. He was hoping to come and do a big concert with her in Miami Beach. He even had a date in mind.

Judy said, "I'm sorry, Plácido, I can't do it, because two weeks before that date I have Luciano."

"Oh," Plácido said, "always he comes before me."

So Plácido really felt quite ill used by Luciano. And by me. There was a great deal of hostility—not open hostility but quiet hostility—between Plácido and myself because he always suspected that I was doing something against him behind his back, which was not true. But he felt that way: as if I was there to promote Luciano and unpromote him. There was one incident where Luciano had a new record out, and an ad announcing a new release from "the greatest tenor in the world" ran in a program at the Metropolitan Opera on a night Plácido was singing there. Someone wasn't paying attention, because that kind of thing really shouldn't happen. But it wasn't malice on our part. We didn't have anything against Plácido, and we didn't need to conspire against him. Luciano was already on top.

LUCIANO PAVAROTTI
quoted in the Italian magazine Telesette, *November 1980*

Domingo seeks publicity. Every time I have a success, he pushes his way in to get attention in one way or another. He's an artist of the highest caliber, but he's not a man of quality. I'll say it plainly and you can write it: he's a black marketeer who unseated Carreras by getting him thrown out of the theaters that he wanted. He always uses the names of Caruso and Björling to create free publicity for himself. And I don't understand why a man whom God gave the gift of being such a great artist can show himself to be so ungenerous.

But there was one place where Plácido did have the upper hand: the Metropolitan Opera.

In 1978, an old friend of Luciano's arrived at the Met: Joan Ingpen took over as artistic administrator. You might think it was the end of all our problems. But you should never take anything for granted in this business.

Joan did express the sentiment that the Met had let things slide with Luciano, and she made a point of scheduling a meeting with him soon after she arrived. She went up to his apartment at the Hampshire House and patiently sat there while Luciano vented all of his resentment of the Met at her. He didn't vent it openly, of course. He just let her wait for him. He kept going in and out.

He would leave the room to go make pasta. He would cut her off to take a phone call. He was deliberately trying to make a point.

To Joan, it was more or less water off a duck's back. She hadn't gotten to where she was by being thin-skinned. But at that point, she tended to share Ricky Bonynge and Joan Sutherland's slightly disparaging attitude toward Luciano's monstrous success. She wasn't impressed by his shenanigans, and she didn't think he had much to say artistically.

"Who wants to hear a little bird sing?" she said. Or at least, that's what I heard.

And she didn't use him all that much. There was one season when she said she had nothing at all for him. There was just no way to fit him into the schedule. And this for one of the greatest tenors—and certainly the biggest box office draw—in the world.

As I said before, Luciano and Jimmy Levine didn't get along so well in the beginning, either. One low point was a *Rigoletto* they did together at the Met. Jimmy was going through a phase of faithfully sticking to the written score. Italian opera arias, you see, have gone through a process over the years not unlike a game of Telephone. Notes that the composers didn't actually write have come to be an accepted part of some arias. There's a certain sense to this. In the eighteenth century, Handel and his contemporaries expected singers to embellish the written vocal line with flourishes of their own devising. This practice continued into the bel canto writing of the nineteenth century. Even after ornament and embellishment were no longer widely utilized, it was pretty much assumed that singers would work extra high notes in at certain places in the music, if they could sing them.

But in the twentieth century, the early-music movement introduced a whole new concept of performance practice. The idea was to strip Bach and Handel of the mannerisms that had gradually grown up around them and play the music the way it originally sounded—or as close to that as one could determine from historical sources. By extension, a number of opera conductors, like Riccardo Muti, decided that all opera scores should be sung exactly as written, without those interpolated high notes. Of course, singers don't like this very much. Not only does it rob them of their traditional big climax, but they worry that people will think that they aren't singing the notes because they *can't* sing the notes. For a tenor, high notes are equivalent to manhood. And it's a very dangerous thing to tamper with an Italian's manhood.

Jimmy wanted to conduct an "original" *Rigoletto* and leave out the high note at the end of the Duke's act 2 aria, "Parmi veder le lagrime." Luciano, of course, wasn't very excited about that idea, but Jimmy insisted. So Luciano called on a piece of time-honored singer tradition. He avoided the high note in rehearsal, and then, on opening night, when the big moment arrived, he swerved his eyes away from the conductor and pounded out his high B-flat.

The audience went wild. So did Jimmy, for a very different reason. He was upset enough that Schuyler Chapin himself, the Met's general manager at the time, reprimanded Luciano, who of course apologized. Nobody seriously thought he was very sorry, though.

But 1982 saw the beginning of a sea change in Luciano's relationship with the Met. It came in a very unlikely form: Mozart's *Idomeneo*.

As I said, Mozart was never really Luciano's forte. He had a wonderful voice for Mozart, but Mozart involves a whole different style of singing than most of the roles Luciano took on. With *Idomeneo*, Mozart was still firmly within the eighteenth-century tradition of opera seria, which involves having a character come onstage, sing some recitative to explain what's going on, then sing a big aria that repeats so that he can add all manner of vocal flourishes to the tune he laid out the first time through. There are wonderful opere serie, but if Verdi or Leoncavallo is your thing, with their big arcs of raw emotion, then this more stylized form takes a little getting used to. Even Mozart moved away from it in the operas he's best known for today, like *Nozze* and *Don Giovanni*, which have more in common with our contemporary notions of drama.

The music of *Idomeneo* wasn't completely new to Luciano, be-

cause he had sung Idamante, the role of the prince, at Glynde-
bourne in 1964. Learning Mozart in 1964 wasn't any easier for
him than it was to be eighteen years later, but he had been very
impressed with the caliber of work that was done at Glynde-
bourne. It must have given him some vestigial memory of a work
ethic that he associated with this piece, because he really worked
very hard to get the title role, which he was singing here for the
first time, under his belt.

It was a lot of work. The Met chose to do the earlier version
of the opera, which was more complex. With one exception. Luciano performed the later, simpler version of the tenor aria "Fuor
del mar." But he did it very well.

The Met put a lot into the production. They cast some top-
flight singers. The raving princess Elettra was Hildegard Behrens,
the eccentric, gap-toothed German diva whose voice was as un-
even as her performances were dramatically compelling. Ilia was
Ileana Cotrubas, a Romanian soprano with a beautiful voice.
Idamante, the role of the young prince that Luciano had sung in
1964, was originally written for a castrato. In the sixties and seventies, castrato roles were often sung by a tenor, an octave below
the range in which they were originally written, but by the eigh-
ties, they were increasingly played by women in men's costume,
who could sing them in the original key; and the Met engaged
Frederica von Stade, America's reigning lyric mezzo. Jean-Pierre
Ponnelle, a well-known and intermittently very fine stage director, was responsible for the production, and Jimmy conducted.
And it was really quite a success. The Met even took the production to the Salzburg Festival at the end of that season, and it
went well there, too, which is no mean feat. It takes chutzpah for
a foreigner to come in and sing Mozart in his hometown.

But even more important, what happened in the course of that
Idomeneo was that Luciano won Jimmy Levine's respect. Jimmy
learned how to work with Luciano and get results from him. And
he saw that he was, in fact, capable of working hard. He really
could make an effort, go out on a limb, go beyond his comfort
zone.

That was really what made that *Idomeneo* so important for Luciano. He was saying, in effect, "Look, I can still be an artist. A real artist."

There weren't too many moments like that left.

The Met didn't engage Luciano only for really big roles. Before *Idomeneo*, he added two somewhat smaller roles to his repertoire there. One was the Italian tenor in Strauss's *Der Rosenkavalier*, which is a big glorious opera about eighteenth-century Vienna. In one scene the Field Marshal's wife (the Marschallin) receives petitioners in her morning room, and while she's having her hair done with all these people running around, she's serenaded by a hired Italian singer. The Italian singer is onstage for about four minutes of this four-hour opera, during which he performs a gorgeous and extremely difficult lyric aria, and then he gets to take his bow and collect his fee and go home. Luciano got very fond of that role. He did it in a lot of theaters for a while.

The other role was Rodolfo in Verdi's *Luisa Miller*. Rodolfo is a bigger role than the Italian tenor, but still you have only one big aria and a couple of duets. It was a lovely role for Luciano, but it's not the largest part the tenor world has known.

Of course, I went to hear Luciano every time he sang in New York. It was one of his unspoken rules. In fact, I heard pretty much every performance he sang in the States, and if I could make it to some of the ones in Europe, too, so much the better.

But during his *Luisa Miller* run at the Met, one of the performances—not the premiere—happened to fall on my anniversary. So for that one performance I sent Merle Hubbard, one of my right-hand men in the office in those days, in my place. And I took Carol out to dinner.

Luciano could hardly fail to notice an omission like that.

"Where were you?" he demanded the next morning.

"Well," I said, "it was our anniversary, and Carol and I went out to celebrate. I'm sure you understand."

"Herbert," said Luciano, in a less-than-friendly tone. "We are all eating from the same pig."

Luciano's idea, you see, was that I was profiting from his performance. That was the pig. That "pig," as he saw it, was feeding me and my whole office. And since I was making money from the things that he did, I had better show up when he was earning the money. Never mind that I worked all day long to set up those performances, to organize events, to keep him happy and keep him in the limelight. The way he saw it, I was making money off him. And he wasn't going to do all the work alone. I had to at least look like I was working for it, too. If I wasn't there when Luciano sang, he thought I was slacking off.

JOAN INGPEN

I'll never forget one experience with the Rosenkavalier *at the Met. In order to get Luciano there to rehearse for* Idomeneo, *I'd engaged him to do the Italian Singer. It was rather a luxury. One member of the board said to me, "I hope you're not paying his full fee for that." He needn't have worried: we weren't.*

Well, one evening Luciano came into the theater and he started clearing his throat. And he couldn't get his throat clear. So his voice was giving him problems, and this went on, and he couldn't make up his mind whether he was going to sing that night or not. My poor cover singer was hanging around, waiting to find out whether he needed to warm up.

Herbert finally came to me and said, "Well, it's for you to tell him whether he's singing."

I said, "Oh, no. Because if I tell him he can't sing, you're going to demand his fee, because I was the one who canceled a contracted performance. He's got to decide himself whether he's singing or not."

This went on until ten minutes before curtain, which is so unprofessional. And in the end, he didn't sing. Of course.

Opera was all very well, but we also needed to keep finding new challenges outside the opera house. For one thing, opera wasn't where Luciano was going to make the big money.

Big money was about to make its way into the picture.

In October 1983, Luciano gave a concert in Atlantic City presented by a fast-talking Hungarian named Tibor Rudas. It was a fateful event, in more ways than one, as I was very quickly to discover.

But one thing it showed me right away was that Luciano could make money on a scale we hadn't yet dreamed of. He could draw 9,000 paying listeners in a heartbeat. Because he could sell out so quickly, it was hard to find a venue big enough to accommodate everybody who wanted to hear him. We already knew that he could draw hundreds of thousands when he performed outdoors. But Carnegie Hall has only 2,800 seats. Avery Fisher Hall, where he sang with the New York Philharmonic, has 2,500.

Then there's Madison Square Garden.

Madison Square Garden seats 20,000 people. It's where the pop stars and the New York Knicks play. It's where the circus performs. Initially, it wasn't clear that it was a great place for Luciano to sing.

But when you start digging back, you find that classical artists used to play Madison Square Garden all the time. Adelina Patti, the world-famous soprano of the late nineteenth century, sang at the Garden. Paderewski, the great Polish pianist (and, later, prime minister), played at the Garden. Even Toscanini played the Garden; with the NBC Orchestra, he had the American tenor Jan Peerce sing the Duke in act 4 of *Rigoletto*. There's been plenty of classical music at the Garden. Back in the days when opera singers were advertising cigarettes, there was no shame at all in the idea: there wasn't even a concept of "selling out"—apart, of course, from selling out all the seats in the auditorium.

Admittedly, those earlier performances were in different, smaller Gardens. The current Madison Square Garden opened in 1968. For a classical performer, the problem it poses is one of what I call acoustification. Classical artists don't usually use sound enhancement—that is, microphones and speakers—but in a space like the Garden, you have no choice. There are a few huge spaces where the human voice carries effortlessly, like the Arena in Verona, Italy, which seats 18,000 people and where you can easily hear a solo singer all the way in the top row, but Madison Square Garden, unfortunately, was built without the know-how of the ancient Roman acousticians who made Verona's Arena so perfect.

Critics make a big fuss about acoustification. They act like they're protecting a great tradition. I'd like to know exactly what they're protecting it from. Caruso sang concerts in bullfight arenas. Ernestine Schumann-Heink (who had sons fighting in both the German and the American armies in World War I) sang "Over There" in Times Square. Those singers didn't need any protecting from their encounters with pop culture. We need to be careful that we don't "protect" classical music right out of existence.

Luciano had nothing against singing into a mike. In fact, he liked it. Believe me, if there had been acoustification in Caruso's day, Caruso would have liked it, too.

So I decided to present Luciano at Madison Square Garden.

My thinking was not all that different from my thinking the first time I presented Luciano in solo concert, eleven years earlier. I wanted him to try his act out on the road before bringing it to New York. In 1984, of course, there was a lot less risk involved. For one thing, Luciano had already pretty well codified his concert repertory: he was not going to be singing a lot of unfamiliar material at this concert. For another, he was so popular that we sold out everywhere as soon as tickets went on sale. So I set up a five-stadium tour, from Chicago to the Hollywood Bowl. The second concert, after a warm-up in Chicago, was at the Garden.

Of course, I got it on television. And of course, it was a huge success. But I don't think we were prepared for quite how successful it was.

It sold out. It sold out so much that we made time to schedule a second Garden concert a few months later, and that sold out, too. It sold out so much that Luciano broke the standing record for a single performer in the venue. He passed Michael Jackson. He passed everything except the New York Rangers: apart from them, he was the Garden's biggest moneymaker of the season. The Garden took note. After those concerts, they even hired someone to help them book more classical acts. I don't think they ever found anything to measure up to Luciano.

And I have to say, we weren't just feeding people junk, either. All right, Luciano may not have sung the most varied repertory. And at the beginning, he was a little stiff. Which was to be expected. He'd given huge concerts before, but there's a difference between singing to 100,000 picnickers in the park and 20,000 people who have paid quite a bit of money to hear you in a cavernous arena.

But he was determined to get all 20,000 of those people to their feet. And he could. He could because of that romantic voice he had, which pulled you in with this incredible sound. To the best of my knowledge, that's something nobody else can do like Luciano: make love to you with the sound of his voice. Luciano could. He could do it every time, if he wanted to. And at the Garden, when he began to sing the Italian song "Non ti scordar di me," that melting folklike waltz that crooningly implores, "Don't forget me, my life is empty without you; don't forget me"—when he came in with that song, 20,000 people creamed in their pants.

So I presented my tenor in sold-out Madison Square Garden. Looking back, you could say it was the peak of our career.

chapter VIII

MONEY MAKES THE WORLD
GO ROUND

*The Real Motivation of Opera Stars—
and Their Managers*

Tibor Rudas tells the story all the time, so why shouldn't I? It's the story of how he came to present Luciano Pavarotti.

I should have known Luciano was too big an act for me to keep all to myself.

Tibor is a mad Hungarian show-biz entrepreneur. The Hungarian part is important. Sir Georg Solti, who was Hungarian himself, said that when a Hungarian goes into a revolving door behind you, he comes out ahead of you. That's Tibor to a T. He's emotional, hotheaded, and a little choleric. And very, very savvy.

When Luciano and I met Tibor, his specialty was presenting acts in casinos. He came by his experience in the field in the most tried-and-true way imaginable: he joined the circus. As a result, there's a little P. T. Barnum about Tibor. He's always wanted to show the biggest and the best. He adores classical music and he longs to be accepted by the classical music establishment, but he's never lost his taste for tinsel. In fact, you could say he has gone right on presenting circuses until the end of his career. I mean, what else would you call The Three Tenors? But I'm getting ahead of my story.

When Tibor entered my life, and Luciano's life, around 1980, he was booking acts for Resorts International, finding the talent for casinos in Atlantic City and Las Vegas. They weren't cheap acts, either. He had put on the New York Philharmonic, under Zubin Mehta, at Atlantic City, and after that he was able to book a number of classical artists. And he wanted to put on Luciano.

Now, as I have made clear by now, I have nothing against so-called crossover, and I was all for getting Luciano the widest possible audience. After all, I went on to present him at Madison Square Garden. But at the same time—and regardless of what people say about me—I have certain standards. Today, it probably sounds naïve, but I thought there were limits to what one could do and still be in good taste. When you're working to build up your artist's name, you don't necessarily want it associated with people gambling and that sort of thing. I said, "Luciano Pavarotti is not singing in a casino."

So Tibor went away. And came back. And came back again. Each time, he was offering more money.

I kept right on throwing him out.

Tibor worked on me for three years. Or so he always says. I wouldn't even let him into my office.

Finally, he stuck his head through the door of my office and yelled, "A hundred thousand dollars!"

There were never any cubicles at Herbert Breslin, Inc. Everyone sat together in one big room, and talked on the phone at the top of their lungs, and met clients, and generally did business very openly. The volume level was a little bit like that at the New York Stock Exchange. To the uninitiated, it was chaos, but we were all used to it. It took a lot to get the office quiet. With that offer, Tibor managed it. I'll be frank: I don't remember exactly how much it was. But it was more than anybody had ever gotten paid for a concert.

I said, "Get in here."

It may have been one of the biggest mistakes I ever made.

Let's face it: money is what it's all about. People criticize me for being in this business for money. Well, listen: it's a business. Everyone is in it for money. You want to be successful? It means you're making money. There are very few poor successful people in this world.

And I'm certainly not alone. Most singers feel the way I do.

Let me give you a little lesson in the economics of singing. Contrary to what many people may think, opera singing is a very inadequate get-rich-quick scheme. In the entertainment industry, it's small potatoes.

Here's what I mean. Top fee at the Metropolitan Opera these days is $14,000, which sounds like a lot of money for a night's work. Well, right away you have to lop off 30 percent in taxes. Then the singer has to pay his agent's fee, which is usually 10 percent in opera, if you can get him to pay it. That leaves him with $8,400. Then he has to pay travel expenses to New York—usually a first-class plane ticket, another couple of thousand—and living expenses while he's here. If he's got a publicist, he has to pay that fee, too. He has to go through a couple of weeks of rehearsal before he can start cashing in on that top fee. And he can sing only two or three times a week. Opera isn't like Broadway, where you can sing every day; you have to rest your voice between performances.

So if you're a big star, you don't earn your big money from opera. It comes through the concert work. For singers like Luciano and Plácido, the advantages of singing at a house like the Met are not so much what they're getting paid as what the perks are for doing it. Maybe they can get a performance on TV, for example. That way they get more exposure and more people are going to want to come hear them sing an open-air concert in Miami, for which they may get a six-figure fee.

As I said, everyone is focused on money. The amount of time that's spent discussing money in this business is almost frightening. That's the reason the Met has to be so strict about its top fee. Not that the amount, in itself, made all that much difference to Luciano. But it couldn't be one single dollar less than they paid Plácido. Luciano isn't alone: nearly everybody feels this way. When he sang *Aida* for the first time, the soprano, Margaret Price, got sick, and the San Francisco Opera brought in the great Leontyne Price as a deluxe last-minute substitute. Miss Price—Leontyne, that is—was reportedly very clear about her salary demands.

"I want one dollar more than you're paying that fat man," she's supposed to have said. I'm sure she got it.

And nobody wants to pay taxes. Taxation without representation is tyranny—and do singers ever believe it. In the spirit of protest that inflamed the American Revolution, everybody tries to find ways to get out of it. Teresa Berganza, a Spanish mezzo-soprano who was in her prime during my first decades in this business, was one singer who simply refused to pay them. That is, she wanted to get a certain amount of money when she sang a concert, and no taxes were to come out of that, thank you very much. In order to get it for her, her manager, Leverett Wright at Columbia, had to jack up her fee considerably. If she wanted $4,000, he had to charge almost $8,000, to cover taxes and his commission. He priced her almost out of competition, and consequently Berganza didn't have as big a career over here as she might have.

In New York in the sixties and seventies, there was an accountant all the foreign singers went to who would get what they called "instant refunds." You came to the Met and this accountant would do your papers, and you'd go down to the IRS office, and they gave you clear sailing, and you left the country that day, and of course your taxes were extremely minor. It was wonderfully convenient. This lasted for quite a few years, until the authorities caught up with that accountant and he went to prison. After that, a number of singers didn't come back to the States very much. Birgit Nilsson, Renata Tebaldi, and a few others made themselves scarce for a while.

Luciano didn't like taxes any more than the rest of them. At one point, when he was on a tirade about taxes and thieves and so on and so forth, he told me that I needed to fly to Washington to meet with the president of the United States. I needed to tell him that he should exempt opera singers from paying taxes.

"Oh, really?" I said. "And why is that?"

"Well," said Luciano, "because we have a very short working life."

Luciano's working life was so "short" that he has appeared on the stage for more than forty years. Of course, you could argue that he wasn't working very hard for some of that time, so maybe his working life was shorter than other people's. But that sure wasn't reflected in his earnings.

Anyway, I didn't go see the president about Luciano's taxes. But I did what I could. To begin with, we formed a corporation in America that would pay him a salary and take care of his business expenses. This is standard procedure for many artists; we had a corporation for Alicia de Larrocha, too. In her heyday, Alicia was earning $500,000 a year in the United States. The only sensible way to deal with her American finances was to have a corporation.

I was president of Luciano's corporation, World Wide Concerts. This meant that my office paid his rent, his health insurance, his credit card bills, his secretaries. We paid my fee, too; when a check came in, I took my commission automatically. This is all open and aboveboard. It did make it easy on Luciano, though, because he didn't actually have to know what money was going out for. He was a terrible skinflint. He acted as though people weren't actually being paid for the things they did for him. He liked to think of the people who worked for him as one big happy family, and you shouldn't have to pay your family. Given the salaries some of them got, he practically didn't.

Whenever he needed money, he'd say, "Herbert, I want some cash."

"How much do you need?"

"I need five thousand dollars."

So I'd go to the bank and withdraw $5,000 and give it to him. Nothing problematic about that. When the accountant came, he saw the record of that money, and that was income to Luciano, and it was taxed. But Luciano wasn't aware of it. As far as he was concerned, the money just appeared, free as the air.

When money needed to be transferred to Italy, we wired it to Adua. We'd call her up and ask if the lasagne was ready.

"*Sì, è bene*," she'd say; the money had arrived. Or, "*Non ancora*," not yet. Then we knew what to do. We didn't want to discuss finances too openly on an international phone line.

So I would take care of all of this, and I would give Luciano a statement at the end of every month. I made sure he understood our own fee structure, too.

"Look, Luciano," I'd say. "You're doing four performances this month at the Metropolitan Opera, but you're getting paid for six performances. That's my doing. So I'm taking a commission for six performances."

Luciano was perfectly agreeable. It was all quite fair.

Because I had to look out for myself, too. If the economics of a singer's life look bad on paper, the economics of a manager's life are at least ten times worse, because we get only 10 percent of an artist's take. And we have expenses. I have to pay salaries. I have to pay rent. When my company was at its largest, the rent on our office was $50,000 a year. I used to tell my staff, that's $500,000 in opera contracts. That's a lot of opera engagements. As I said, the music business is small potatoes, and if that's an Idaho potato the singer is getting, you, the manager, are getting a french fry. If you aren't careful, it's gone in one bite.

And I was a small company. I didn't have other resources to back me up. The big agencies can afford to take a loss. At Columbia Artists or CAMI, I hear on good authority, their Accounts Payable amounts to a couple of million dollars. That's a couple of million dollars in artists' fees that nobody has been able to collect yet. You want the tough part of an agent's job, you try collecting your 10 percent after your artist has sung. Before they get the engagement, when you're breaking your ass to land them the job, you're the Second Coming. After they've sung and had a big triumph, they forget all about you. They think it was all their great voice that did it. The fact that you worked hard to get them that money is often forgotten. They forget that some of that money belongs to you.

"Oh," they say, "I have a mortgage to pay off. I had to buy a new suit. I had to get this and that and the other thing."

"Well," I would say to that, "you can have whatever you want, but that's my money, and you cannot spend it on yourself until you pay me. We do not print money of our own in this office. I cannot say to my landlord, 'Oh, I have to wait with the rent until I get my commission from this singer.' "

Sometimes these conversations would get quite heated. I would have to get on the phone at the start of every month and pound it into some of them. "I want my money!"

Then people would say, "Oh, the Breslin office is very aggressive."

Well, we are. We have to live on what our artists pay us.

Compounding the difficulties of a manager's financial life is the fact that everything is booked so far in advance. You're working your ass off now to get an engagement three years in the future. So you're always getting paid way, way after the fact. In the spring of 2003, I got a great engagement for one of my singers, the French coloratura soprano Natalie Dessay: a starring role in a new production at the Metropolitan Opera. But it wasn't until 2008.

Someone in the office said, "I hope she's still singing in 2008."

"I hope I'm still alive!" I said. "It's too bad if she can't sing anymore, but what about my being alive? I want to be there to collect my commission! That's more than five years from now!"

And then, of course, when opening night rolls around, she'll probably get sick.

As a businessman, how do you begin to deal with that kind of time lag? And all of the everyday costs of running a business that went into getting that contract in the first place?

Because the economics of the business are so tricky, I was the first agent to institute the practice of a retainer. I asked certain artists to pay me a monthly fee for representing them. Some classical agents hold that this practice is immoral. It's not ethical, they claim, to take money out of the hides of young singers before they've actually started earning it. Traditionally, the agent business is supposed to be a gamble: you find a young talent that you believe in and you work to promote it on the chance that you're right and it will make you money. Well, I'm not a big gambler. I don't like to discover artists; I like other people to discover them. And it's easy to throw around words like immoral, but it's not so easy to keep your head above water in this business.

I looked at it this way: nobody was forcing any artist to work with me and my office. Quite the contrary. Artists were eager to work with me because of what I represented. That cachet was worth something to them. And I was incurring operating costs by working for them, whether I landed them a job or not. Why shouldn't I get paid for my work like everybody else?

One of my models was the legendary impresario Sol Hurok. Hurok was an immigrant from Russia who came to New York as a penniless teenager and ended up presenting most of the important musicians and dancers of the twentieth century. He was famous for saying things like, "If I would be in this business for business, I wouldn't be in this business." That was disingenuous because, believe me, Hurok was a businessman, and a smart one. Working with him was very advantageous for any artist because he had a big name and being presented by him pretty much guaranteed you an audience. Of course he made money off his artists. What he would do is pay them a certain set fee for a concert, then sell them for whatever he could get for them. For example, he might pay Victoria de los Angeles $2,500 and then get her a booking for $6,000, and he would pocket the difference. I don't think she felt she was unfairly treated. He did a lot for her career, and she knew it. Hurok had all the best artists. In my heyday with Luciano, I think I had a little bit of a similar reputation.

Payment is always about what the market will bear. Everyone does whatever he can get away with. The really big singers wouldn't put up with paying me a retainer. Some of them don't even want to put up with paying the going commission rates. The standard rate is 10 percent for opera and 20 percent for concerts, but there are a lot of singers who find those figures far too high. Mirella Freni, for instance, isn't interested in paying 10 percent for opera anymore, so she pays her manager 5 percent. She probably isn't interested in getting a mere $14,000 a performance from the Met anymore, either; I would hazard a guess that she got more than that for her last appearance there in 2002, although I don't know for sure. Mirella is in her sixties and a living legend, so she gets to do whatever she wants.

It's the 20 percent for concert fees that particularly sticks in those golden throats. Somebody like Hildegard Behrens would never pay 20 percent. She would pay 10 percent. Luciano would never pay 20 percent, either. So I took 10 percent. Sometimes I even settled for 5 percent. Look, they were earning me money anyway. I'm a realist. If you're talking about somebody who is grossing a million dollars, and you get 5 percent of that, that's $50,000, which is a hell of a lot better than getting 20 percent from somebody who makes $50,000. I'm not going to walk away from that. I'm as much of a whore as anybody.

The point then becomes to make sure that the amount on which you're getting that 5 percent is as large as possible. And it was amazing how high those amounts went. When Luciano started out, we were talking a few thousand dollars. Within just a few years, we were talking twenty thousand, fifty thousand. Then a hundred thousand. In fact, Luciano and I single-handedly transformed the whole fee structure in opera. Everybody else looked at what he was making and said, "Why can't I earn like that?" Some of them tried. Now, they tell me, Kiri Te Kanawa wants $70,000 for a concert. Renée Fleming, the soprano star of the moment, wants $50,000. Nobody used to get that kind of money. If you got $15,000, that was considered very, very good.

Luciano appreciated his popularity, of course. We were both a little amazed by how easy it became to make money. All the opera companies wanted him to do benefits, because you could go a long way toward making up your deficit in a single night when Luciano Pavarotti sang. They all needed him. They were happy to pay what it took.

I admit I enjoyed it. It made me laugh when I could go to Luciano in 1983, after Tibor and I had come to an understanding, and say, "Hey, I got you your first hundred-thousand-dollar contract."

He enjoyed that, too.

But you know what they say: money is the root of all evil. There's truth to that. Luciano's concern about *soldi*, money, began to supplant his concerns about other things, like learning his music, or rehearsing his roles, or changing his concert repertory, which basically stayed set in stone from the time he started doing concerts. What happens when that kind of money enters the picture is you start to believe that you must be something really special. You begin to believe your own publicity. And you have the feeling that if you really are that good, then you don't have to work so hard.

This is what gradually happened to Luciano. Whatever he asked for, he got. The challenge became to see how *much* we could get.

I came up with a term for the kind of golden handshake Luciano liked. I called it a "giftola." "What can you offer us in the way of a giftola?" I'd say. Very often there was something there to be gotten. As I said, people were eager to get Luciano—at any price.

Luciano had his own concept of a giftola. A horse, for example. By now you know that Luciano adored horses. His horsing around caused us any number of headaches. Once, in Florida, he had to cancel a performance at the last minute.

"Luciano has a cold," I told Judy Drucker.

Judy, by then, was well embarked on her career as a big-league concert presenter. Luciano never forgot his special relation to her from the days of his U.S. debut. He came and sang for her almost every time she asked him.

"A cold?" Judy said skeptically. "He didn't have a cold last night."

"Well, he's got one now," I said.

Actually, it wasn't exactly a cold. It was just that he'd gone out riding, and a dog had run under his horse's nose, and the horse had thrown him. It's a miracle that he wasn't seriously injured. We bundled him on a plane and got him back to New York to recover from his bruises and lecture us on horsemanship.

Despite that, Luciano continued to go riding every chance he got—at least, whenever he had seen enough results from his diet of the moment to enable him to get on horseback. Horses were always galloping off with Luciano. And when he was too heavy to ride himself, he could always collect them. It began with two Irish horses named Herbie and Shaughran and ended up with a stable of something like sixteen horses and Luciano's founding, in 1991, the Pavarotti International Horse Show in Modena. And Luciano was always looking to add to his stable. So he hit upon the bright idea that if people wanted him to come sing somewhere, they should give him more than a fee. They should give him a horse.

Sometimes this ploy actually worked. It made for yet another set of complications our office had to deal with. Luciano was once presented with a horse in Oklahoma, and Hans had to arrange for it to be flown to Kentucky to be bred and then shipped to Italy. It's a good thing Hans likes horses, because not everybody in my office would have known how to go about something like that. That was a pretty deluxe horse. When she was presented to Luciano, she was swaddled in a mink horse blanket. That night, Luciano slept under the mink blanket himself.

On another occasion, however, Luciano didn't like the horse that was offered to him. He looked it over and turned up his nose at it. So we never picked it up. But then, of course, there were ruffled feathers (or manes) to be smoothed over, as well. If someone is ready to give you a horse and you don't take it, it's a bit of a snub.

When he saw how well it worked with the horses, Luciano got it into his head that he wanted a boat. Poor Judy Drucker knocked herself out one year trying to find somebody in Florida who would give Luciano a boat. Nothing came of that, but Judy was great that way. You'd say, "He wants a boat," and she'd say, "OK," and she'd go out there and try to find him a boat. She knew how to keep him happy.

Keeping him happy, especially about money, was not that easy a proposition. The more Luciano earned, the more suspicious he got. He wanted to make very sure he wasn't being taken advantage of. It wasn't just me; other people were "eating from the same pig," too, people like Judy Drucker. It didn't help to explain that presenters like Judy were scrambling to make all the arrangements and meet all his requirements so he'd be willing to sing in their halls. From his point of view, he was the one doing all the work, because it was his singing and his fame that were bringing in the money.

After one Miami concert, Luciano got very angry at Judy. "I never come to that girl again," he said.

Judy and I were reminiscing about it a few months ago.

"You never know why he gets mad," she said. "You bend over backward to try to get everything perfect. You check the hotel rooms, and you install the refrigerators, and you get all the food he wants, and then you've done something wrong."

"You don't remember why?" I said.

"Maybe I didn't compliment him enough or something," she said.

"But it was about that time that Luciano began to get very preoccupied with money," I said. "Don't you remember?"

"I do remember," said Judy, "but I would never have said it myself."

What I remembered was this. Judy had Luciano come down

to give an open-air concert on Miami Beach. Visually, it was pretty memorable, because it was so windy that Luciano wouldn't put on his evening clothes. He didn't want to catch cold. So he gave the concert bundled up in his windbreaker, while the soprano Cynthia Lawrence, who was singing with him, wore the beautiful evening dress I had purchased for her especially for the occasion. Anyway, after the concert, Judy set up another tent and gave a big gala dinner, as a fund-raiser. That's the way it works: you have a benefit dinner and everybody comes and pays a lot of money for the privilege of eating under the same tent as Luciano, and that's how you raise money to give similar concerts in the future. Judy brought in tables, and chandeliers, and plants, and fabulous food for 1,150 people, and it cost a bloody fortune.

Of course, Luciano had done the same kind of thing many, many times before. I think his first tent dinner was in San Diego. But on that particular evening, he saw all the opulence around him, and all he could think was, My God, they're making so much money. So he decided that Judy was using him. Of course, his concert fee had taken this whole appearance into consideration and was accordingly tremendous. But don't try to present that kind of reasoning in the face of Pavarotti logic.

"This is increasingly what he was like," I said to Judy.

"Look," Judy said, "these things happen. It's true, I went through a couple of bad times with Luciano. But you always knew that in a year or two he would be back, and he would have forgotten all about it. And he was."

"Did *you* forget all about it?" I said.

"I did," Judy said, "until you just reminded me."

Well, that's how all of us more or less got along with Luciano. There would be these flare-ups, and then he would come back and everything would be forgotten. I'm not sure it was always so easy for everybody else to forget as Judy says it was for her. But when he was being nice, he could still be so lovable and charming that you would just shrug and keep moving ahead.

After a concert, sometimes you'd look at the presenter with a sigh of relief: "We made it." Sometimes it was Judy you'd sigh with. Sometimes it was Tibor.

The difference with Tibor is that nobody else could offer Luciano what Tibor was offering. Not in terms of perks, and certainly not in terms of money.

Tibor's whole operation was set up to accommodate very big, Las Vegas marquee–type stars and give them all the big-star perks you can imagine: the cars, the catering, the private planes, you name it. When I said that Luciano didn't want to sing in a casino, Tibor's response was, "Fine." Then he went out and built a big tent venue on the beach that could seat 9,000 people. That way, Luciano could sing in Atlantic City, but he didn't have to sing in a casino. Very few singers mind that kind of accommodation of their wishes—or get it, for that matter.

Tibor was also able to pay Luciano amounts of money I couldn't match, in ways I couldn't even begin to think of.

In some respects, you could say that Tibor and Luciano were alike. Gambling, for example. For someone who supposedly had compunctions about singing in a casino, Luciano is pretty serious about gambling. He's a terrific poker player, and he plays for big money. He's also a very big winner. He's very shrewd. Sometimes you'd think, Oh, if he's betting $2,000, he must have something really great. Then it would turn out that he had nothing. The next time, you'd call his bluff, and that time he wouldn't be bluffing. You were always off base.

As I said before, I'm not really a gambler. I like a sure thing. I'm not interested in betting $1,000 on a card game. Of course, I'm interested in winning $1,000, but I'm certainly not interested in losing it. And I'm not a good bluffer. I played poker with Luciano a few times in the early days, and he would always be very critical of everybody at the table because nobody else played with the reckless spirit he did. Everybody was a little shy about betting $5,000 on a hand. Luciano came up with a special nickname for me because of my timid betting. *Cappuccetto rosso*, he called me. Little Red Riding Hood.

But Tibor and Luciano played exactly the same kind of poker game. They were great foils for each other. Neither of them wanted the other to get the better of him. Luciano was fearless. I'll see you for five hundred, he'd say, and then raise another thousand, and before you knew it, the bet was up to several thousand dollars and Tibor was right in there with him. In the end, though, Luciano usually won. He likes to win. He plays hard. I wish that determination to win came out a little more in his artistic side.

The way Tibor gambled was a bit like the way he did business. He played for very high stakes, and he'd go out on a limb, and he'd put all his resources in one direction, presenting Luciano. Whereas I, in business as in poker, like to preserve myself. I don't like to put all my eggs in one basket. I had a whole roster of artists who needed my attention. Furthermore, even if I had tried, I couldn't possibly have done all the things for Luciano that Tibor could do—the perks, the huge events, the money—from my small office. I didn't have the manpower, and I didn't have the connections.

So the handwriting was on the wall.

It wasn't long before Luciano let me know that Tibor was going to be taking over and handling all of his concert work.

Of course, I didn't think that was a very good idea. But there wasn't a lot I could say. Luciano and I had been together for nearly two decades. And I was still making a lot of money from Luciano. I still got my commission. I still handled all the opera contracts. I couldn't necessarily bite the hand that fed me. As Luciano says, we're all eating from the same pig.

I kept running World Wide Concerts, his American corporation, for quite a long time. I still serviced all of Luciano's contracts for appearances within the United States. And I still got my commission on whatever Tibor paid Luciano. At least, on what the contract *said* Tibor paid Luciano. Whatever the perks were, the extras on the side—and there were plenty—I didn't know about most of that.

Chapter IX

ANOTHER OPENING, ANOTHER SHOW

Getting Luciano Onstage

I've said it before: Luciano Pavarotti is the heir to a great Italian musical tradition. He's happy to let everybody know it himself.

The tenor roles he sings are his birthright. He learned most of his arias in childhood, through his father's incessant playing of his great tenor precursors: Caruso, Pertile, Schipa, Gigli. You could say it's in his blood.

At least, the arias are in his blood. What may not have made it into the bloodstream are all the words to all those arias. Nor did he learn the parts of the roles that weren't arias: the dialogue, the recitatives, the ensembles, and all the other things that make an opera an opera. For those, he needed a little help. Well, all right, a lot of help.

And it's not always easy to help Luciano. How can you help somebody who always knows best about everything? To judge by the way he treats what's written in the score, Luciano even knows better than many of the composers who wrote the operas in the first place.

So how does the greatest tenor in the world prepare to go out onstage? It's a question I've gotten a lot. It's hard to give a concise answer, except to say that it involves a lot of people and it's a long process.

The first step is to bring a coach in to teach him his roles. We did that all the time. Gildo Di Nunzio from the Met and Leone Magiera, Mirella Freni's ex-husband, whom we often hired to accompany Luciano's recitals or conduct his concerts, were practically fixtures in Luciano's homes.

But in order to be effective, a coach needs to sit down and work with you. That was the tricky part.

Luciano is not very good at programming his time. There are always a million things to do instead of work, and when you do finally start to work, there's always something to interrupt. The phone will ring and require Luciano's immediate attention. A couple of unexpected visitors will drive up. Some young singer will arrive, pleading that the maestro (that's Luciano) promised to hear him sing, so of course Luciano has to oblige. Then, and most important, it's time to prepare lunch. You can't work without a good lunch. So Leone Magiera might show up at Luciano's house at nine or ten in the morning and sit around until four o'clock in the afternoon without actually getting any coaching done. The fact that other people might have other things to do with their time than wait around for him is not a very big consideration for Luciano.

To get him to do what's required of him, you have to insist a little. That's something about me that was probably very helpful to him, although he may not have felt as if it was helpful at the time. I know how to insist.

"Come on, Luciano, let's do this book project. Let's do this TV production. Let's have you sing *Ernani*."

If you pound Luciano enough, he'll agree. Then, once he's agreed, there's the next step: trying to make him follow through.

"Luciano, do you think you could give the guy a half hour of your time so he can work on the script for the show? Do you think you could sit down with Bill Wright, the author of your book, for half an hour without any interruptions? What do you think he's here for?"

Of course, that generally went over like a lead balloon. But nevertheless I had to keep trying it all the time. Sometimes it worked. We did, for example, manage to get Luciano to sit down with Bill enough times for Bill to produce *Pavarotti: My Own Story*, a book that was on the best-seller lists for a while.

Sometimes my pounding didn't work.

"I had a summer vacation," Gildo Di Nunzio said after one two-week sojourn at Luciano's beach house in Pesaro. "But I might as well have stayed at my own country house, for all the work we got done."

Gildo's country house, I might add, is in Pennsylvania.

Another step in the process of getting Luciano onstage is figuring out what roles to sing. As I said, Luciano was gradually moving into heavier repertory, the meat and potatoes of the Italian tradition: Cavaradossi in *Tosca*, Radames in *Aida*, Calaf in *Turandot*. Not everybody thought these bigger roles were for him. A lot of people will still tell you that Luciano should have stuck with the lighter, more lyric repertory. I had to insist with a lot of opera houses, too, to get them to give him a chance.

People may have said Luciano was taking on too much, but Luciano was very smart about saving his voice. After his first staged *Turandot*, in 1977, he called Sir John Tooley, then general manager of Covent Garden, where he was also supposed to do it. He asked to be let out of his contract.

"I have just sung it once," he said, "and it is a killer for the tenor."

Tooley said, "But you are thinking of singing other heavier roles, like Radames in *Aida*."

"Ahh," Luciano said, "there are certain heavier roles you can sing lyrically. But you cannot sing Calaf that way."

That was a pretty savvy observation. And he followed his own advice. He sang Calaf in *Yes, Giorgio*, but he didn't sing it onstage again for more than twenty years.

There were other roles he avoided for reasons that had nothing to do with his vocal estate. *La Forza del Destino*, for example. Although it's saddled with a rather convoluted plot, *Forza* is one of Verdi's greatest operas, and I thought that Luciano would be perfect in it. I was always trying to get him to do it. The problem was that Luciano wouldn't even let you say the name of the opera in his presence.

Forza is to opera what Shakespeare's *Macbeth* is to spoken theater: bad luck. Actors avoid saying even the name *Macbeth*; they refer to it as "the Scottish play." Everybody dies at the end, and it traffics in the supernatural, and all kinds of terrible things are said to have happened during performances. *Forza* has the same reputation. Its very title, The Force of Destiny, hints at the problem: all the lead characters tempt fate, but fate catches up with everybody in the end. Then everybody dies. Of course, you could point out that dramatic death is a prominent feature of many other operas, but the superstitious can counter with a raft of stories about the bad luck *Forza* has brought down on people. The most infamous took place in 1960, when the tremendous American baritone Leonard Warren collapsed and died onstage while singing *Forza*. What further proof do you need? Any time you mentioned the word *Forza* in front of Luciano, he would immediately touch his balls to ward off bad luck.

Another bad-luck opera is *La Juive*, by Fromental Halévy. *La Juive* is not done all that often these days, but it used to be a major vehicle for a star tenor, most famously Enrico Caruso. But it was also, famously, the last role Caruso ever sang, and for Luciano it was "the role that killed Caruso." Pleurisy and the effects of smoking forty Egyptian cigarettes a day are more likely culprits, but there's no countering superstition with mere fact. *La Juive*, too, has an array of bad-luck stories. Adolphe Nourrit, the tenor who first sang the role (and who even wrote the words to its most famous aria, "Rachel, quand du Seigneur"), killed himself, although not until four years after the opera premiered in 1835. Richard Tucker, who dreamed of singing it at the Metropolitan Opera, died, it's said, the very day the Met offered to stage a new production for him. José Carreras was diagnosed with leukemia during the time he was working on a recording of the opera. And there are other stories. I never managed to get Luciano anywhere near *La Juive*.

In fact, I never managed to get Luciano in any French opera at all. Which I think is a great shame. Luciano, you see, has a natural voice for French music. People often sing French with what's called a white sound, which is easy to recognize when you hear it: it's rather straight, and pale, and even brittle. But the music isn't necessarily supposed to be sung like that. The distinctive liquid brightness of Luciano's voice would have brought some of those roles to colorful life. It was tailor-made for parts like the Chevalier des Grieux in Massenet's *Manon*, which Luciano sang once at La Scala, in Italian, in 1969, and never touched again. Maybe it was just too long for him. It's true that French grand opera, which always extends over five acts, can be a real test of endurance—at least for the audience. When Leonie Rysanek, the great Austrian soprano, went to her first *Manon*, she said, during one of the intermissions, "And they say *Wagner* is long?"

We came close a few times. Massenet's *Werther*, for example: I almost got him to do that one. We even had an actual contract to sing it in Pittsburgh. Unfortunately, he never got around to learning the role. They substituted a *Tosca* instead, and then he came down with a cold or something on opening night and canceled the whole run after singing two-thirds of a performance.

And I would have loved to hear Luciano sing Charles Gounod's *Faust*, based, like *Werther*, on a work by Goethe. Luciano would have been a gorgeous Faust—but he wouldn't go near it. Terry McEwen, who was a great raconteur and a great embellisher, said it was because Faust traditionally wears medieval costume and Luciano wouldn't appear onstage in tights. It's true that Luciano in tights is quite a thing to contemplate, but I don't think that was the reason he didn't do *Faust*. I think it was just that for Luciano to learn the French language would be a little bit like pulling every single tooth out of his head. The costumes wouldn't have been that much of an obstacle. After all, if he had done a *Faust* they could have modified the costumes. People modified everything else for him.

This is a reason stage directors weren't crazy about Luciano. He never really understood the role of the stage director. From his perspective, the whole point of a staging was to help him get through a performance as comfortably as possible. After all, the ticket buyers were paying to hear him sing. He had no illusions that they were paying to see him do anything else, and he didn't even consider that they might be paying to see other members of the cast, or the opera itself. So he couldn't have cared less about a director's vision of the piece. His primary interest was ensuring his maximum comfort. Over the years, as he got arthritis in his hips and an old soccer injury acted up in his knee, he got less and less mobile, and comfort—what he called "safety"—became increasingly a concern.

Stairs, for instance, were extremely "unsafe." In a *La Bohème* he did in San Francisco in 1988, the bohemians were supposed to climb up from downstairs to enter their attic garret. No stairs for Luciano. The stage crew had to cut a hole in the wall for him. So Marcello, Colline, and Schaunard, Rodolfo's pals, all climbed up from the street below, and Rodolfo strolled onstage, presumably levitated through the skies of Paris to get there. There were plenty of performances where that kind of thing took place.

Very few opera houses protested, though, partly because Luciano was right about who the people were paying to hear. A Pavarotti performance was always a sold-out performance. Once Joe Volpe took over as the top administrator in 1990, the Met became particularly accommodating. Joe is not necessarily someone most people think of that way. He worked his way up at the Met from carpenter to general director, and he's kept a tough-talking, street-smart, bullheaded attitude that scares a lot of people who work for him. Getting Joe and Luciano together, two ultratypical Italians, is something to see. Frankly, I prefer not to get between them. They both change their minds so much you can't believe a thing either one says. But when it came to changing stagings around for Luciano, Joe wasn't bothered. His attitude was, "You want a rock onstage to lean on? We'll give you a rock. Just sing the goddamn performance."

JOE VOLPE

We were doing a piano rehearsal for Tosca, *and we had the set. And Luciano saw the stairway in act 3, leading up from Cavaradossi's prison.*

He called me and said, "You know, those stairs, they look pretty dangerous."

"Yeah," I said.

"I'm going to tell you right now," Luciano said, "I will go up and down those stairs, but when I die—and I will die—it will be your fault."

Of course, I killed the stairs.

You know why he said that? Because he didn't want the press to say that the Met changed the set because of him. He didn't want it printed that Luciano Pavarotti wouldn't go up the stairs. So he didn't refuse to do it. He never said he wouldn't go. He made sure I was the one who changed it. Now, that is an Italian.

Since Luciano didn't care all that much about staging, his attitude about rehearsals could be a little cavalier. Rehearsals, after all, are a lot of effort. They involve a lot of sitting around and waiting. And if Luciano is going to sit around and wait, he'd rather do it in the comfort of his own home.

The Met might call a rehearsal at 10:00 in the morning. At 9:20, my phone would ring.

"Herbertino," Luciano's voice would say, "see if they'll come over to the apartment and rehearse here. Then, we can have something to eat."

His colleagues were generally very nice about coming over.

They would all share a plate of pasta before getting down to business. I'm not sure if they worked as efficiently as they might have in the focused atmosphere of a rehearsal studio, but as Luciano always said, "In order to sing well, I have to be happy. And in order to be happy, I have to eat." So they kept him happy.

For Luciano, the hardest part about rehearsing had nothing to do with, say, learning about the inner motivations of his character. Luciano, remember, didn't go to the University of Modena; he was no intellectual. He was not somebody who, if he was preparing Verdi's *Otello*, would go out and read the Shakespeare play. For Luciano, the hardest part of learning a role was remembering the words.

I never understood it. It wasn't as if Luciano changed his repertory very often. In concert, especially, he's been singing the same selections for years and years and years. How many times can you sing "O sole mio" and still need cue cards to get the words right?

"What have you got," I'd say, "a hole in your head?"

That never went over too well, but I wouldn't have cared if it had inspired Luciano to apply himself and learn his words. He never did, though. Part of the secretaries' job was writing out the texts on cue cards and sometimes holding them up in the wings during a performance. If it was a foreign language, they would have to write out the syllables phonetically. In concerts, of course, it was never a problem, because he just read the words off his music stand. Sometimes he wore bifocals to help him see them better.

Maybe this, too, is part of the Italian tradition. I remember, years ago, putting on the legendary Golden Age tenor Tito Schipa in a recital at Town Hall, when I was young and he was quite old—in his seventies, in fact. (What is it with me and aging tenors?) In his prime, Schipa's voice was exquisite—very small and very sweet. He was well past his prime when I put him on, and he had all the traditional Italian mannerisms: you strike a pose, you sing, and you move your hands to emote along with the music. In Schipa's case, there was method behind that motion, because he had palmed the texts of his songs. So he'd start singing,

"A-a-a-veeee," and as he sang, his hand came up toward his face so he could glance down to get the next line, "Marii-ii-aaa." Once a tenor has attained the stature Schipa had, nobody is going to question whether he should be able to remember the text to "Ave Maria," even though it's a prayer that every Italian has been saying since the age of three. He didn't have the words only in his palm, either. He had them written all over his body—his sleeves, his chest, you name it. So Luciano was in good company.

Another Italian tradition is superstition. The theater is traditionally a very superstitious place to begin with. Everybody knows you're never supposed to wish anybody good luck before he goes onstage. In the theater, you say "Break a leg"; in the opera house, you say "*In bocca al lupo*"—in the mouth of the wolf—or "toi-toi-toi," which is supposed to be the sound of someone spitting three times over your shoulder for luck. Then there's some superstition about the color purple. Luciano didn't let it near him. When a friend of his showed up backstage in a purple jacket, he made her take it off before she could enter his dressing room.

Add to that the specifically Italian superstitions, like fear of the number seventeen. In Italy, thirteen is a lucky number; it's seventeen that's missing from elevator buttons, seating rows on airplanes, and Luciano Pavarotti's calendar. He preferred to spend the seventeenth of any month in bed.

The most famous Pavarotti superstition is the bent nail. There's a saying that you should carry a bent nail in your pocket for luck. Luciano took this to such an extreme that he had to find a bent nail backstage before every performance. Time was when bent nails were always lying around the flies of a theater, but today's stagehands tend to be a little more careful. Consequently, Luciano's secretaries had the unofficial responsibility of placing a bent nail on the floor where he would find it on his way from his dressing room to the stage. His fans knew all about this, and they sent him bent nails in profusion. He even got one cast in solid gold.

One reason for all these superstitions and contrivances to help him get through the evening was that Luciano was just plain scared. Most singers suffer from stage fright to some degree or another. Rosa Ponselle, an American soprano who rose directly from the vaudeville circuit to the Met in 1918 and of whom Maria Callas said, "We all know Ponselle is simply the greatest singer of them all," claimed she used to walk to the theater as slowly as possible before a performance, hoping that she might be run over by a bus so she wouldn't have to go out and sing. The more highly regarded a singer is, the harder a time he or she is likely to have. The audience arrives with huge expectations, and you feel you have to live up to them. Nobody was more aware of this than Luciano.

I remember one time when he was standing backstage ready to go on. His eyes were wide as saucers, and he was dripping with sweat. But all he was going to do was say a few words before the final round of the Pavarotti Voice Competition in Philadelphia. He was on the jury. He wasn't even going to sing.

"Luciano," someone said, "how can you be nervous?"

"That is the difference between a performer and a nonperformer," Luciano said. "Those people out there, they are my life's blood."

I think that fear made his mind go blank sometimes. It certainly got him to condition everyone around him to the idea that getting him onstage comfortably was the most important thing possible. He trained his secretaries and, as time went on, his whole entourage to make sure that all he had to do was think about singing. Everyone was willing to do whatever it took to enable Luciano to sing comfortably. And "whatever it took" came to be more, and more, and more.

Giovanna Cavaliere, who in 1984 took over the secretarial portion of Madelyn's duties, used to carry what she referred to as the "diaper bag," with all the things that Luciano had to have around him. His makeup, for example. Of course, opera houses have their own makeup artists, and they would come in and do Luciano's makeup before a performance, and as soon as they were out the dressing room door Luciano would take it all off and do it over again with his own makeup, his way.

Giovanna also had to save the corks any time they had champagne. Luciano used burnt cork to darken his beard, and mustache, and hair, and to cover the bald spot that was starting to appear at the top of his head. Half the time he just looked dirty. It didn't endear him to the hotels he stayed in, either, because all his sheets and pillowcases were black from the stuff every morning.

Fear didn't make Luciano the best of colleagues onstage, either. He was sometimes capable of fairly extreme measures to make sure that he remained the center of attention. If the soprano and the baritone, say, were singing, he'd find a way to get in between them. I don't think it was malice; I think his nerves kept him from knowing quite what he was doing. Not everybody agreed with me.

Once, when he was doing *I Puritani* with Joan Sutherland, he put her hand across her windpipe when she was singing a high D during their duet. Maybe he just wanted to make sure that he himself was heard. You can be sure that only happened once. She reamed him out when they got offstage, and he behaved himself for the rest of the run.

That opera must have brought out something in him, because he had a *Puritani* incident with Beverly Sills, as well, when they were singing it in Philadelphia in 1972. At the end of their duet, they were greeted with a huge roar of applause, and Luciano wanted to break character and take a bow, but Beverly didn't. The two of them were standing motionless onstage, locked in a passionate embrace, as the applause continued. So Luciano bit Beverly's ear. She jumped, of course, which meant that she had broken character and therefore there was no reason not to take their bow, as Luciano wanted.

His colleagues were a pretty select bunch. Luciano wasn't too particular about whom he sang with—as long as they were the people he wanted. Theater managers wished to keep Luciano happy, and so they would generally make an effort to accommodate him by engaging the singers he liked.

Madelyn, for example. Luciano made great efforts to launch Madelyn's career. Back in 1980, he arranged her professional debut. The opera house in San Diego gave her a cover contract as Mimì when Luciano was there singing *La Bohème*. Of course, Luciano didn't just want her to be the cover; he wanted her to sing a performance. At many houses, it's not unusual for the cover singer to get one performance late in the run, but there were only five performances in this run, and Diana Soviero, a very respectable American soprano, was contracted for all of them. Luciano figured out a way to get around this. The final dress rehearsal is often open to the public; Luciano simply arranged for the house to turn the rehearsal into a "performance." That way, Soviero could sing all five of her contracted performances, but there would be a sixth for Madelyn to sing.

The theater went along with this, but Soviero was rather miffed, and it didn't take long for the media to pick up on the situation. As a result, Madelyn, at twenty-four, had to make her debut at the center of a maelstrom of publicity that focused a lot more on the nature of her relationship with Luciano than on whether she could sing the role.

Luciano angled to get Madelyn other parts, as well, although he couldn't always bring her front and center at the bigger houses. He finagled her into the role of the Sacerdotessa, or High Priestess, in *Aida*, for example. It's a small role, sung offstage, but it got her her first—and her last—appearances at the Metropolitan Opera.

Where Luciano really managed to get Madelyn into the spotlight was at his recitals and concerts. Whenever he thought he could get away with it, he would have her join him onstage, billing her as his protégée and only student. It was doubly advantageous for him, because if she sang a few numbers he didn't have to sing as much. So Madelyn appeared with Luciano in recital all over the world—even in Modena, before his family. She was only his student, after all.

Madelyn's biggest moment came in 1986. To follow up on Luciano's success at Madison Square Garden with something a little different—since having him learn new repertoire in any big way was basically out of the question—I had the idea of putting him on with Joan Sutherland in a few arena concerts. The idea was ill-starred from the start. Luciano wasn't crazy about sharing the billing, and, as it turned out, tickets for Pavarotti and Sutherland together didn't sell as well as tickets for Pavarotti alone had. Don't think Luciano didn't remark on this, loudly and often.

"You see," he said, "you don't help me when you put me together with somebody else."

And then Joan got sick. She really did get sick. Joan was not a canceler: when she had contracted to do something, she did it. However, I don't imagine that she was heartbroken that she didn't have to do the arena concerts. She still looked down her nose a bit on the whole idea of singing in an arena. She didn't think that was in the best of taste. Of course, she had no problem singing her arias to a group of puppets on TV. To her, that was perfectly OK.

Anyway, Joan canceled, and Luciano thought it would be a fine idea to have Madelyn substitute for her. I'll say this for Madelyn: she had nerves of steel. Imagine getting up there onstage at Madison Square Garden in front of 20,000 people who want to hear Joan Sutherland and are about to hear you instead.

It didn't exactly catapult Madelyn to superstardom. But at least Luciano got to sing with whom he wanted.

In the years after *Yes, Giorgio*, the biggest problem getting Luciano onstage was—simply getting Luciano onstage. For one thing, he began to cancel more often. And then it became more difficult to find him a place to sing, because some houses got tired of putting up with him.

One obstacle was Luciano's discovery, in 1982 or 1983, that he had an allergy to dust. Theaters, of course, are very dusty places, especially when you have to lie on the floor pretending to be dead, which is where more than one tenor hero, like Cavaradossi in *Tosca*, ends up. We had to cancel a number of appearances, among them a run of *Tosca*s at Covent Garden, where he was scheduled for five performances, all sold out.

"If I sing any more, I run the risk of being unable to sing again," Luciano said.

Sir John Tooley received more documentation than he ever wanted on the subject of Luciano's allergies. But something must not have completely convinced him. Possibly it was the fact that Luciano went onstage with Joan Sutherland in Sydney the day after he announced his London cancelation, then went off to Honolulu with Madelyn for a rest. Believe me, the guy needed a rest, but of course there was quite a hue and cry in the trigger-happy British press. The upshot was that Sir John let it be known that he was not inviting Luciano to return to Covent Garden.

The same thing happened in Chicago in 1989. Luciano was supposed to open the season there with *Tosca*, and he pulled out of the production. According to Ardis Krainik, the house's indomitable general director, that brought his total up to twenty-six cancelations out of his last forty-one scheduled performances. She announced that she was firing Luciano.

Many members of the public applauded. For it wasn't only theater administrators who were souring on him; there were murmurs in the opera public, as well. At La Scala, there were more than murmurs. Italian audiences are notoriously tough, and the climate at La Scala is especially treacherous because of the infamous claque, who can be paid not to boo you but whose applause cannot be bought. I don't think the claque was responsible, though, when in 1983, singing an old standby of his, Edgardo in *Lucia*, Luciano was booed. It shook him up. His philosophy about booing is fairly direct. "If an artist is booed," he says, "he has usually done something to deserve it." I'm not sure how he reconciled that with being booed at La Scala, but the reception would surely have been more positive if he hadn't cracked in his final aria.

Another theater where Luciano stopped appearing, at least with any great frequency, was his old artistic home, the San Francisco Opera. In 1981, after a quarter of a century, Kurt Herbert Adler stepped down from his post there. For Luciano, though, there were mitigating circumstances. Kurt's replacement was Terry McEwen, our old friend from London Records.

This could have been great news, a sign that Luciano's close relationship with San Francisco could sail ahead on the same friendly footing as before. Indeed, Luciano opened Terry's first season, at his own request, with Verdi's *Ballo in Maschera*, which for a while was Luciano's favorite opera for the tenor.

Unfortunately, Luciano became indisposed and canceled a gala concert he was supposed to do in Golden Gate Park the day after the opening, and Terry had to scramble to fill in for him. And Luciano wasn't pleased with the way Terry handled the cancelation. The concert was televised live, and Luciano was sitting in the airport watching it as he waited for his flight back to New York, so he heard Terry make the announcement. No general manager likes to announce a Pavarotti cancelation. Anthony Bliss once borrowed a shield from the prop department before coming out in front of the curtain to face the wrath of the audience. Terry's way of handling it was to keep right on talking, without giving the crowd any time to react, and to distract them immediately by offering them Montserrat Caballé instead, which drew a great wave of applause.

According to Terry, Luciano called him the next day from New York and said, "You are a monster. You should have given them time to show how disappointed they were."

Of course, that was the last thing Terry wanted them to do on live television. But it meant Luciano and Terry got off to a slightly rocky start in Terry's new position.

Terry had difficulty in his new position with or without Luciano. You'd think that with his great contacts at London Records he would have been ideal. That's certainly what Terry thought when he took the job. But it's funny how your friendships with singers can fade when you don't have as much to offer them. Not every big singer is as excited as you might think about going all the way out to San Francisco. You have to really offer them something great, and Terry wasn't always in a position to do that.

Part of the problem was that Terry wasn't a very good administrator. His job at London Records in New York was perfectly suited to him because it wasn't a big office, and he could go out late every night and entertain his artists, and everyone was happy. But running an opera house is something else. One issue was that Terry liked to sleep until 2:30 in the afternoon. He'd get to the office around 3:00, then do some work until 4:00. This was quite a change from Kurt Herbert Adler, who had been there all the time, morning to night. Kurt ran a tight ship; Terry's ship was always on the verge of almost not sailing at all.

And there were other, outside factors that got in the way of Terry's working relationship with Luciano. In 1984, Luciano was scheduled to do Verdi's *Ernani* in San Francisco, and he brought some of his family over. They stopped off in New York on their way, and I couldn't help noticing that something was wrong with Giuliana, their youngest daughter, who was then about seventeen. She was slurring her words, as if she couldn't control her mouth.

"Luciano," I said, "what is wrong with that child?"

"Oh," he said, "we took her to the dentist and she needs new braces. She's going to get them when we get back."

I had never heard of anything like that, but I didn't say a word. Luciano is the world's leading expert on medicine.

But in fact, Luciano was very worried about Giuliana. When they got to San Francisco, during the rehearsal period for *Ernani*, the family arranged to have their old friend Ernie Rosenbaum, who was a doctor, see Giuliana. Ernie took one look at her and said, "That child is gravely ill."

It was lucky Ernie was around because at that time many doctors didn't recognize myasthenia gravis. It's a disease that causes the autoimmune system to attack nerves and muscles, it's degenerative, and it used to be potentially life threatening.

One thing you have to say about Luciano: he's great in a crisis. He swung right into action. He got Giuliana appointments with the best doctors he could find. He flew back to New York with her for further tests and, finally, an operation. Then he flew back to Italy with the family, and he stayed with Giuliana until she was on the road to recovery. I'm happy to say that Giuliana never looked back. She recovered completely and grew up, without further incident, into a warm and lovely woman.

Of course, Luciano didn't sing *Ernani* in San Francisco. He had to cancel performances of it in Chicago, too, when he flew back to Italy. But that was one time his cancelations were completely, unquestionably warranted.

TERRY MCEWEN

When I was head of the San Francisco Opera, I had worked out that Pavarotti would come in the even years, Domingo in the odd. I just figured I wouldn't be able to afford both of them in the same year, although I learned later that I could have. But it was all right; I usually had the one who wasn't appearing in a production give a concert for the opera's benefit.

Anyway, in 1984, Luciano canceled Ernani *because his daughter was sick, so in 1985 I was going to have both tenors. Domingo would come only if we did an opera that he could televise. He had caught the Karajan-Bernstein disease: everything I do must be immortal. Everything he did had to be televised, preserved on film. So the only opera that we could find that we could do, and that we had a beautiful production of, and that he hadn't already committed to television, was Verdi's* Ballo in Maschera.

We hadn't decided what opera Luciano would sing, but he was pushing for Mefistofele, *by Arrigo Boito. He wanted to do an opera he hadn't done before; he had a tradition of doing operas for the first time in San Francisco. And he'd recently recorded* Mefistofele. *Well, he sure chose an expensive opera for me to put on, but I love the piece. So I engaged James Morris as Mefistofele and a wonderful Rumanian girl called Maria Slatinaru as Marguerite. I engaged them late, which was why it was Morris and Slatinaru; they weren't my ideal, but I wasn't unhappy.*

One night I was in New York, in Luciano's apartment, and we were walking in the kitchen—where else—and I put my arm around him.

"Listen," I said, "I want to explain something to you. You know, we have an old friendship and I wouldn't do anything to upset you, personally. But I want you to know that Domingo will be there while you are in San Francisco. You sing with him at La Scala, Covent Garden, the Met; you appear at the same time when the other one's there, so I presume it's no problem. But I know that you have problems with each other, and so," I said, "I want you to know that he's going to be there. And his show will be televised. Plácido had a deal with some British outfit, and he set it up."

Luciano said, "You are so sweet to tell me this. Tu sei il solo che mi considera—*you are the only person that would be so considerate as to tell me."*

And fine. We kissed and cuddled and that was that.

About four or five months later, Luciano called me and said, "I don't want to do Mefistofele.*"*

"Ouch," I said.

I had thought of the possibility. That's why I hadn't engaged a basso profundo to sing Mefistofele. *I engaged a bass-baritone, because it's much easier to cast a bass-baritone in another part.*

"Then what I suggest, Luciano," I said, "the easiest thing for you and the easiest thing for me is Tosca. *You've done it before in San Francisco, but only once. And it's an opera the public loves."*

"Ah, Tosca," *Luciano said. "I'm not so crazy about* Tosca. *You know what opera I want to sing in '85?"*

I said, "What?"

*"There's only one opera," he said. "*Ballo.*"*

I said, "Luciano, I already told you: I'm doing Ballo *with Domingo. And televising it."*

He said, "You didn't tell me."

"Come on," I said, "I told you, and you thanked me and said only I would have been considerate enough to let you know. Come on, Luciano."

"You never told me!" he said. "I am not coming to San Francisco!

You love Domingo so much, you make him film a Ballo. You don't care about me!"

"But I told you," I said.

"Bah," he said. "I don't come."

And he didn't. I had to put on Tosca *with another tenor, Giuseppe Giacomini.*

After that I tried very hard to make peace with Luciano, without humiliating myself. But my attitude about him as a person changed.

Luciano never quite got back on his old footing with Terry during Terry's six years in San Francisco. In fact, apart from the opening *Ballo,* he hardly performed at the San Francisco Opera at all. One of the last things Terry set up with Luciano was planned for the fall of 1988, which actually took place after Terry resigned from the company, at the end of the 1987–88 season, and retired to Hawaii. Terry conceived of a double bill of two one-act operas: Leoncavallo's *Pagliacci* and Puccini's *Suor Angelica.* It's an unusual pairing, but Terry wanted to present Mirella Freni in her first-ever *Angelica* and Luciano as his first-ever Canio in *Pagliacci.* As it emerged, however, neither Luciano nor Mirella felt quite ready to take on those roles by the time the production date rolled around, so the theater substituted their old standby, *La Bohème,* instead. (Terry's successor, Lotfi Mansouri, went ahead and staged the *Pagliacci–Suor Angelica* double bill a couple of years later.)

Then we learned that there were plans to televise the production. Now, neither Luciano nor I could quite see why Luciano should agree to appear on television for free. After all, the San Francisco Opera would be able to take that broadcast and promote it, and market it, and make money off it. And I'm not there to sweeten the pot for the San Francisco Opera. I'm there to sweeten the pot for Luciano.

So I made sure they paid him a little extra something. I don't remember how much. Some say $50,000, but I think that's exaggerated. I don't think it was more than $35,000. But Lotfi wasn't very happy about it.

In fairness, I have to say that, for all his foibles, Luciano was very honest with himself about his art. "Don't always tell me that I'm great or that I sang well," he used to say. "I know better than you whether I sang well tonight."

That's not to say that he ever wanted to hear that he sang badly. No singer ever wants to hear that, no matter how much he may beg you to tell him what you really thought.

It's a perennial problem for those of us in the music business: what do you say to someone about a bad performance? I used to work for the Belgian mezzo-soprano Rita Gorr, who was quite a wonderful singer; but no singer, wonderful or not, is above an occasional bad night. One night, Rita sang in Mascagni's *Cavalleria Rusticana*, and she simply was not very good. So I went backstage afterward with a certain amount of trepidation, partly because, like Luciano, I'm not very good at concealing what I think.

I got to Rita's dressing room, and she was sitting there with her head on the table, crying like crazy. Then in walked Robert Lawrence, who at the time was the head of an organization called Friends of French Opera.

"Oh, Madame Gorr," he said like a bloody fool, in his pidgin French, "you were wonderful, simply wonderful!"

Rita lifted her head to see who was saying that and took a good look at him. Then she put her head back down on the table and began to cry even harder.

So lying is stupid. But not everyone is thrilled about honesty, either. In the early years, I might twit Luciano about a particularly bad performance. "What were you doing, phoning in that Verdi Requiem with Leontyne Price," I might say. He would take that, for a while. But there got to be a time when criticism became a bad idea.

Criticism of himself, that is. He was very open to criticism of others. I remember when he saw a TV broadcast of Mirella's *Aida* from Houston. He called up Mirella afterward.

"You know," he said helpfully, "that's not a role for you. And where did you get those costumes? La Standa?" La Standa is the Italian equivalent of Woolworth's.

He could dish it out, but he couldn't take it. This may have been at the root of the problem Luciano tended to have with conductors. It was one of the biggest problems in getting Luciano onstage at all.

In the opera house, a conductor is supposed to be the ultimate arbiter of the musical performance. Luciano, when he was singing, saw things a little differently. He thought he was the one who knew best how everything should go. He would beat time with his foot to correct the conductor's tempo. He would tell the orchestra how to play. This did not make him a great favorite with many conductors. Opera houses were happy to have Luciano, but very few conductors went out of their way to ask to work with him. Even fewer asked more than once.

This all has to do with the Italian tradition. It's hard to say exactly what the Italian tradition consists of, in Luciano's mind. Being Italian is certainly not a prerequisite. Herbert von Karajan, Luciano's early champion, was German, but he seemed to do just fine with the Italian tradition in Luciano's eyes. But Luciano's coach-accompanist and sometime conductor, Leone Magiera, who actually is Italian, doesn't know a thing. Given that fact, it's very kind of Luciano to allow him to teach him so many roles.

Another titan who came out of the German tradition but represented the Italian one perfectly well to Luciano was Carlos Kleiber. Kleiber is the son of another legendary conductor, Erich Kleiber, and he has a rather untouchable reputation in the music world. Kleiber only enhances his mystique by keeping his appearances few and far between. He just isn't crazy about conducting, unless someone makes it worth his while by offering him a new car or something to go along with his fee. (Luciano, you see, isn't the only artist who works with the concept of the giftola.)

Anyway, Luciano worked very successfully with Carlos Kleiber, and they had a nice relationship. So when the Met was thinking of how to lure Kleiber over to conduct in New York, Luciano took the bull by the horns.

"If we let the Met get involved," Luciano said, "he will never come."

So when he was in Germany one time, at the home of a doctor friend of his—Luciano had a doctor friend in every city he ever went to—he had Kleiber come over after dinner and join them for dessert and coffee.

Kleiber asked Luciano what was coming up on his program.

"Well," Luciano said, "I'm going to do a Verdi Requiem with Zubin Mehta, and then Zubin is taking a sabbatical."

"Oh," Kleiber said, "that's what I should do. Take a sabbatical and go off fishing."

Luciano said, "But you never conduct. You're just wasting away doing nothing."

Not too many people could talk to Kleiber like that. But, evidently, he would take it from Luciano. And Luciano talked to him a little more, and the upshot was that Kleiber came to New York in 1988 to make his Metropolitan Opera debut with *La Bohème*. I don't know how they financed it, but Bruce Crawford, who was the general manager at the time, must have found a sponsor to pay the additional fee. The normal fee at the Metropolitan Opera certainly wouldn't have satisfied Carlos Kleiber. I think his going rate was around $50,000. But that was how it worked in those days. If you wanted to get Kleiber and you knew that you had to pay for him, you found the money somewhere.

Of course, it was worth it. The Kleiber *Bohème* is still remembered as a highlight of recent Met history. Luciano and Mirella sang beautifully, and the orchestra loved Kleiber, not least because he didn't make them rehearse too much. And Jimmy Levine is supposed to have stood backstage every night, just to see Kleiber in action.

"Every time I watch this man conduct," he said, "I learn something else about *Bohème* I didn't know."

Jimmy Levine was another conductor Luciano worked well

with, after a rocky start. Jimmy is famous among singers for being the most supportive conductor you can imagine. He understands voices better than any other conductor alive and knows how to lead the music so that singers have an easier time. He was always there for Luciano. That is to say, he could always let him know when to come in, and he anticipated every place where he might make a mistake. This was wonderful for Luciano. He might make a lot of mistakes with Sir Georg Solti, or Riccardo Muti, or Claudio Abbado. But with Jimmy, he didn't make mistakes.

"Luciano's chances of success," Joe Volpe once said, "are greatly reduced if Jimmy's not conducting."

So Jimmy knew the Italian tradition. The same couldn't be said of Sir Georg Solti, whose conducting, Luciano said, was too square, too heavy, not Italian enough. Some people would agree with him, but it doesn't change the fact that Solti was a very important conductor. Sir Georg was also a real stickler for learning every detail of the music, and that was an area in which Luciano was, as we've seen, somewhat laissez-faire.

Yet it was with the supposedly un-Italianate Solti that Luciano had his most daunting encounter with the Italian tenor tradition, in 1991. Verdi's *Otello*.

Otello is the biggest challenge in the Italian tenor repertoire. It's a killer role that calls for a huge, powerful voice and acting ability to match. Only the very largest voices—and talents—have taken it on. It became a vehicle for Plácido, but some maintain that even Plácido's tough sound wasn't big enough or wasn't as ideal for the role as that of great Otellos of the past: Mario del Monaco or Francesco Tamagno, who created it in 1887. Singing Otello is almost an act of hubris. And it's not a role one would generally associate with Luciano Pavarotti.

But there it is. You're an Italian tenor at the peak of your career—or coming down off that peak, as the case may be. And there's the greatest role in your literature, staring you in the face. So Luciano tried it.

Luciano was never going to be a big heroic Otello. But I

thought he could bring something new to the role by singing it his way. With his beauty of voice and his declamation of the Italian language, he could have brought a whole new dimension to a role that many singers simply bark. I thought it could be a new artistic highlight of his career. And we hadn't had many of those lately.

As fate would have it, Luciano had two offers to sing *Otello* the same year. One came from Riccardo Muti, head of La Scala and, at that time, the Philadelphia Orchestra; the other came from Solti. Solti wanted to give *Otello* as his farewell concerts to mark the end of his twenty-one-year tenure at the head of the Chicago Symphony Orchestra.

Solti was a former client of mine, but that wasn't the only reason I thought Solti's was the offer we couldn't refuse. It would be a historic performance, a great maestro's farewell. You had Solti. You had the Chicago Symphony, one of the top orchestras in America. You had Kiri Te Kanawa as Desdemona—say what you will about Kiri, she has a lovely voice and a lot of people like her, even if she's boring. You had Luciano Pavarotti. To top it off, Solti was also a Decca/London artist, so there were immediately plans to do a recording. In the classical music world, it doesn't get any better than this.

So I convinced Luciano to do the performance with Solti.

Luciano was very pumped up about learning *Otello*. "Verdi is a genius," he told us. "Everything you need to know is right there, in the score."

"So how come you don't *know* the score, Luciano?" Hans and I nearly asked. But we didn't.

The fact was, though, that Luciano wasn't prepared. He arrived in Chicago, and he basically was not ready to sing. Of course, this wasn't the first time that had happened. And he had Leone Magiera with him, to pound the music into him. But it didn't seem to be going in, at least not fast enough for him to be ready by opening night. And because these were concert performances, the rehearsal period wasn't very long. We suddenly realized we were going to have to make some adjustments or we weren't going to have a performance at all. Luciano needed a prompter. We had to figure out a way to get Leone onstage with him. And I got to go tell this to Maestro Solti.

These are the moments when a manager's job is the last thing you want to do on earth. There's Solti, one of the greatest living conductors. You want to go to an artist like that and say, "My tenor can't learn his part"? You want to take your life in your hands?

But Solti was a realist. I'm sure he didn't like it very much. But he's not a stupid man, and he knew that something had to be done. I think by then we'd all realized this wasn't going to be the *Otello* we had hoped for.

To compound everybody's problems, by opening night Luciano had come down with a cold. It wasn't altogether clear whether he was going to sing. Meanwhile, Solti got a touch of the flu. At least now, he and Luciano had one thing in common. They were both sick. You couldn't blame them for not feeling well, although they may have had slightly different reasons. So spirits at this festive gala were not quite what they might have been.

The setting, though, was imposing. We had Luciano sitting on a kind of throne, near the other singers, at the center of the orchestra. Next to the throne was a little table, and on that table Luciano had some handkerchiefs, and some water, and a little plate of sliced apples, to help lubricate his voice. He looked like a king, waiting to eat dinner. The real reason for the throne, though, was that underneath it, hidden from view, sat Leone Magiera. There, huddled ignominiously at the orchestra's feet, he sat with the score, screaming the cues up at Luciano so Luciano would know when to come in and what to sing.

Solti's concert opera performances were always a big event. After Chicago, he'd take them to Carnegie Hall, and they were artistic highlights of the New York season: Wagner's *Rheingold*, Strauss's *Salome*, Berlioz's *Damnation de Faust*. Now he was standing up there conducting something that looked like a great big joke. I'm sure he must have felt, How the hell did I ever get involved with anything like this?

In fact, I don't think the performance was all that terrible. The Chicago Symphony, for one thing, is a force to be reckoned with. And Luciano, for all his health problems, did his best with the role. But I can't say that it was an evening that set the world on fire.

The *Otello* performances went on to Carnegie Hall, too, but they didn't improve very noticeably. What everybody noticed, of course, was all this stuff Luciano had onstage with him. So instead of being a peak of his career, *Otello* was remembered as a bit of a laughingstock. I thought the recording was OK. But it wasn't exactly one of Luciano's greatest hits.

Luciano himself always knew, afterward, what had gone wrong. As you might expect, it was all my fault.

"I should have done *Otello* with a conductor who understands the Italian tradition," he'd say. "I should have done it with Muti."

chapter X

CITY OF WOMEN

Luciano's Entourage

Late one night in 1987, the sound of the ringing phone tore through our apartment. By then, I was used to it.

But this time was a little different. Luciano was beside himself.

"I'm going to kill myself," he said.

"Calm down," I said. "What's going on?"

It was Madelyn. After seven or eight years of a very turbulent relationship, Madelyn had decided that she wanted something a little more—like a life of her own. And on Luciano's historic tour to China in 1986, she had hit it off with one of the Italian journalists who was along to cover the event. Everyone on the tour had been abuzz about it. Now it was out in the open, and it was final. She was leaving. She was going to get married. And Luciano was coming unglued.

"She has left me," he moaned. "I am going to throw myself out the window."

It was impossible to soothe him. I started to get worried.

"Don't do anything, Luciano," I said. "I'll be right there."

Nothing like a little excitement in the wee hours of the morning. I got myself on a red-eye flight to Chicago and went straight to Luciano's hotel and rang Giovanna Cavaliere—who, you'll remember, had taken over the purely secretarial portion of Madelyn's duties—from the front desk.

"I'm coming up," I said.

"What do you mean?" Giovanna said sleepily. "Where are you?"

I said, "I'm here, in the hotel."

"What are you *doing* here?" said Giovanna.

I came up to her room, where she repeated the question.

"Well," I said, "I got this frantic call from Luciano, saying he was going to throw himself out the window."

"How could he throw himself out the window?" Giovanna said. "He wouldn't fit."

"Oh, for Christ's sake," I said, "just let me into his room."

"You know how he is about being woken up," said Giovanna.

There's a reason Luciano has secretaries. They protect him. Giovanna was an especially good watchdog. She kept me out of his room until nine o'clock.

I went in—and came out again, fast.

"Who the hell was that?" I said.

"Don't you know?" Giovanna said.

"Why didn't you tell me he had a woman in there?!" I said.

"Well," Giovanna said, "it's not *my* place to tell you he has a new girlfriend."

So that's how I met Judy Kovacs. Luciano's next secretary.

To be honest, I never wanted to know too much about Luciano and women. There are some things you'd rather not know. All right, I suppose I was a little curious. I've sat with Luciano in the steam room at the New York Athletic Club and, believe me, it's quite a sight. It's very hard to sit there and imagine that this is a figure capable of any great sexual prowess. Put it this way: he's hardly the answer to a maiden's prayer.

He certainly did appeal to them, though. He was almost as great a flirt as he was a singer. Onstage, he would find a way to bring the audience to its feet. Offstage, he found ways to sweep women off theirs. The line was quite something to see after a performance. They may not have literally thrown themselves at his feet, but they tried. There were gifts, there were phone numbers, there were panties: you name it, it was offered up to Luciano. But for the most part, he kept everything right out in the open. He'd offer them a big smile but no hanky-panky.

I do remember one time, after a concert at Wembley Stadium, when there was this handsome woman by the dressing room who was trying very hard to be close to him. She was really rather attractive.

"Come into my dressing room," Luciano told her. And he closed the door.

I was on that like a shot. I was pounding on that door in a minute.

"What are you doing, Luciano?" I said. "Do you know this woman? You can get yourself into a lot of trouble with this kind of stuff. Because you don't know who she is, or what she wants, or anything like that, and the likelihood is that she wants something, and you're not aware of it, and consequently you're going to get screwed.

"Please leave, madame," I added.

Luciano was a little bit sheepish. And of course, he yelled at me for a while. But I'm used to that. He did it mainly to save face. The most important thing is, the woman left.

You can't be too careful. I could just imagine us getting slapped with a lawsuit; it's been happening to big tenors since time immemorial. In 1906, Enrico Caruso was visiting the Central Park Zoo, and he made some kind of contact with a pretty woman in the Monkey House. She construed it as a pinch and made a huge stink, and he was arrested and had to go to court. The Monkey House scandal was in the papers for quite a while. Some people said he'd been set up; others said, "Typical Italian." He got off with the minimum fine of ten dollars for disorderly conduct. But it was terrible publicity. And think of all the stars of our own day who have gone through the wringer because they were accused, rightly or wrongly, of making indecent advances toward women. The last thing we wanted was a Monkey House incident of our own.

But I didn't need to worry. I never encountered a woman who minded Luciano's advances. To be honest, I'm not convinced it was all about sex, either. I'm sure he wanted sex, although it's very hard to say how much of it he got. He had the steady girl-friends, like Madelyn and Judy, but what was going on on the side, I don't know. Of course, there were plenty of other women around, but I don't think they were there for serious screwing. Some women tell of being invited up to Pavarotti's room for a private dinner, which he would cook for them, and then saying a warm good night and going home. Sometimes he'd have four or five women around him, eating dinner, and then go to bed alone. Just food, no sex. Of course, in Luciano's universe, that's probably how priorities are ordered.

The thing to remember about Luciano is that he was raised by women. His grandmother had lost her daughter shortly before Luciano was born, and she lavished on him all kinds of feminine attention, as well as spoiled him rotten. This upbringing conditioned him to love the company of women and to expect them to wait on him hand and foot. Another result, in my opinion, is that Luciano developed something of a feminine side himself. Maybe I'm wrong, but to my mind, if you're a man, you take certain responsibilities. If you say you're going to do something, you do it. A woman, meanwhile, will change her mind 500 times. And that was Luciano. He avoided responsibility, and he had a kind of slyness I think he learned from women. And changing his mind was his specialty.

He had a man's eye for a pretty woman, sure. But funnily enough, if someone was too big or beautiful, he'd shrink away.

He got a little out of his league sometimes. There was one beautiful young Italian model named Lucia Debrilli. I think she thought the press attention would help her career, and she was playing him for all she could get. They worked each other, those two. She would always call up and want tickets, and he was very friendly to her. I don't think it was a big sexual thing, though. I could be wrong.

One night, they arranged to meet up at her apartment, and he enlisted me to drive him over.

"You come with me, and don't leave me," he said.

So we went over to her place in New York. She was really a very beautiful girl. At a certain point, I got some sort of signal from Luciano and I knew it was time to make myself scarce. So I went out and walked around the block a few times. Then I went back and got him, and we went home.

I would be very surprised if anything actually happened, though. Maybe he wanted me to think that something did.

As I remember, Adua found out about that one, and Luciano got her a very expensive bracelet as a peace offering. I've read in the press that it cost $200,000. I have trouble believing it cost him that much. But I've learned to keep my mouth shut.

Even with the women he was deeply involved with, Luciano didn't have what you'd call adult relationships. There was an imbalance there. He needed them to take care of him, and they did. But you have to ask what was on their minds. What were they doing with this big, hefty, overweight tenor who was so egomaniacal that it was hard to have any kind of real relationship with him? The connection that his long-term "girlfriends" had with him was not based on a reciprocal adult relationship. He attracted needy women, and they became kind of enslaved by him. They became dishwashers and laundresses and cooks: they were there to service him.

The closest he came to a genuine romance was with Madelyn. He and Madelyn had a real glow when they walked into a room. There was a kinetic energy between them. I didn't see that happen again.

Lovers or no, they all said they were only secretaries. In Giovanna's case, it was true.

"I do everything but sex," she used to say.

"Did you join him in bed at all?" I asked her.

"No way," she said. "Too much there. Besides, I had to do the packing. That came first."

"Did he ever make a pass at you?" I said.

Giovanna said, "No, because he used to say I was old enough to be his mother. The thing is, I'm six years *younger* than him. But I treated him like a child. Because he loved that."

"Oh," I said, "so you started as a virgin and you ended as a virgin."

"A virgin with Luciano, definitely," Giovanna said.

She sounded somewhat thankful.

Luciano's way of showing he was close to you was to treat you badly. He'd say whatever was on his mind, without very much thought about how it would come across. As he saw it, anything he wanted to say was perfectly all right.

He'd look at me and say, "Oh, you're getting so fat."

"*I'm* getting fat," I'd say, looking at his impressive girth.

"You're popping out of your jacket," he'd say. "The buttons are bursting."

Of course, I could have said something like, "Take a look at yourself. You're a mess. Your hair is all dirty from burnt cork, and your shoes are scuffed, and you look like a big fat slob." But that would have devastated him, which was not to either of our advantages. So I kept my mouth shut. Meanwhile, he remained the ultimate fashion arbiter for everyone else. The Dior of fashion. The Mr. Alexandre of hair. It got a little tiresome after a while.

He didn't change his tone one bit when he was talking to his girlfriends. Even Madelyn. As I said, Madelyn was a very attractive woman, and she had flair. When she was performing, she would get herself ready to go out onstage, in her glamorous costume, and of course she wouldn't stint on the makeup, because when you're under those lights you need a lot of makeup. Luciano wore a lot of makeup out there, too. But he saw only hers.

"Why do you get yourself all made up like that?" he'd say. "You look like a transvestite."

Yeah, Luciano really knew how to build a girl up. Especially when she was about to go onstage in front of I don't know how many thousands of people.

Judy Kovacs was a very different kind of person. She was Hungarian, at least by origin, and she lived in Vienna. Like Madelyn, she was studying voice when she met Luciano, but she didn't meet him as an opera singer. She had a part-time job as a librarian/archivist at the Vienna State Opera, doing things like writing the conductor's notes into the orchestra parts, and this meant that she got to sit in on rehearsals if she wanted. In 1986, Luciano was in town rehearsing *Ballo in Maschera* for several weeks, and that's how they got to know each other. Very quickly, Luciano was treating Judy like family. At the end of one of the final rehearsals, she was standing in his dressing room observing the tumult as various people, led by Giovanna, went about the enterprise of getting Luciano ready to go on, and he realized he'd left his wig in his hotel room. Don't ask me why he had brought his wig home from the opera house, but he had. He handed Judy, still nearly a stranger, the key to his room and sent her to pick up the wig. Call it training for her future position.

Judy may have been a singer, but when she first came on the scene she was a little mouse. She was very shy, and she stayed in the corner and watched. There was a lot for her to digest. Giovanna was ruling the roost—and ruling it pretty aggressively. And I think Judy was unsure about joining the three-ring circus of Luciano's life.

She was a little mysterious about her background, too. At the beginning, for some reason, she and Luciano decided they needed to concoct a story about her past.

"Her name is Tamara," Luciano told Giovanna. "You met her when you worked in retail." (Giovanna was a buyer for Gimbel's in New York before Luciano lured her away—at, please note, a much lower salary.) "Now she's here as your guest."

Giovanna wasn't too thrilled about that. I don't think she was too thrilled about having Judy around at all. She went along with it, though, while they were in Chicago. But then Luciano popped down to Tampa for a concert.

"You can't pass her off as Tamara in Tampa," Giovanna reminded Luciano.

"Why not?" Luciano said. "You're always trying to start trouble."

"No, I'm not," Giovanna said. "It's just that Emerson Buckley will be there, and he already met her in Vienna, when we were still calling her Judy."

"Ahhh," Luciano said. "Thank goodness you have such a good memory."

Gradually, Judy settled down into just being Judy. Giovanna never quite acclimatized to her, though. Giovanna took her job very seriously. Being ordered around by Luciano was one thing, but being ordered around by his bed partners was another. Giovanna, of course, had come in to replace Madelyn, who decided she'd had enough of being chief cook and bottle washer a couple of years before she decamped altogether. Of course, Madelyn had her own ideas about how things should be done, and she and Giovanna had a few run-ins before they established their pecking order. After that, they got along just fine.

With Judy, though, it was another story. Judy just rubbed Giovanna the wrong way. The web of jealousy backstage is a hard thing to penetrate. Before Judy came along, Giovanna was the chief caretaker and babysitter. She sat with Luciano every night and kept him company. When Judy first got to Chicago, Luciano saw no reason to change his habits, even if Giovanna may have felt less like part of the family than part of the furniture, sitting there in her chair while Luciano and Judy canoodled on the sofa.

Giovanna finally had enough and got up.

"Where are you going?" said Luciano in surprise. "It's early; it's not even nine o'clock."

"I'm going to my room," said Giovanna. "Do you think I want to sit here and watch this?"

Things didn't get any easier between Judy and Giovanna. I

think Giovanna found it especially difficult on the South America tour, since Adua came along, as well. Adua, as I said, claims
not to have known anything about Luciano's extramarital activities, but at the very least she had to have sensed something.

"What exactly does she do?" she kept asking Giovanna about
Judy.

Giovanna was trying to claim Judy as her assistant, but it was
clear Giovanna was doing all the work. That's partly because Giovanna is not the kind of person to relinquish any work. At some
point, she had started ironing Luciano's shirts. He loved to watch
her do that. She washed his socks. She was a real workhorse. The
more work you gave her, the more she liked it.

"He was spoiled before," Adua used to tell her, "but you have
absolutely ruined him."

So there wasn't a lot for Judy to do, even though Giovanna
kept asking her to at least look like she was doing something.

Eventually, though, Giovanna's brother was taken ill and she
had to leave on short notice, and Judy was left with all the work
to do herself. After Giovanna's brother got better, she was ready
to come back, but Judy didn't like dealing with Giovanna any
more than Giovanna liked dealing with her. That was the end of
Giovanna.

What did Adua think? I honestly don't know. Luciano and
Adua had a very touching ceremony on their twenty-fifth wedding anniversary: they went to church and, in front of the priest,
renewed their vows, and then gave a big party afterward. I flew
to Modena myself for the event. It was a lovely ceremony. It almost convinced me that these were two people who were terribly much in love with each other. Even though I'm sure they
hadn't been to bed together for ten years before that.

Years later, after they were divorced, Adua still said she hadn't
known anything for a long time. Luciano had always looked into
her eyes and sworn there was nothing going on. Madelyn had
also denied their involvement.

"What about Judy?" I asked her.

"Judy, too?" said Adua. "Judy was also his, his—"

"She was his secretary," I said quickly.

"So. She was a girlfriend, too," said Adua, laughing dryly to herself. "Even Judy."

ADUA VERONI

In '81 or '82 he fell hard for Madelyn Renée. It was the first time there'd been somebody else. But he always denied it, denied, denied, and she denied, denied, denied, just like him. And I foolishly believed them.

I had my suspicions, of course, but he was always so sincere.

And perhaps because this was such a strong emotion for him, he began to have a completely different attitude.

The year before our divorce, I finally confronted him about it.

"I was younger," he said. "Maybe you would have done better, if you were in my position. I loved her as I loved you. I'd like to know what you would have done if you'd been in love with two people at the same time."

Now he's told our daughters that I knew all about Madelyn Renée, and that we only stayed together because of them. He's an expert at twisting the facts to make them appear the way he wants.

Judy stayed with Luciano for more than six years, which was a long time to put up with him. At least Madelyn could argue that by staying she was helping her career, although I would question whether being with Luciano really helped her career very much. Leaving him certainly didn't. I heard from several people that after she left him, Luciano called up a number of theaters and told them not to engage her anymore, and the theaters complied. I can't prove this or disprove it; I just heard it. Without Luciano, Madelyn might not have gotten all that many engagements in any case. But he certainly didn't make it any easier for her.

Judy wasn't an opera singer, and she wasn't getting any career help at all from working with Luciano. All her position offered was the satisfaction, such as it was, of enabling the world's greatest tenor to function. And I use the word *enabling* advisedly. I don't know what else she got out of it, but there must have been something, because she stayed for a long time.

When Judy eventually decided to leave, it took her almost two years to make the final break. Luciano is very good at exerting low-key emotional blackmail when he wants something, and he wanted her to stay. He said he needed her. One thing Judy did offer, certainly, was a knowledge of music and languages that was very helpful to Luciano. They worked a lot together on his parts.

But Judy finally had enough of living Luciano's lifestyle. She called it "the golden globe," a world of limousines and hotels and private planes that was always a little bit separate from the world outside. So she went back to Vienna.

JOE VOLPE

We were doing one of our galas, the twenty-fifth anniversary of Luciano's and Plácido's debuts at the Metropolitan Opera. Luciano was singing act 1 of Otello, *Plácido did act 1 of* Die Walküre, *and then we did act 3 of* Trovatore, *with Plácido and Luciano splitting the role of Manrico. That is, Plácido sang the aria, "Ah sì, ben mio," and then he went off and Luciano came on and sang the cabaletta, "Di quella pira."*

So there we all were, and then, after the five-minute call, Herbert came to me and said, "Joe, Luciano is feeling tired and is going home."

I said, "What the hell are you talking about, he's going home? Going home. Baloney."

I went back to his dressing room. He wasn't there.

So I found out what was happening. His assistant, Judy, was going to the airport, leaving. She'd had enough of him. And Luciano had gone after her.

So Luciano was out on Sixty-fifth Street, chasing Judy, in his Otello costume. He's running down Sixty-fifth Street in plain view in that costume, a sight I've never seen in my life.

I went racing out there, and I grabbed the two of them.

"First of all, Judy, you're coming back to the Met," I said. "And you, Luciano, are, too."

And I got them back inside.

Miraculously, nobody saw them. It was never in the paper, it was never anywhere. I don't even know whether Herbert knew what happened. All he knew was that Luciano wasn't there.

chapter XI

TRAVELS WITH LUCIANO

Around the World in Eighty Suitcases

L uciano is a homebody. He's a nester. Wherever he is, he wants to be surrounded by all the comforts of home.

It's true in Modena. It's true in Pesaro, at his summer house. Many stars as well-heeled as Luciano would buy villas on remote Caribbean islands. Luciano stuck to the values he grew up with. Owning a house in Pesaro is the dream to which every factory worker and tradesman in Modena aspires. Pesaro is the Jersey Shore of Italy. It's overrun in summer with Italians plashing in the lukewarm wavelets of the Adriatic and eating in cheap restaurants. Luciano's villa overlooks not spectacular tropical vistas but a stretch of dusty beige coast almost hidden by orderly ranks of beach umbrellas.

And it's true in New York, at the Hampshire House, which you could call another example of Luciano's impulse buying. He was renting the apartment of Sophia Loren's husband, and he liked it so much he decided he wanted to buy it. But the price was too high, so he bought the exact same apartment one floor up. When his traveling entourage got too big for that, he also bought the apartment next door.

In all these places, Luciano is "home." But, of course, he spends a large part of his life away from home, on the road. And for the people who work for him, his need to have the comforts of home transported from one place to another is not so much a charming quirk as a big nightmare.

Exactly what are the comforts of home? Naturally, many of them involve food. Luciano is always worried when he travels that there won't be anything to eat that he likes or any way to prepare it properly if there is. As a result, he travels with a whole arsenal of kitchen supplies: espresso machines, prosciutto slicers, pots and pans, table linens, you name it. When he arrives at a new hotel, a bedroom of his suite is immediately commandeered to serve as a kitchen. He draws the line at a refrigerator. He doesn't travel with that. He just makes sure the hotel has it in the suite waiting for him.

No one who was there will ever forget Luciano's trip to China in 1986, when he went to perform *La Bohème* with the Genoa Opera Company and a group of winners of the Pavarotti International Voice Competition and to give a solo concert in the sold-out Great Hall of the People. For outsiders, the trip was legendary because this great Italian tenor was bringing opera to hundreds of thousands of ecstatic Chinese. It was a rare example of international friendship, of breaking down boundaries through art. It was even documented in a film, *Distant Harmony*, by De-Witt Sage, which included footage of Luciano getting fully kitted out in the makeup and costume of a character from Chinese opera. (This process, believe me, is a lot more fun to watch on film than it was to experience live over several hours, with a hot and restless tenor under the lights.)

For those who went, the trip was unforgettable for other reasons. Primary among these was the food.

Simply marshaling all of those forces to go to China was a huge endeavor. The kids from the competition, which had its finals in Philadelphia, had first flown over to Modena, where the *Bohème* production was remounted as part of the celebrations of Luciano's twenty-fifth anniversary on the stage; then had continued on to Genoa; and, together with the whole Genoa Opera Company, were now going to take the first-ever direct Alitalia flight from Italy to Beijing. For Alitalia, it was excellent publicity to have their first Beijing flight carry Pavarotti and a veritable cultural embassy, and so they donated the whole thing. This meant that in addition to the cast, crew, and staff, Luciano was able to bring along a couple of dozen family members and friends, whom Giovanna, in her dry way, had dubbed the "screaming Modanesi." They were, at the very least, a kind of insurance that Luciano would have somebody to play cards with in his free time.

The logistics of all this were mind-boggling. Still, everything was moving along very well until Luciano came back to his hotel room in Genoa one day and pulled the plug.

"We're not going to China," he said.

"What do you mean, we're not going?" said Giovanna, looking up from whatever she was doing—probably washing Luciano's underwear by hand or some task equally deserving of her time and energy.

"We're not going to China," Luciano repeated.

It seems that Luciano had encountered Katia Ricciarelli, the soprano, on a flight to Milan. Ricciarelli was a lovely-looking if slightly vacant woman with a very pretty voice that didn't have much muscle to it. She had evidently just returned from a concert tour of China and informed Luciano that she had found nothing decent to eat the whole time she had been there. A worse nightmare, from Luciano's standpoint, was unimaginable.

"They don't even have water," he said.

"They don't have water in China," said Giovanna.

"No food, no water," said Luciano, impervious to irony. "We're not going."

Giovanna pointed out that canceling the trip at this point would involve overturning the plans and hard work of hundreds of people. But such considerations bore very little weight with Luciano.

"*Non mi importa*," he said. "That doesn't bother me."

Just when it seemed that Luciano's whim might be on the verge of turning into a serious action—which would have been an event not without precedent in the annals of Pavarotti history—a deus ex machina appeared in the form of Zeffirino, one of Genoa's better eating establishments, where Luciano ate twice a day when he was in the city. Zeffirino's motto is *Ci pensa noi*: We'll think of it. It soon became apparent that this was no idle boast. What they thought of, in this case, was nothing less than a full-scale plan of culinary assault on the country of China. They would bring food. And they would feed the company.

It's amazing the plane even got off the ground. There were the sets and costumes. There was the luggage. There was the food. There were more than 300 people on board, including the screaming Modanesi, who were already living up to Giovanna's nickname for them. In fact, the plane almost didn't get off the ground. After we were all loaded and strapped in and ready for takeoff, there was some kind of bomb scare, and everyone had to get off and be searched and get back on. Some people on the plane immediately began ascribing the call to Plácido Domingo. All in jest, of course.

We didn't quite realize the scale of Zeffirino's operations until the plane had landed and it was time to get everything to the hotel. The restaurant had done itself proud. There was, of course, pasta. There were crates of garlic, lemons, potatoes, onions, tomatoes, melons. There were raw chickens and cuts of veal and sausages and Parma hams. There were wheels of Gorgonzola, Parmigiana, and Pecorino cheese. There were 1,500 bottles of mineral water and a comparable amount of Lambrusco (already starting to lose its fizz). There were hot plates to cook on, a refrigerator to preserve everything, and an oven to make bread.

There were plates and cups, silverware, glassware, and tablecloths. There was so much stuff that Giovanna had to give up her bedroom so there would be somewhere to put it all. She ended up sharing a room with Adua's secretary, Checca.

Of course, after the long flight and the rigors of the baggage compartment, all of this bounty quickly began to go bad. Giovanna spent a certain amount of time every day just throwing things out. She also took it upon herself to clean up after everybody, until I came along one afternoon and found her doing dishes in what should have been her bathtub.

"What are you doing?" I said.

"Washing dishes," Giovanna observed.

"If I see you do another dish again, you're fired," I told her. "This is not in your job description. If they want to come over here and do all this cooking, then let them do the dishes."

I'm not sure I convinced Giovanna, but she did get away for a little while every day. She may have simply wanted to escape the screaming Modanesi, who were keeping up their card games and decibel level; or maybe it was the smell of decaying food that drove her out. In any case, she soon happened upon a market that sold wonderful fresh fruit and vegetables. Luciano refused to believe that she'd found such things in China until she brought him out and showed him herself—taking particular relish in an array of string beans that looked very much like the ones we'd brought with us, in bulk, from Italy (except that the Chinese ones were considerably fresher). By then, of course, we'd also located all sorts of Western delicacies—smoked salmon, roast beef—in the restaurant of our very Western hotel.

The Italian cooks lasted about a week and a half, cooking two meals a day for dozens of people in a hotel bedroom, and then they gave up in disgust. We tried to give some of the food and other accoutrements away to the Chinese, but even our generosity ran into problems. Nobody was willing to take our refrigerator; they thought they'd be jailed as traitors by accepting such a lavish gift. So in the end we just left the refrigerator there in the room, and a lot of the food, as well. Who knows what happened to it.

Luciano would never admit he's wrong, but he must have learned a bit of a lesson. When he went to Japan with the Metropolitan Opera, he brought the prosciutto slicer and the espresso machine and set up the ovens and the refrigerators and the hot plates in a hotel room. But he relied on the local produce, rather than bringing it with him. As Joe Volpe soon learned.

When singers go on tour with the Met, they get a per diem: a sum of money over and above their regular fee, to cover living expenses. On that particular trip, Joe Volpe held back Luciano's per diem until I arrived in Japan a week later, and gave the money to me, since I generally kept track of Luciano's spending money. Luciano hardly ever had money in his pocket. His favorite words were, "Herbert will pay." Or, "Giovanna will pay," or whoever happened to be in his entourage at the moment with ready cash. Of course, it was his cash, but somehow he kept up the illusion that he didn't have anything to do with it.

On this particular occasion, for some reason or other, I handed the money on to Luciano, and I happened to do it in Joe's presence.

Luciano said, "What's this?"

Joe said, "Well, Luciano, that's your per diem. That's the money that you get for your food, and your dry cleaning, and expenses like that."

"Oh," said Luciano, looking at the money in his hand. "This is for my food."

"Yes," Joe said, "that's right."

Not long after that—I think it was on a night that Plácido was singing—Luciano invited everyone up to his suite after the performance, for dinner. In true Italian style, the first course he offered was prosciutto—freshly sliced in his machine—with melon. Unfortunately, when Joe Volpe tried to cut into his melon, it was as hard as a rock.

"What the hell is this?" said Joe, never one to mince words.

"In this country, you should buy muskmelon, those wonderful ripe melons. What is this?"

"Well," said Luciano, the picture of innocence, "that's the kind of melon you get for two hundred yen a day."

And then, of course, he got Joe some fresh, ripe melon out of one of the refrigerators. A melon that, in Japan, probably cost $40. The Met's per diem is a drop in the bucket for a singer like Luciano. He just wanted to drive the point home.

It isn't only when Luciano goes on tour that he has special culinary requirements. Whenever he packs, wherever he's going, there's some kind of food item that needs to go along. As I mentioned, from America he has to have garlic, as well as Coffeemate, Carter's liver pills, Head & Shoulders shampoo, and so on and so on and so on. That's if you're coming over to see him. If he's traveling himself from New York back to Italy, one of the requirements used to be porterhouse steaks. The day before he left, Hans would go down to Ernest Klein on Sixth Avenue, where there was a butcher who knew exactly how Luciano liked his steaks cut. Hans would pick up eight of them and pop them in the freezer. Then he and Giovanna would go to Lamston's and buy a few of those soft picnic carriers, and then they'd buy blocks of dry ice. The next step was to run to the hotel, wrap up the steaks—by now frozen hard as rocks—in towels, pack them up in the dry ice, and schlep them to the airport along with Luciano's dozens of other bags. By the time Luciano got to Modena, the steaks were almost thawed—ready to be cooked up for his first dinner at home.

But food, important as it was, was only a part of the worries of anybody responsible for Luciano's packing. Packing for Luciano is no joke. Not only does it involve dozens of bags, but it has to be completed when Luciano wants it done. It used to be that Giovanna would have to come home after the final performance and then stay up all night packing so that everybody could leave on time the next morning. These days, Luciano sometimes wants to leave right after he sings, which means that somebody

has to stay in the hotel and pack frantically during the performance, so that the plane can take off exactly when Luciano wants.
You can't really get started with the packing while Luciano's
around, because it disturbs him.

Of course, there are clothes to pack, and shoes, and that kind
of thing. There are also Luciano's desk supplies. Giovanna, at
least, used to carry his desk blotter around with them. Anything
that he had on his desk, he wanted with him: scissors, stapler,
pens, you name it. He also wanted all his music around him, so
Giovanna would Xerox all his scores and his concert music.
When they arrived, she'd put the music on the piano and the
blotter on the desk. Of course, Luciano never actually touched
any of that stuff. Giovanna would dust it sometimes, and then,
when it was time to go, she'd put it right back in a suitcase.

And don't forget the medicines: there was a whole bag just for
them. Blood-count machines, cuffs to measure blood pressure,
thermometers, bandages, and every kind of pill you can imagine.
All the pills got dumped into a drawer and then dumped back
into the suitcase, and maybe sometimes he'd take a few of them.
Luciano goes in cycles with his medications: he'll take anything
from one pill to twenty a day, depending on his mood. Of course,
the pills aren't only for him. If something's wrong with somebody
around him, he'll always know what pill the person should take.

One medical professional whose services he can't do without
is his dentist. Luciano spends more time at the dentist than anybody I know. His mouth is worth more than his estate. I don't
know how he manages to have enough teeth to give Dr. Sendax
as much business as he brings him. He arrives in New York and
he's got to go to the dentist.

"Giovanna," he'd say, "call the car."

"Luciano, it's a block away," she'd say. "Walking is what you
need to do." (Giovanna was always trying to get Luciano to lose
weight.)

"No, no, no, we take the car, it's easier," Luciano would say.
"Walking makes my teeth hurt."

As with everything else, Luciano is convinced he knows best about teeth. His dentist is clearly the best dentist, so everybody else has to go to him, too. That's why we all go to Dr. Sendax. He might as well have set up a branch in our office for all the work he's done on us over the years. Luciano had him do his father's teeth. He paid for all the dental work for his good friend Dr. Umberto Boeri, which was a real favor. Luciano sent all kinds of other people to Dr. Sendax. A lot of them got treatment and never paid their bills. I guess they believed that Luciano was serving as the health and dental service.

That's how generosity works with Luciano. He has a real generous streak, but it's unpredictable; you are not always sure if he means to give you something or not. And his generosity is not necessarily based on what he thinks you might like. It's based on his own latest enthusiasms. If he's discovered something and he thinks it's the best, everybody should have one.

Believe me, I'm not knocking it. One time he called me up to say, "Herbert, I have gotten a Saab, and it's the best car ever. You must have one."

And he bought me one. I still have it. He was right. It's a wonderful car.

As a matter of fact, Dr. Sendax did my teeth, too. But I paid for that myself.

Luciano's enthusiasms are so powerful that, as I've said, he tends to buy in bulk. If he finds something he likes, he'll buy five of it. Come to think of it, it's kind of like his approach to opera roles. Once he finds one that fits, he'll keep doing it over and over and over again.

One thing he likes are Mephisto shoes. He tried to charge four pairs to the Metropolitan Opera's costume department. He said he needed them for the performance. When he got caught, he told the department to go ahead and order them anyway, and he would pay for them himself. And he did. But because the Met is a not-for-profit organization, he was able to avoid the sales tax.

That's Luciano. One moment he's buying you an expensive

car, and then he's turning around and trying to avoid fifty bucks tax, or whatever it is, on a few lousy pairs of shoes.

And then again, he'll see something he likes and decide he has to have it right away. Like the suite of hotel room furniture at Caesars Palace.

"Herbert. I must have this."

Giovanna was perusing the bedspread, absolutely deadpan.

"It looks like a big blood clot," I said to her, nudging a corner of it with my foot.

But Luciano loved that bedspread. He wanted the bedspread, he wanted the drapes, he wanted the whole thing. What am I going to say, "No, you can't have it"? It's his money. He wants the furniture, he gets the furniture. I went to whoever was responsible at Caesars Palace and arranged to have the whole suite— drapes, bedspread, TV cabinet, and all—shipped to Modena.

Don't ask me what he did with it when it got there. Italian homes tend to be full of stuff anyway. Don't be fooled by the sleek, minimalist pictures in the high-end design magazines: the average Italian home looks like something on Queens Boulevard, crammed with trinkets, tchotchkes, anything and everything. Luciano's house in Modena was no exception. And he must have warehouses full of all the other stuff he gets. So I don't know what happened to the Caesars Palace furniture, except that I can almost guarantee he had forgotten about it by the time it arrived. I think Giovanna gave the bedspread to the maid.

In addition to all the stuff Luciano bought on his travels, there was the stuff people gave him along the way. Huge stuffed animals. Silver platters. More different things than you can even imagine. Sometimes you had to draw the line. Once in Houston he was presented with a live pig named Rigoletto. But Giovanna put her foot down.

"There's only so much I can carry," she said.

Another big consideration when you're traveling with Luciano is moving Luciano himself. It's not just his mobility, although, as his hips and knee became increasingly troublesome over the years, simply having him walk from one place to another became more and more of a problem. But arranging for him to get from one city to another can be equally difficult. To Luciano, nothing is so set in stone that it can't be changed if he wants it to be. And that includes airplane reservations.

"I will leave Monday," he'll say. "Or maybe Tuesday. In the morning. Or maybe in the afternoon. I will decide later."

Our poor travel agent, Jay Lazarus, had to perform prodigious feats on the computer to keep all the possible travel dates open for him. Normally, when the computer notices that the same person has multiple bookings, it automatically deletes them, so I'm not quite sure how he did it.

Finally, two days in advance, Luciano would decide. He would travel on Monday. So Jay would scramble to issue the tickets— this was in the days of paper tickets—and messenger them over to the office.

But you could count on it: the next day Luciano would decide he'd fly on Tuesday, instead.

On the other hand, certain things in Luciano's world may not be altered by even a hair. For instance, when he flew the Concorde, he had to be seated in the first seat, first row. That's the seat of honor on the Concorde, and it's reserved for dignitaries like the president of France, so of course it was the seat Luciano had to have. Sometimes there was a problem getting it. Sometimes the president of France actually was on the same flight as Luciano. But try to explain that to Luciano.

"Oh, it's no problem," Luciano would say affably. "Ask him to switch."

Luciano had some reason to be choosy about where he sat on a plane: he was a slightly nervous flyer. His anxiety dated not from childhood but from 1975, when he was in a plane crash; the plane he was in broke up on the runway as it was landing. Fortunately, nobody was killed, and Luciano walked away unscathed, but he was understandably a little edgy about flying after that. And he always insisted on sitting at the front of the plane. Another long-range effect was that, several years later, he decided to "suit" the airline. He said he had sustained hearing loss in the accident that made it difficult to do his job. I don't remember how that finally turned out, but it never went to trial. I guess the hearing problem must have gotten better, since his would-be suit was more than twenty years ago and he's managed to sing more than a few times since.

There was also a reason for another of Luciano's unchanging demands: he always wanted to be driven in a Mercedes-Benz with bucket seats in the front. When he's driving himself, Luciano's car preferences are strong but variable; for a while he swore by Maserati, then he switched allegiance to Saab. But when he's being picked up somewhere, his requirements are always the same. Luciano sits in the front of a limo—it's too difficult for him to get in and out of the backseat—and he wants to be able to adjust the seat to his liking—go backward, go sideways, turn the thing over, whatever the hell he wants to do. So it has to be a Mercedes-Benz. With bucket seats.

The only problem is, not every limousine service in the world has a Mercedes-Benz with bucket seats. But again, try to explain that to Luciano. When he goes to the car and sees it's not the kind he wanted, he blows his top. First, he throws his hands up—his favorite gesture—and then he starts in. I'm *stupido*. Thomas—who used to do all his travel arrangements for Tibor—is *stupido*. Everybody is *stupido*. Once he's got that off his chest, long-suffering as he is, he gets into the car and we can go.

Luciano's list of demands grew ever longer with the years—not least because whatever he wanted Tibor and his staff seemed able to provide. Not only did he want his hotel rooms to replicate the comforts of home, his dressing rooms had to as well, down to a full buffet that looked more like an imperial banquet. It was more food than one person could possibly eat; it was more food than ten could possibly eat. That didn't matter, because when the concert was over Luciano had someone on his staff pack the whole thing up and bring it back to the hotel. Of course, the hotel was also stocked, but you never knew when you might need a midnight snack. The hotel was also furnished just the way he wanted it. The chairs had to be a certain height. The bed had to be a certain height.

Tibor's staff spent a lot of advance time going through the hotel suites—with a tape measure—to make sure all their specifications had been met.

"I am a very simple man," Luciano used to say. "I ask for only two things: a private car and a private plane."

Would that we were all so modest in our needs.

He wasn't always unappreciative, though. Judy Drucker became an expert at getting places ready to put up Luciano. One time, she got him a magnificent villa at the hotel on upscale Fisher Island, right on the water. Luciano arrived and surveyed the premises to make sure everything was to his liking, while Judy followed him, hoping that she'd once again managed to make the grade.

He got to the refrigerator and threw it open. Judy had filled the refrigerator with everything Luciano liked. There was smoked salmon, there was roast beef, there was champagne.

Luciano broke into a broad smile. Then he threw back his head and began to sing "God Bless America."

BRUCE CRAWFORD
(former general manager of the Metropolitan Opera)

None of the big stars ever wanted to go on the Metropolitan Opera's annual tour, which is why I ultimately canceled it. Luciano was the exception. He was always willing to go. But of course he didn't stay at the same hotel as the other singers. In Boston, he stayed at the Ritz-Carlton, the fine old Boston hotel. Everything is top of the line there; even the elevators are perfumed. For the other singers, it was too expensive.

Well, one night Luciano arrived with his baggage, and one of our people from the Met was helping him. I don't remember why Luciano didn't have anybody traveling with him. Anyway, our staff member had to get thirty-two pieces of baggage into the elevator, because Luciano used to pack all his utensils for cooking—pots and pans—and olive oil. Something had clearly broken, because olive oil was oozing out in that perfumed elevator.

Our staff member wrangled all the luggage onto the elevator and off the elevator again and down the hall into Luciano's room, olive oil dripping on the carpet. And he got all that luggage into Luciano's room. But something hadn't met with Luciano's approval, and he lost his temper.

He turned to our staff member and said, "I don't ask for much."

THE THREE TENORS

Opera's Greatest Franchise

Luciano's success in Madison Square Garden got me dreaming. I dreamed of other ways to present classical music to a mass audience. I dreamed of putting on Handel's oratorio *Messiah* at Madison Square Garden, with dancers enacting movement while singers sang at the side; I even had the well-known designer Rouben Ter-Arutunian come up with a set that would have turned the Garden into a kind of cathedral. It would have been spectacular. I dreamed of doing a version of Wagner's *Ring* in the Garden—an abridged version, of course, because the whole thing lasts four nights, and you wouldn't want to do that. But you could cut it down to a manageable length, and engage the greatest singers, and very, very beautiful people to act everything out, with Sir Georg Solti conducting. I went so far as to talk to Georg and he said he was interested, though we never got far enough with it for me to find out how interested he really was. None of these things ever actually happened.

I dreamed of a lot of things. But I never dreamed of The Three Tenors. I wish I had. A lot of people wish they had.

You could say that the genesis of The Three Tenors went back to 1987. Well, a part of it, anyway. One day that summer Luciano and his entourage were in Pesaro, and Giovanna was reading the *International Herald Tribune*, a paper that wasn't on Luciano's media list. Luciano was very specific about his news intake. Wherever he was in the world, he had to have *Corriere della Sera* and *La Gazzetta dello Sport*, a publication printed on pink paper and devoted entirely to sports.

"Luciano," Giovanna said, "is there anything about José Carreras in the Italian papers?"

"No," Luciano said. "What about José?"

Giovanna said, "It seems he's ill. In a hospital in Seattle."

"Let me see that," Luciano said.

He grabbed the paper. Then he picked up the phone and called Carlos Caballé, Montserrat's brother, who was José's manager.

"Tell me what's going on," he said.

What was going on was that José had leukemia.

José was a wonderful young singer. He had a beautiful strong tone and a melting way of singing that was really very affecting. The best way to get an idea of what his voice was like is to hear some of the live recordings from the mid-1970s: a gorgeous, exciting sound.

Perhaps because José was a little younger, Luciano didn't feel as competitive with him as he did with Plácido. Or maybe it was just clear to him that José, as good as he was, wasn't quite in his league. Whatever the reason, Luciano adored José. And the news that he had cancer galvanized him to action.

As I said, Luciano is terrific in a crisis. The first thing he did was get on the phone to Ernie Rosenbaum in San Francisco, the friend who had flagged the problem with Luciano's daughter. Ernie's specialty is oncology, so he seemed like a good candidate to help. I don't know how much Ernie actually did or how much help was necessary, but Luciano certainly let it be known that he was there. He called José every single day.

"You have nothing to worry about," he told him. "Whatever you need, there is money for you, anything you want."

And he kept calling, to make sure José was OK, to see if there was anything he could do, and so forth.

José underwent a bone marrow transplant, which is a pretty harrowing thing to have to experience, but it worked and he got better. He was back onstage by 1988. He was changed, of course. You could say his voice lost some of its resiliency. He might have lost some of that before he got sick, as a result of taking on increasingly heavy roles. But he was singing, and people were thrilled that he was better, and they welcomed him back with open arms.

So as José continued to sing and it gradually became clear that the crisis had passed, an idea started to develop that it would be nice to do something to celebrate his recovery.

In 1990, the World Cup was to be held in Italy, so all eyes would be turned on that country—all eyes, at least, of the majority of the world's population to whom the words *World Cup* instantly summon up the idea of soccer. It seemed like a good time to do a concert in Rome. It seemed that way, at least, to Mario Dradi. Mario was Carreras's manager in Italy. He represented most of the Italian artists. He liked to give the impression that he was a very big deal, and while that may not have exactly been true on an international scale, he was very tight with all the theaters in Italy, which is why all the big singers kept working with him.

It was this character, Mario Dradi, who presented the world's three leading tenors, Luciano, Plácido, and José, together for the first time in concert at the Baths of Caracalla on July 7, 1990, with Zubin Mehta conducting.

It was a feel-good event all around. For one thing, it was a charity concert. The official idea was that the tenors would sing for free and then donate the proceeds from the television rights, the recording, and the like to a charity of their choice. Singers love to do charity events. Luciano did more benefit concerts than I can keep track of. But as sure as God made bananas, there's something in it for them. No singer ever sings for nothing, no matter what he claims.

Financially, the concert was a one-off deal. Instead of signing contracts that would entitle them to royalties on future recording sales and the like, all three tenors agreed on a flat fee. Mind you, it wasn't a modest fee. That was not a contract I did through my office, since everything was handled with Mario in Italy, but I think each of them got something like $300,000. In 1990, for a classical artist to get that much money for one night's work was pretty impressive. I bet those tenors had never seen money like that before. They were so enchanted with this huge figure that none of them even thought of taking it up with their legal people to see if it was actually a good deal or not.

This is a lesson in what can happen when a singer operates on his own. I like to think that if I had been involved I would have said something. I would certainly have been interested to know what the presenter was getting, and what kind of deal he had with the record company, and that sort of thing. But at this point I was in a secondary position and Luciano was inflamed with the ardor of a good cause, and he signed the contract. Of course, he made a big, big, big mistake.

Because—as I hardly need mention—the Three Tenors concert was the biggest blockbuster hit in classical recording history. It was a pretty major hit, period. The record sold something like 11 million copies. Luciano's "Nessun dorma" gained the status of a pop song. All three of those guys became household names. They thought they were famous before, but it was nothing like what happened after that Three Tenors album hit the stands.

You'd think they'd have been delighted. But, of course, all three of them had signed those flat-fee contracts and gone off with their $300,000. Now, millions and millions of dollars were being made, by Mario Dradi and by Decca/London, Luciano's very own record label, and the tenors weren't getting even a tiny piece of it. All of their proceeds were supposed to go to charity in any case, but they were so good-hearted that they must have been very frustrated to miss this chance to give millions, rather than just hundreds of thousands, to the charities of their choice. And believe me, they didn't suffer in silence. The racket they made about it could be heard from Rome to California.

It was at that point that I, Luciano's trusty agent, got called on to come in and clean up my tenor's mess.

That was about what my role had become to Luciano. I was the one who went in and did the dirty work. Luciano, you see, is very reluctant to confront people directly. So if things weren't going well, he'd call me. I was the person, for example, who'd argue with Tibor about paying him more money. Luciano and Tibor would make nice together, and then Luciano would grouse to me, "He's not paying me enough. Go tell him to pay me more." For his part, Tibor had some things he wanted me to say to Luciano, too. He kept after me to get him to change his concert program and sing something different every once in a while. As if anybody could get Luciano to change his concert program by the 1990s. I'm good, but even I couldn't work that kind of miracle.

It wasn't only Tibor, either: it was everybody. That was my role. Once, I had been Luciano's creator—not in the sense that I actually created him but in the sense that I kept coming up with new things for him to do, and new objectives, and new ideas about how to present him. Now I had been reduced to his foil. My role was to act as a buffer and, most important, to get him more money.

So my task, after the success of The Three Tenors, was to go back to Decca and negotiate with them. It had been a long, long time since Luciano and I had gone to Zurich together to talk to Mr. Rosengarten. Luciano was far beyond accompanying me to talk business with Decca by now, and Mr. Rosengarten was no longer with us. The head of Decca now was a guy named Roland Kommerell, so I met with him and made my case.

"Look," I said, "you guys have made a bloody fortune, and it's all over the press how much money you're making and how many records you're selling. You just can't expect to have that kind of publicity on the Three Tenors records that you're selling and not have them want some more money."

Now, did Luciano have a legal right to more money? Of course not. But on the other hand, he was an exclusive artist with Decca and he sold a lot of records for them, especially now that The Three Tenors were such a success. If they didn't keep him happy, that was not going to be very good. So they couldn't really afford to piss him off.

I suspect that they wanted to figure out how to pay Luciano without Plácido knowing or José knowing, because they didn't want to pay them the same thing. It had to be a big subterfuge. Plácido is no fool, and he always suspected that Decca was doing something for Luciano that they didn't do for him, because Luciano was exclusive with Decca and Plácido is not exclusive with anybody. So Plácido was extremely suspicious. He always knew that they gave Luciano some kind of cut.

A lot of people talked about it, in fact. The rumors were that Decca paid Luciano $1 million. Well, that's wrong. It wasn't $1 million. It was $1.5 million, paid out over eight years, in relatively modest chunks of $187,500. I have to say that that was our best giftola ever.

I don't believe that Decca gave that to Plácido or José. But they must have given Plácido something. Plácido would never have stood still knowing that Luciano was getting some kind of payout and he was not. The Three Tenors concerts were all very friendly on the surface, but there was not exactly a trusting atmosphere behind the scenes.

The next Three Tenors concert took place in 1994, in Los Angeles, for the next World Cup. It was a whole different ball game. There weren't going to be any $300,000 mistakes made here. The negotiations that went on before that concert were on a par with the Camp David accords in terms of sheer complexity.

For one thing, there was the question of who was going to release the recording. All the major labels bid on it, but as the bidding went up into more and more millions, they gradually dropped out, except Decca and Warner/Atlantic. Warner, in the meantime, had signed José Carreras to an exclusive contract, leaving Plácido as the only one of the three without a major record label behind him. Plácido had sworn he would never again work with Decca, because he kept supposing they had given Luciano some big payoff they hadn't given him. And Tibor was good friends with Ahmet Ertegun, who cofounded Atlantic Records and continued to hold sway there even after Warner bought the label. Not surprisingly, Warner ultimately got the rights. They paid so much money they figured they would have to sell 6 million copies of the record to break even. I'm pretty sure they didn't.

Then there was the question of who was going to produce the concert. Again, there was a deadlock. Luciano, of course, wanted Tibor, but José and Plácido had been working with a German concert promoter named Matthias Hoffmann. Tibor wanted to do it, but the financial commitment for that concert was so heavy that I think it put even him off. Hoffmann had all the money that was necessary. No one asked too closely how he got it. What they worked out in the end was that Hoffmann was the producer, the big mucky-muck, and Tibor got paid some very nice amount of money to actually create the production—the staging, the lighting, the visuals, all that kind of thing. Which was no mean feat, because that production was very spectacular: the concert was held in Dodger Stadium in front of 56,000 people.

Hoffmann kept the financial control. He had a way of handling money that was very appealing to artists. He was always on the lookout for that extra dollar. At one of José's concerts in Florida that Judy Drucker put on, he went up to her backstage at intermission and said that she should pay José more money because the concert was going so well.

That's how this business is. Nobody would ever come up to a presenter at intermission and say, "Hey, my artist is not so great tonight; let me refund part of your money." But if the concert is going well, they think, Oh, the presenter got a fantastic deal.

After that, Judy wasn't very impressed with Mr. Hoffmann.

Luciano called her up to ask her what she thought of him, and she said that he should stay away. So of course Luciano went ahead and worked with him. It's almost a guarantee that if you say something's black, he's going to turn around and call it white, if only to show you who's boss.

Anyway, the negotiations around that second Three Tenors concert were an unbelievable headache for everyone involved. Just dealing with these three people at one time, or even at separate times, was very difficult. Simply getting them in one room together for a press interview was a major logistical challenge. Before the concert, they all flew over to Monte Carlo, which allowed them to do a kind of run-through, and prerecord the album, and pick up their fees in advance. Tom Brokaw wanted to come over to do an interview with the three of them, but nobody could manage to get him any of the information he needed to set the thing up, so he canceled the trip. I think the prevailing attitude was that it was his loss. Those guys were so big by that point that they didn't think they needed national TV coverage. They may have been right, because it would be hard to get a larger TV audience than they got for that concert in Los Angeles. It's supposed to have reached something like 1.5 billion people.

When you're dealing with an event on that scale, the most important thing becomes to protect your own interests. This led to a lot of backbiting and mistrust behind the scenes, although nothing was ever spoken aloud. At least, not publicly. A lot of things were certainly spoken out loud to me. Tibor would complain to me about Hoffmann, Hoffmann would complain to me about Tibor, and both of them would complain to me about Luciano, who would complain to me about both of them right back. And Plácido and José were doing their own share of complaining, to Hoffmann or Tibor or anyone who would listen. It was a real round-robin of complaint that went on back there.

That's inevitable when that kind of money enters the picture. Each of those three tenors had a lot to protect. The fees they were getting for that concert were considerably higher than the

measly $300,000 they had gotten in 1990. I think it was some-
thing like $2 million apiece. I heard that Zubin Mehta got $1 million, and they certainly got more than Zubin.

I don't know exactly how much they got, because I didn't see
the check. All the money from the Three Tenors concerts went
straight to Luciano's lawyer. At that point, I was taking commission on a figure of my own choosing. I made up what seemed like
a reasonable figure, and they paid it. It certainly wasn't 10 percent. If I had taken $200,000, it would have blown everybody's
mind. I don't think it was even $50,000. I think it was less. It was
still a lot of money. I didn't do so badly.

That second concert wasn't as good as the first one. Some of
the fun went out of it when the money started pouring in. To a
tenor, big money is a very serious thing indeed, so the concert itself was a little stiff and formulaic. But who cared? Certainly not
anybody behind the scenes. It was clear that there was a lot more
money to be made out of the Three Tenors shtick, and nobody
saw why they should wait around four years for the next World
Cup to start making it. So for 1996 and 1997, Hoffmann set up
an international Three Tenor tour.

The biggest difference between the first concerts and that tour
was a new conductor. Zubin had had enough. In the music
world, Zubin gets a lot of criticism for his conducting—people
call him uninterested, uninvolved, or simply not very good—but
in his own mind he's a very important artist. He sees himself as
up there with Karajan, Solti, and the rest of them. He had earned
some good money from The Three Tenors, and now he wanted
to concentrate on what he regarded as real music. To replace him,
Hoffmann and Rudas brought in Jimmy Levine, the upholder of
artistic standards at the Metropolitan Opera. Like I said, every
artist has his own idea about what constitutes artistic standards,
and if you wave half a million dollars at him for conducting one
night's performance, that definition has a way of stretching. You
would have to be a very big fool if somebody offered you that
kind of money and you turned it down. And Jimmy is no fool.

So The Three Tenors went around the world, and raked in the money, and got perks galore. Hoffmann was even better at that kind of thing than Tibor. He had Wolfgang Joop, the German fashion designer, whip up a couple of suits of evening clothes for Luciano. That was the sort of perk that arrived unbidden in Hoffmann's world. All three tenors enjoyed that kind of thing very much, but Luciano enjoyed it even more than the others. Although there were three of them, Luciano always felt he was number one—as did many, many people in the audience—and he acted the part. He would have a little golf cart to get him around so he didn't have to walk too much, and he would sit there backstage with his feet up and have someone pour his Perrier, and someone bring him his towel, and someone serve him from what amounted to the entire kitchens of food they would keep for him backstage. I wouldn't even say he was treated like a superstar. He was treated like some extraordinary being who had no relationship to anybody else. Plácido was in his dressing room cooling off, José was in his dressing room cooling off, and Luciano was in his dressing room with forty-five people taking care of him.

Rather quickly, people began coming up with Three Tenors knockoffs, trying to latch onto even a tiny crumb of their success. There were The Three Countertenors, and The Three Irish Tenors, and The Three Mo' Tenors, who were black. I had another idea. I thought that someone should do a Three Sopranos.

Tibor was just thrilled with that idea. Because of Hoffmann, Tibor had been forced into a somewhat secondary role in the Three Tenors enterprise, and he didn't like it. The Three Sopranos was a way for him to do something on his own.

So we went out and found three sopranos, all of whom, coincidentally, happened to be represented by my office. Their names were Kathleen Cassello, Kallen Esperian, and Cynthia Lawrence. Although they were my artists, I think the selection was a mistake from the start. If you really want to do The Three Sopranos, you should take three like Montserrat Caballé and Joan Sutherland and Beverly Sills, or whoever the hell was still singing by the mid-nineties: really big stars. But the three sopranos we ended up with were all young singers who weren't very well known. They had done quite a bit of stuff in the opera world, and they had all won the Pavarotti competition, but their accomplishments were light-years away from those of Luciano, Plácido, and José.

The Three Sopranos quickly became Tibor's baby, which was perfectly all right with me. He was paying them a lot of money—well, a lot of money by their lights, $20,000 a concert each—and I was getting my commission, so everybody was content. The idea was that these glamorous women would appear in glitzy costumes—which Tibor's wife designed—and sing like a million dollars, or at least like $20,000, which they were very happy to do. For them, it was such good money that they didn't even care that the concerts were artistically ridiculous. Tibor negotiated a deal for their first album with his old pal Ahmet at Atlantic Records, and tried to get a lot of A-list journalists in to cover their first concert in Los Angeles. They made a splash for about fifteen minutes. They sang in L.A. and London and Atlantic City and all kinds of places, and they had this record, which some people bought, but not all that many. The fact of the matter is, nobody was very interested in listening to these three ladies they'd never heard of shrieking out all these high notes. Let's face it: the sound of three sopranos singing together can be a little grating on the ears. So the act gradually fizzled out.

But that was the kind of thing that was going on all the time. People saw all that money being made by The Three Tenors and they went a little bit crazy. Sony Classical tried to get a piece of it, too. They made a Christmas album with them in Vienna, and I'm sure they paid them millions. I don't know, because that contract didn't go through me, either. I just know that it didn't sell particularly well, so Sony suffered terribly on that one.

The contracts that were handled in Europe never came through my office at all. None of Luciano's recording contracts ever went through me, in fact, even though I negotiated with Rosengarten and Kommerell and those guys; I saw all the royalty statements, but the money went straight to Luciano in Europe. And the Three Tenor contracts were all Tibor and Hoffmann, and Hoffmann had it all worked out. He tried to take care of everything for those three. He even took care of their taxes. By 1996 and 1997, they were supposed to be earning something like $2.3 million a concert, and he divided it all up for them into salary and royalties and taxes, and he took care of their taxes for them. At least that's what they said he said a couple of years later.

Soon enough, though, the whole enterprise began to run into trouble. One flap, in Germany, was a rather amusing debate about royalty payments. Presenters have to pay royalties to the composers of any music that isn't in the public domain, and in Germany, at least, pop and classical concerts are charged at different rates. It would hardly be fair to make the presenter of some little chamber concert in a church basement pay 10 percent of his gross in royalties, but if you're talking about a stadium concert for 50,000 people, the presenter is not going to find it quite so hard to come up with more money. Hoffmann naturally claimed that a concert by the world's three leading operatic tenors was "classical," not "pop," and paid the lower rate on the tenors' 1996 concerts in Munich and Düsseldorf. But the German authorities noticed. The case ended up in court, where the discussion revolved around whether "O sole mio" was a pop or a classical song, much to the amusement of everyone except the participants, for whom the answer to that question meant a difference of about a million dollars. Hoffmann lost.

That wasn't all he lost. It turned out Hoffmann hadn't exactly been playing by the book about the tenors' taxes, either. Mind you, I have no idea if he really told them he was going to pay taxes for them on their money, but they all said that he did, and said it vociferously, when he came under investigation in 1998. During the proceedings, Hoffmann made the shocking claim that the tenors were being paid extra under the table. Just imagine that.

The upshot was that Hoffmann was sentenced to five or six

years in jail. The tenors were hit with a pretty big bill for back taxes to the German government; Luciano had to pay something like $900,000. And Tibor, now that Hoffmann was out of the picture, got to take over as principal promoter of The Three Tenors. When the smoke cleared, the happiest person, of course, was Tibor, who now got to do everything himself, without Hoffmann to veto his ideas.

It was a mixed blessing, though, because the concerts gradually got less and less popular. Ticket sales were already falling off during the 1996–97 tour. Sales were so bad for a New Year's Eve concert they did in Vancouver that the promoter tried to cancel the event. Hoffmann had to sue him to make sure the show went on. Perhaps to reward the public for their reluctance to buy even hastily discounted tickets, the tenors ended the concert at 11:45 so they could ring in the New Year with their loved ones backstage, leaving the audience to ring it in on their way to their cars in the parking lot. Vancouver, evidently, was not amused. The next time Luciano was scheduled to sing there, only 25 percent of the tickets sold. He had to cancel that one.

Still, they kept on churning those concerts out. By the time they did one in September 2003, Luciano was about to turn sixty-eight, and none of the three of them was exactly exuding what you could call youthful vigor.

A children's book came out in Germany in 2002 about The Three Tenors traveling to give a concert for the penguins at the South Pole. The penguins are delighted, but the real reason the tenors have deigned to pay them a visit is that nobody else wants to hear them.

It wasn't so far from the truth.

chapter XIII

HOW TO MANAGE A TENOR:
THE ADVANCED COURSE

Everything Your Advance Strategy
Didn't Prepare You For

Managing an artist can be like serving a life sentence in Alcatraz.

People think it's some kind of dream job. You get to meet the artists, and befriend them, and go backstage, and hear this fantastic music. I can't tell you how many people come to work in this business with stars in their eyes. Very sweet people, who love opera. A lot of them even worked for me. But you know something? That attitude gets you about as far as the exit door. For one thing, it's not income producing. Being friends with singers doesn't get you very far if you can't pay the rent.

And the word *friend* is relative. You're not the singer's friend; you're working for him. All the other stuff is great, but it's gravy. The bottom line is, you have to produce for the singer or he's going to go off and find some other manager, however strong your so-called friendship. This was true of Luciano. It was true of everybody.

Sometimes it's impossible to produce for a singer, because the singer isn't really very good. But the singer never thinks that's his fault. It's always your fault.

If a singer sings badly, there's always an excuse. He had a cold, he had to go to the toilet, he didn't sleep well. Artists tend to take very little responsibility for anything that goes wrong. On the other hand, you, the agent, are seen as responsible for everything. You hear it all the time. You shouldn't have booked them with this or that theater, in this or that role. They wanted a different airplane seat. They didn't like the hotel. The toilet paper was too rough.

If you're not careful, a lot of your job can get caught up in that kind of little detail. A singer likes it best if you meet him at the airport, take her out to dinner, bring over his mail, and so on. I had employees who were happy to do those things. But not me. I'm in business. I don't do anything unless there's a return on it. With Luciano, there was a big return. I had eight people working for me at my peak, and at any given time three or four or five of them might be busy with Luciano. We had one part-time person who came in just to answer his fan mail.

A worst-case scenario is what happened between Merle Hubbard, who used to work for me, and the soprano Carol Vaness. Merle had a number of people whom he basically represented himself. I let my employees have that kind of autonomy, and they got their own cut on the people they represented, which was 20 percent of what I got, on top of their salaries. Merle was a wonderful, warm man who adored singers and dancers, and a lot of them adored him right back. He brought some great people into the office, too. He had a young soprano named Renée Fleming, back when she was starting out; of course she went on to become, supposedly, this great American diva and the darling of the press, although her story would be very different if there were some good soprano competition out there to give her a run for her money. And he had Carol Vaness. He and Carol were so close that she gave him control of some portion of her money. I don't know what he did with it, but she ultimately accused him of mismanagement—of absconding with some of her funds—and there was a lawsuit against my office that created some notoriety for a while. We ended up settling. I've had relatively few lawsuits in my time, and I don't even think that one counts, because it was really about Merle, not me. But it does show what happens when you get too caught up in your artists' personal lives.

DAVID PATRICK STEARNS
(journalist)

I broke the story about the Carol Vaness lawsuit, and of course when I was writing it I called up the Breslin office to get a comment. Herbert was in Europe, and I got his assistant, who said he didn't want to bother him.
I said, "Well, I just wanted to ask him about Carol Vaness's suit."
He said, "Oh, Herbert doesn't care about her clothes."

There's a lot of mistrust between singers and agents. They always think you're out to make money at their expense. They always think it's in your power to do everything for them. If you don't do enough for them, they leave. Then they say you were terrible. Nobody has ever left and said, "I'm leaving because I realize I'm not that good."

I may have engendered more mistrust than some, first, because I had this reputation as being very focused on money and, second, because every singer thought I had it in my power to make them into the next Pavarotti. But the fact is, you can't create those careers single-handedly. You can help them along. But the artist has to have a certain spark, and a certain drive, and a certain understanding of the business. And a lot of artists don't have it. Especially the business understanding part.

I used to represent a Russian soprano named Nina Rautio. Ever hear of her? I thought not. Madame Rautio was someone who was very clear about where she belonged.

"I want to enter *par la grande porte*," she would say. Through the big door.

In other words, she wanted to make a big splash. No modest entrances for Madame Rautio.

Her husband, a little Russian man, used to come around the office. "What is she doing next? Remember, she wants to enter *par la grande porte*."

"Well, I'm afraid *la grande porte* doesn't exist," I said.

I did get her a contract for *Aida* at the Met. The first performance was very good. The rest of the performances were very bad. She eventually left my office. I guess no other agent managed to find her a *grande porte*, either.

I could make a long list of people I worked with who had this odd psychological misconception about who they were and where they fit in the big picture. I'd call it "Where Are They Now?" Nina Rautio. A mezzo-soprano named Markella Hatziano. Kathleen Cassello, of The Three Sopranos. And the list goes on.

It can be frustrating working with artists because as an agent you can't control a lot of the things that determine whether or not they are going to be successful. Are they learning their music? Are they getting coaching? Are they taking care of their voices? Are they singing the right parts? Of course, you can give advice, but they're the ones who ultimately have to tell you if they're capable of singing something or not. And if you give too much advice, they will probably take offense.

I remember trying to advise the Bulgarian soprano Anna Tomowa-Sintow, known for dramatic roles like Aida and Elsa in Wagner's *Lohengrin*, when the Met asked her to do *La Traviata*. I said, "You know, this is a very strange house, and a very strange *Traviata*; you have to be careful in this place."

But to an artist, that's tantamount to saying, "You're incapable of doing it." Madame Tomowa-Sintow drew herself up.

"What's the matter," she said, "don't you have confidence in me?"

Well, all the confidence in the world doesn't take away from the fact that you might be trying to caution her and say, "Do something supremely well, that you do superbly, and don't go out of your comfort zone." But many singers will just think you're undermining them.

I've heard some artists criticize me for not doing enough. Many people had the impression that, although I represented a lot of people, my main focus was Luciano. Of course he was my main focus; who do you think was paying my rent so I could represent other people at all? My practice of charging a retainer wasn't very popular, either. Singers would be happy to go along with it, but then, when their careers didn't get off the ground, they would turn around and gripe, "That Herbert Breslin is a big con artist." But I never heard a singer say, "Gee, I made a really dumb decision."

Take Kathleen Cassello. Kathleen lived in Austria with her husband and was very eager for more American exposure. After many, many, many tries, I managed to get her a contract for *La Traviata* at the Metropolitan Opera. I was very happy to have gotten it. She, however, was more concerned about whether she was going to get to sing the first performance.

I said, "Look, who cares? Just go sing it, and sing it fabulously, and then they'll offer you the first night in the next contract."

She was hardly somebody in a position to demand first night or second night from the Met, or third or fourth night for that matter. But she insisted on doing the first performance. Of course, they didn't give it to her, so she wouldn't sign the contract. She's still waiting to make her Metropolitan Opera debut.

Take the Romanian soprano Angela Gheorghiu. I represented Angela and her husband, the tenor Roberto Alagna, for a while. Angela has a fantastic voice, one of the best in the business today. But she's so difficult that people are reluctant to work with her.

Joe Volpe once fired her from a production of *Carmen* when she refused to wear the wig for her character, Micaëla. He's supposed to have said, "That wig is going onstage whether you're in it or not." And, of course, it went on without her. That's not an isolated incident, either. She told off Riccardo Muti at La Scala, and now he won't touch her. Neither will the Vienna Staatsoper. I worked very hard to get her and Alagna a contract at the Vienna Staatsoper, for Gounod's *Romeo and Juliet*. I had to make a special trip over to Vienna and really work on Ioan Holender, the general director. But then Angela got her hands on a video of the production, and she announced that she wouldn't appear in it. So I didn't get my commission on that contract. And Holender won't have them back; be sure he won't. He doesn't have a vendetta against them, but on the other hand, he's Viennese, at least by adoption: he remembers.

This is what the opera world, and opera singers, and opera administrators are like. So how do you, as a manager, work with people like this?

EXCERPT OF A LETTER FROM HERBERT BRESLIN
TO A LEADING OPERA ADMINISTRATOR

Please resist as much as possible your own stupidity and maliciousness.

FROM A MUSIC BUSINESS PROFESSIONAL

I plastered the wall in my office with nasty letters from Herbert. It was a joke. Everybody came in to look at this wall. He wasn't about writing long letters; it was always one nasty sentence like, "You're doing everything all wrong." And that was in the days before faxes, so they were all sent through the mail.

I didn't take him that seriously when he started yelling and carrying on and doing his Herbert shtick. I was in his office once in New York when he was just yelling at someone, reaming them out, and he put them on the speakerphone so the whole office could hear it. I didn't know if this was for my benefit or his daily entertainment.

One cornerstone of my philosophy, as I've said before, was to get singers out of the opera house and into giving concerts as quickly as possible. There are a number of reasons for this. It makes you more money, and it buys you independence. Opera houses are very tricky places. You don't want to be too dependent on them.

But a lot of work goes into organizing a concert tour, as well. First, your artist tells you, "Oh, I have two weeks free. I'd like to do some concerts." You, the manager, have to sit down and figure out what that means. Two weeks: that means you can do about five concerts. Are you going to do one in New York and one in California, and if so, how is travel time going to impact the schedule? And are there enough people who want to hear that singer to put on five concerts?

And when they go off to Podunk, U.S.A., and some presenter wants them to sing a couple of opera arias on a program of lieder, the singer will say, "No, I won't compromise my art." To the mind of a singer like Soile Isokoski, a very distinguished Finnish soprano I represent, it's not artistic to perform opera arias on the same program as art songs. Never mind that the audience in Podunk may not be familiar with all the wonderful lieder and Finnish folk songs Soile has it in mind to sing. And Soile is not exactly a household name at this point. You have to draw the audience in somehow.

What singers like Soile don't seem to understand is that they're not getting paid for their art. They're getting paid because somebody like me has succeeded in twisting some presenter's arm practically out of its socket. That thought doesn't enter anyone's brain. No artist has ever asked me, "Gee, Herbert, what did you have to do to get them to engage me?"

HANS BOON

Herbert is so dynamic. You walk in there, and you're in this tornado. The mind goes so fast. When I first got there, in 1979, Merle Hubbard was working there as well, and I would say to Merle, "What does he mean?" Merle would have to translate. Because Herbert doesn't finish a sentence, because he's already thinking of the next one, which might be on a completely different subject. He gets going like this. You begin to anticipate what he's going after. It was a hard adjustment sometimes.

I never knew another person who had so many ideas pouring out of his head at the same time. He might have ten ideas in ten minutes. Two of them might be awful, six mediocre, but there'd be two or three that were really sensational. Sometimes he'd articulate them before they were fully formed. But the ideas were fantastic. The trio concert with Horne and Sutherland and Pavarotti was, in my humble opinion, one of the most amazing concerts that ever happened in my life.

The thing is this: if somebody has a terrific amount of talent, I can package and merchandise it brilliantly, probably better than anyone else in the business. But if somebody has only a moderate talent, you do what you can. I accomplished a lot of things for a lot of singers. But I never managed to create or oversee another career like Luciano's. There aren't any other singers like Luciano. You can't create that kind of career. You can help it along. In my case, I helped it a lot. But we won't see another Luciano in our lifetime.

To be honest, I wasn't so interested in finding the next Pavarotti, even if such a thing were possible. I already had one Pavarotti, and that was plenty. I was more interested in finding the next Herbert Breslin. I wanted someone I could groom to take over more of the business so I could step back a little. I wanted someone who could keep the money coming in while I rested on my laurels. I put a lot of time into this business, and I wanted a reward, as well.

Finding a successor is not as easy as it sounds. As I said, my office was filled with nice, smart men who loved opera. But those are not necessarily successors. Merle Hubbard was terrifically intelligent and extremely capable, but he had a handicap: he was too flighty. I don't mean that he was nervous; it's just that he was a tremendously social person and could spend hours on the telephone, and he didn't always know when to stop. He would become overly friendly with the ladies and replace the work that he had to do with the social part of the equation. It happened with Carol Vaness; it happened with Natalia Makarova, the ballet dancer, whom we represented for a number of years. It happened with Barbara Cook, the cabaret singer.

Barbara Cook was another person whose career I helped kickstart. That is, her second career. I had heard everything she did on Broadway for years in the sixties, but then she dropped out of sight. One night around 1975, I heard she was performing and I raced over to hear her in a real dive, a place called Brothers and Sisters, on Manhattan's West Side. And she was like a different Barbara Cook. Actually, she was like five Barbara Cooks, because she'd put on some weight. But she was still terrific. I was blown away. So I did the kind of thing I used to do in those days. I went backstage and said, "Ms. Cook, you don't know who I am, but I am an artists' manager, and I would like to put you on at Carnegie Hall." And I did. It was a good gamble. The concert was a huge success, and it catapulted her back into the spotlight, and she's stayed there ever since—by now, almost thirty years.

I kept working with Barbara for a while, even though I was outside my field of expertise. But I did quite a few things for her. I had Merle on her account, and another employee of mine, Marvin Jenkins, who also loved the whole Broadway and cabaret scene. I called Merle and Marvin the Mavens of Broadway.

Merle and Barbara got very friendly. But she walked into the office one day and looked at him and Marvin, who were sitting there at their desks.

"You know," she said, "you guys don't know what you're doing."

And she left. At least, that's the way I remember it.

That kind of thing wasn't very satisfactory as far as I was concerned. Ultimately, replacing the work part of the job with the social part of the job is not satisfactory to the clients, either, and they become annoyed. Look what happened with Carol Vaness. So I didn't think Merle had the right mentality to take over.

Then you have someone like Hans, who has been working for me ever since he came to me from London Records in 1979. Hans is a walking opera reference book. He knows everybody who ever sang a role and when, and he knows all the recital repertory, and when you're a singer planning a concert Hans is the person you want to plan it with. But that knowledge doesn't necessarily translate into the ability to run a music management firm.

So these people weren't really capable of being groomed. Not the way I had in mind.

There were a number of others over the years whom I did try to groom. There was a kid called Steven Marcus, who was very good, and there was Marvin, who ended up moving out to Hawaii with a friend. And there was Olivier Wilkins.

Olivier was working for an architecture firm when I met him, but he wanted to work in the music business. He had all kinds of ideas. He wasn't just a fan, as so many of them are; he had a sense of the business, like I did. He could be aggressive, like I was. Right away, he had a very good understanding of what went into making a career. We thought the same way about things. I believed Olivier might be somebody who could be a real successor. And I brought him into my office.

It was a great hire. Olivier was extremely energetic and very proactive. He's half French, and he went right off to Paris and brought in a bunch of new European clients, like Natalie Dessay, whom I still manage. And he had all kinds of ideas about how to make the office run more efficiently. He developed the office as a team, and he tried to decentralize it so that it wouldn't all be concentrated around me. The idea was that I would be able to delegate a little bit more of my work. This was all great, but inevitably the fact that I was so willing to follow Olivier's advice caused resentment among the people who had been working for me for a long time.

The upshot was that a lot of people who had been working for me left. Merle left, and took his clients with him, and went into business on his own. Neil Funkhouser left, and Harvey Rosenstein left. The dynamic of the office changed considerably.

Olivier had a great run. But after a while, he decided it was time to move on. He left the business altogether and went to law school. Let's face it: the opera world is not what it once was. There's been a retrenchment, and it's been marginalized in the bigger scheme of things. Everyone is interested in events like The Three Tenors, and they turn to singers of that ilk, like Andrea Bocelli, but they seem less and less interested in opera itself. It can feel like a very small, rather limited world. I wonder if I would stay in it, myself, if I were thirty years younger.

If there was one lesson I tried to communicate to the people who worked with me, it was this: keep your eye on the bottom line. You can't dance attendance on all these singers, all the time.

Except Luciano. With Luciano, you had to dance attendance because he was extremely demanding, and if his demands weren't met he could become extremely difficult. So there were a lot of things that had to be done for Luciano that became time-consuming for everyone. Some of them had to be done without telling him. If Luciano had known everything that I actually did, he would probably have had ten heart attacks.

The best example is complimentary tickets. When singers appear at the Met, they are entitled to two tickets, to give to friends or family or whomever. Sometimes a singer can get four. Beyond that, he or she has to pay for them. Luciano wanted at least twenty-four and sometimes thirty. And he certainly didn't want to pay for them.

We all decided that what he didn't know wouldn't hurt him. It was much easier to just get him his twenty-four tickets and say to the theater, "Look, send me the bill." Then I would pay the bill. Luciano never had to know.

Of course, I kept my client's best interests at heart. I never missed a chance to let Joe Volpe know I thought he was making us pay too much. Joe didn't charge us gala prices—we paid the regular box office rate, even when everyone else was paying $1,000—but it still added up to a rather large sum, and I never gave up trying to see if I could work out a discount. I was very conscientious, you see. I didn't want to throw away money, even Luciano's money.

Luciano had an obsession with those tickets. He would sit at his desk and fan them out like a poker hand and go through them to see which ones were good and which ones were not.

"Ah, these are no good," he would say. "I don't want those, I want a different pair. More central. Or nearer the stage."

Of course, all the other tickets in the theater were already sold, because Luciano's performances always sold out. But that didn't matter a bit to Luciano. We had no choice but to find a way to get him the tickets he wanted.

Once he was satisfied with the tickets, he gave them out like candy. His doctor, his dentist, somebody he met on the street. People were always calling him to ask for tickets, and he didn't ever want to say no; he decided it was his role to be Santa Claus. They went fast. Someone needed four, someone needed six, and before you knew it he would be calling me up to demand four more, sending everyone scrambling to try to squeeze them out of a sold-out house.

It was difficult for the Met because there was always the fear that other singers would find out that Luciano was getting all these tickets. On the one hand, the Met couldn't tell them that he was really paying for them, because Luciano had to be kept from finding that out at all costs. On the other hand, if another singer thought that Luciano was getting twenty-four free tickets and she was getting only two, Joe Volpe would have a riot on his hands. It was always a problem because Luciano was so generous. A singer would come into his dressing room and complain that she couldn't get extra tickets, and Luciano would say, "Oh, you need tickets? Here's a pair."

It was a big headache for Joe. If you want to get Joe Volpe to look nervous, which is not a very easy thing to do, just ask him about Luciano's free tickets.

TERRY McEWEN

I don't envy Luciano. He may be the richest man in the music business, but he sure isn't the happiest. He never has a moment to relax. But then, if he had a moment to relax, maybe he'd start thinking about what he's doing. And it's very often true of a lot of people in music—it's becoming like business in this sense—that if they don't have twelve appointments in one day, they consider themselves a failure.

The same thing happened to Herbert. Herbert became the most powerful manager in the business because of his tenor. Herbert is not stupid. He's very bright. But Luciano called the shots. And Herbert is so useful to Luciano because Luciano can have an absolutely ruthless idea on how to make a half a million dollars in one night, and Luciano never has to say it directly to the person involved. He just tells it to Herbert and tells Herbert, "Do it." And Herbert does it.

A MUSIC BUSINESS ASSOCIATE

Herbert was always very quiet when he was around Luciano. Luciano became the boss.

Luciano's whole act with me was a kind of test. Luciano had been testing me from the beginning, from the days when he experimented to see how much caviar I could pay for without squealing. He had a lot of different ways to test people. He always liked to make sure everyone was up to speed, particularly in their ability to satisfy his needs.

We'd all be in the back of the limo after a concert, and he'd be up in the front seat, and he'd say, "Herbert, what is my schedule for next Wednesday?"

Well, of course, I would have it all written down at the office, but maybe it wasn't something I could summon up accurately off the top of my head. Then he would be on me for not keeping on top of the situation.

"Ah, you should know these things," he would say.

At other times he would be even more critical. He would kind of hack at you for a while, but as soon as he saw you were getting annoyed, he would pull back.

"Ah," he'd say, "I was only kidding."

Sometimes I was on the verge of saying, "Look, I couldn't have been so stupid. Look at your status now. You became number one in the world of music. Is that what you wanted? If that's what you wanted, that's what you became. You became the greatest singer of the day, you became the greatest earner of the day, you had all of the new productions, you had the greatest conductors, you had everything like that. That is the essence of what a good manager is supposed to do. You had all of that."

JUDY KOVACS

There is something very gentle inside Herbert. He can act like a real bastard. I saw him send someone away once, at the Met, and I still remember it. His "No" is very impressive. But he has a good heart. He was always fine with me. I think he respected me.

And he really loves music. In that, he and I agreed. We were doing it all for this voice. Not every night, but some nights it was perfect. So whatever Luciano wanted, we did it, for that voice.

chapter XIV

TWILIGHT OF THE GOD

The Last Decade

er name is Nicoletta Mantovani. She's thirty-four years younger than Luciano. The story is that they met at the Pavarotti International Horse Show in 1993. The fact is that since then she's dominated his life.

Nicoletta is a cipher to me. I'm really not sure what Luciano is doing with somebody like that. She's not the most glamorous person in the world; I think she's dull as dishwater. And she doesn't seem to have any particular interest in what he's doing as an artist. She seems very interested in his fame, though, and what to do with that. She certainly has him wrapped around her little finger.

Nicoletta began working for Luciano as a secretary when she was still a student. That's "secretary" in every sense that Pavarotti watchers have come to understand the term. With one key difference: she was perfectly open about her relationship with Luciano. All the other secretaries had been a little circumspect, at least when Adua was around. But Nicoletta would literally sit at his feet and gaze up at him. Adua could walk right through the room and she would never even blink.

Adua didn't keep walking through for very long.

It was early in 1996 that an Italian gossip magazine published pictures of Nicoletta and Luciano in flagrante—well, kissing, at least—on a romantic beach vacation in Barbados. Luciano even gave an interview. He called Nicoletta "the favorite in my harem." How's that for a touching proclamation of love? It was enough for Adua, though. Adua's response was an open letter to Luciano in the Italian press, warning him that one risk of going too far would be an unhappy and lonely old age. I think that the way Adua saw it, by going to the press she was playing the same game they were.

ADUA VERONI

Do you think an Italian newspaper would really send a correspondent to Barbados unless someone had called to tip them off?

She must have known it was too late to reconcile, though. She wouldn't have taken such a step if she hadn't, because she of all people was aware that the best way to get Luciano to do something is to tell him not to. The next thing we knew, Luciano and Adua had formally separated and Luciano and Nicoletta had moved in together and were billing and cooing all over the place. The press was full of items about how Nicoletta wanted six children and read Luciano bedtime stories every night.

"She is giving me a second childhood," he said in one interview.

That was what it looked like to me, too. But perhaps not in the positive sense he meant it.

ADUA VERONI

Luciano has always been a coward. If somebody comes to the house he doesn't like, he'll say, "Hi, how are you, have a glass of wine," and then when they're out of earshot he'll say to someone else that he doesn't ever want to see the person again.

So after this thing happened in Barbados, the next time he came home, I said, "Let's put our cards on the table."

He just whined.

So I said, "Look, do you love this person, or not?"

"Ah, but I . . . Well, yes—but it will never be the love I had for you."

"Well, thank goodness! Just think where we'd be if you had hated me!" I said.

I was very busy at that time. I had my own agency for singers, and I had other responsibilities, like the horse show, where I had to sit in a box with local government officials, and meanwhile I knew that Nicoletta would be walking around with her friends as if they owned the place. Those months were a terrible period of my life.

Finally I reached a point where I said, "OK, fine, that does it. I've had enough."

Around this time there was a concert in London where some of the singers I represented were appearing as well. I called up Luciano and said, "Hey, reserve me a room at the Hyde Park Hotel."

"There aren't any rooms in the Hyde Park Hotel."

"Where are you sleeping?" I said.

"Ah—at the Hyde Park Hotel."

"Fine," I said. "Then you go to another hotel and leave me your room."

So they managed to find a room for me at the Hyde Park Hotel, where he was in a suite with her. I had the room right across the hall. I felt like a prisoner. He was trying to keep us from running into each other. I had to go to their room to bring him some papers, and she wasn't there. "Where have you hidden her?" I said.

Finally, after a day or so of this, he came into my room and said, "Listen, Nicoletta wants to talk to you."

Nicoletta came in. He left, of course. It wouldn't have been nice if he were there. And Nicoletta told me that they were in love.

I didn't have much to say to that.

Then they left in a private airplane and went back to Pesaro, which is a house that belonged half to me and half to him. I should have followed the advice of a friend who told me to go there and throw all his stuff out the door.

Nicoletta was young—she was twenty-six when the affair began—but she was very, very savvy. I can't say with any authority whether theirs is a relationship based on great love. I truly hope that it is. But it was certainly conducted with an eye to the public. Maybe it had to be. Adua wasn't the only one to notice how well informed the press was always kept about Luciano's latest activities.

Nicoletta had some professional goals, as well. She wanted to be a music producer, for example. And since her lover was one of the most famous singers in the world, she wanted to produce him. The problem was that she had no interest in opera. She found classical music, and the whole classical world, a little boring. She liked pop music. And Luciano was as famous as any pop star. She thought his pop image was something he should develop.

Luciano had already started the Pavarotti and Friends concerts in 1992. The idea itself was not bad. He would get together a group of really big stars, from every branch of music, and put on a big benefit concert for charity. He had some very good people, especially at first. He had Sting, and Elton John, and Bono, and Anita Baker. He had a slight problem with Anita Baker. I think she wasn't happy with the hotel arrangements. In a little Italian city like Modena, where the concerts were held, you don't have the Excelsior, or the St. Regis, or the Ritz-Carlton. They can't pick you up in a forty-five-foot stretch limousine. I'm sure they treated her as well as they possibly could, but I guess that wasn't good enough, and there was a bit of a dustup. Which just goes to show that Luciano isn't the only artist who's very exacting in his demands. In truth, compared with many pop stars, he's modest.

Anyway, there were these Pavarotti and Friends concerts, and Decca would record them every year, and Nicoletta began producing them. She loved cultivating her pop contacts. Every year, she would come over to New York and spend thousands of dollars buying Christmas presents for everybody: for my office, for the family, for Bono, for Sting, and so on. That was her special thing. She was very enthusiastic about those concerts, but I think that for everyone else they became something of a burden. They were certainly a burden for Decca, because it cost an incredible amount of money to get the releases for all the different artists, and the orchestra, and the recording equipment; and then hardly anybody bought the albums. And it was a burden for Luciano, because he tried to make a point of singing personally with every single artist, and it meant a lot of unfamiliar music to learn.

The real problem with these Pavarotti and Friends concerts is that Luciano is not a pop singer. He doesn't have the right approach. He doesn't know how to sing that music and doesn't bring anything fresh to it, and standing up there with rock stars and roaring away at some song or other, checking his words every five seconds, he looks a little bit like a clown. At one of the very first concerts, he demonstrated that he can't even lip-synch correctly. He didn't have time to learn all the music he was supposed to sing with all these people, so he prerecorded it and mouthed along with the tape. But even from the fiftieth row, people in the crowd could tell he wasn't actually singing. He got a tremendous amount of flak for that. To his credit, he apologized quite openly and moved on. That's all you can do. But it didn't stop him from doing more of these concerts.

Just try talking him out of it. Believe me, I did.

"Ah, you don't know what you're talking about," he'd answer.

Maybe I didn't. I certainly didn't understand what he was doing in this pop world. To me, as the years went on, it looked more and more like he was taking this gorgeous career of his, which we had worked so hard to build up, and flushing it down the toilet.

I don't think Nicoletta saw it that way, though, and increasingly her opinion seemed to be the only one that mattered. And she, at first, was insecure. We had been around a lot longer than she had and knew Luciano a lot better, and I think this was very threatening to her. I suspect that she also wasn't thrilled about her older lover being advised by all these even older men. I'm eleven years older than Luciano, and Tibor has another four years on me. To Nicoletta, we did not represent anything very compelling. She thought we were out of touch.

I don't know why he listened to her. I don't know why he decided he needed her so much. Maybe it was because *he* was getting older. Up to that point, women had always been in plentiful supply. There was always a sense that there was tremendous female interest in him and that he would always have another chance. But as he got older, he may have felt as if his options were narrowing: that there wasn't always going to be a new chickadee at the door every time the old one got fed up and left. And he had burned his bridges with Adua. So he had nowhere else to go.

He was also more dependent on people in general, because it was harder for him to get around. As the years passed, he spent more and more of his time just sitting in one place. He had a hip and knee replacement operation in 1998, and that may have helped to a certain degree but he didn't seem very much more mobile. I had my hip replaced, too, by the same doctor, and I'm still walking around fine. But after an operation like that, you have to do physical therapy, which is quite a bit of work, and work, of course, was something Luciano was not very interested in doing. The upshot was he didn't move very much, which made him more like a king on his throne than ever.

His entourage had grown accordingly. He had always liked to have people along with him when he was on the road, but by the 1990s, between Tibor's people and his own, he had a whole staff. I've already mentioned that he always picked up things on his trips: a pig, a horse, a suite of hotel furniture. Well, on one trip he picked up Tino. Edwin Tinoco, nicknamed Tino, was working in a hotel in Peru where Luciano stayed on one of his South American tours. Luciano got to be on such good terms with him that he offered him a job as majordomo or indentured servant or chief cook and bottle washer or whatever you want to call it, and Edwin joined up and has been with him ever since. Then there's Veronica, who was working as a nutritionist and masseuse at a spa Luciano stayed at in Merano, Italy. Her therapy must have been pretty good, because Luciano enlisted her, too. I'm sure people winked and nudged about that, but the fact is that there was no hanky-panky between Veronica and Luciano. For one thing, Nicoletta was there to make sure nothing happened, and for another, Veronica and Tino quickly became an item. They've been together for years now. I'm not sure why they haven't gotten married, because if they did, Edwin's legal situation as a foreigner in Italy would get a whole lot easier. I'm not sure why they're both still there, either. Veronica did try to cut free once and returned to work at the spa, but before long she was back in the "golden globe." Breaking free of Luciano's orbit is not easy.

There was also Thomas, who started out working for Tibor, taking care of Luciano's travel arrangements. He eventually stopped working for Tibor, but not for Luciano. So he's still there on trips. And Martin, who acts as a driver or bodyguard or what have you. I'm not really clear on the nominal titles of some of these people, but it seems they're all absolutely essential to keeping Luciano functioning.

Anyway, as I said, the pop concerts had nothing to do with me. My job was supposed to be finding things for Luciano to do in the world of opera. But it got harder and harder to find something that he could do. Certainly it was hard to find something he could do well. He wasn't exactly at his artistic peak. And he was more capricious than ever.

The Met, especially, had to put up with a lot. There was 1992, when they contracted him for a new production of *Lucia di Lammermoor*. But then Riccardo Muti invited him to come open the season at La Scala with a new production of Verdi's *Don Carlo*.

That *Don Carlo* was a tale unto itself. Whenever you get two Italians together, you're setting yourself up for trouble. With Riccardo and Luciano, it was even worse, because they were famous for not getting along. I'm not sure exactly what that was all about. Riccardo has a reputation as being very, very egotistical and very vain. In other words, he's a conductor. At La Scala, he's developed a reputation for giving chances to young singers. People say this is because he can't stand working with any star big enough to compete with him.

There's an old joke you hear from time to time that Muti is stuck in a desert, crawling across the sand, gasping, "Water, water." Finally he looks up and there, ahead of him on a rock, is a little cup of water.

"Oh, thank God," says Muti. And he takes the water and uses it to slick down his hair.

You can imagine that this might not be the best personality type to get along with Luciano. And I know they had some choice things to say about each other over the years. But then some kind of thaw began to take place. After all, Muti was one of the leading Italian conductors, and Luciano was the leading Italian tenor. So I guess it made sense to bury the hatchet.

You'll remember that Muti invited Luciano to do *Otello* with him, and Luciano turned him down to do it with Solti. In lieu of that, however, he did his first *Pagliacci* with Muti, in concert with the Philadelphia Orchestra, and then Muti asked him to do *Don Carlo*, another Verdi role Luciano had never done and one that fit his voice a lot better than *Otello* did. It was one of those offers you couldn't refuse. You had Muti conducting. You had Franco Zeffirelli directing. You had the opportunity of a recording, be-

cause Muti and La Scala had a contract with EMI. You had opening night at La Scala, which is one of the most important evenings
on the Italian calendar. It was a question of national pride. So of
course Luciano blew off *Lucia* and the Met. Joe Volpe was furious, but what could he do? You can't sue (or "suit") Luciano. You
can't afford to alienate him. You need him to sell your subscription series. If Luciano's name appears in a subscription performance, people will rush out to buy the whole series, including
another ten operas they otherwise would not buy tickets to. A
manager can't afford to lose that kind of revenue. So Joe released
Luciano from his contract. The official explanation was that Luciano had decided to retire the role from his repertory.

Now, *Don Carlo* is not exactly one of the most difficult tenor
roles. In fact, although the tenor has the title role, there's very little meat to his part. *Don Carlo* is a big, long opera, but it has six
main roles, and the tenor really has only one aria and a few ensembles. It seemed as if Luciano should be able to manage to learn
that.

That assumption turned out to be overly optimistic.

At some point, Luciano no longer seemed able to take in any
more music. Something in him just shut down. It was as if his
brain had reached its capacity. I don't know what it was. Maybe
he didn't have the same fire in his belly to learn new things.
Maybe he let his mind get as flabby as his body. True, the music
of *Don Carlo* may not have been as familiar to him as that of some
of the other big Verdi operas. But it's not like we didn't have people trying to pound it into him. We pounded and pounded, and
it just wouldn't go in.

The premiere was not a fun occasion. There was a sense of un-
ease from the moment the tenor walked out onstage. Usually, a
great singer comes out and you have the feeling you can sit back
and relax and enjoy yourself. When Luciano came out, you had
the feeling he might not make it. And this in spite of the fact that
we had Judy Kovacs standing in the wings, holding up the words
on big sheets of paper.

When a singer isn't comfortable, you hear it right away. In one of the big recitatives, early on, Luciano cracked. At La Scala, they don't take that lying down. There was a big shout from the gallery, and eventually people began booing.

So the whole thing became something of a fiasco. My soprano Daniela Dessì was singing the lead role of Elisabetta. Her big last-act aria is a prayer to her ancestors, and one line is, "*S'ancor si piange in cielo, piangi sul mio dolore*"—If you still shed tears in heaven, weep for my sorrows. She got as far as the first part of that phrase, which of course everybody in the audience knows by heart, and a voice boomed down from the balcony, "*Verdi piange*," Verdi is weeping in heaven. The audience enjoyed that very much.

The only silver lining to the *Don Carlo* experience was that the *Lucia* at the Met turned out to be a big disaster. The very modern production was the young director Francesca Zambello's first one there, and didn't turn out to be among her best. Met audiences still talk about it as if it were some kind of outrage. So it was a good thing Luciano didn't appear in that.

A couple of years later, Luciano had another bright idea about something he could do at the Met. He announced that he wanted to revisit what was arguably his greatest Met triumph, more than twenty years before: *Daughter of the Regiment*.

"Why the hell would you want to do that?" I said.

It had been a long time since Luciano had had easy command of the high C. And that aria, you'll remember, has nine of them. Of course, Luciano could follow a great Met tradition and transpose the aria down to a lower key. Singers have done this since time immemorial. By 2002, Plácido was transposing Giordano's *Andrea Chénier* down so far it was practically a baritone part. They don't call it transposing per se. They always say they're doing "an alternate version," which implies that the composer sanctioned a transposition for some other singer who couldn't hit all the notes. The Met is very accommodating about alternate versions. But even nine high Bs is not exactly a walk in the park.

But Luciano was adamant. "I want to do *Daughter of the Regiment* for my sixtieth birthday."

Well, of course Joe Volpe put it on for him. By this point, Joe was very amenable to whatever Luciano wanted to do. He would have put on Schoenberg's *Erwartung* if Luciano had wanted to do that. Of course, the likelihood of that was very small, since *Erwartung* is an atonal opera written for soprano.

Then again, you could say that Luciano's doing *Daughter of the Regiment* at age sixty was almost as ludicrous as taking on *Erwartung*. But it's very difficult to set yourself up as a judge of what Luciano can or can't do. When you think he can do a good job, like in *Otello*, he messes it up. But when you say, "You can't do it," he may turn around and give a great performance. He might be making up half the words as he goes along, but he can pull it together when he puts his mind to it.

And Luciano seemed convinced he could do *Daughter of the Regiment*. It was hardly likely that he would have insisted if he was going to make a fool of himself, since nobody wants to fall on his face in front of thousands of people (even if Luciano had done so a few times by this point). Of course, it was hard to tell in rehearsals exactly how it was going to go, because many singers don't sing full voice in rehearsals. Hell, Luciano sometimes didn't even sing full voice in a performance. So we waited to be surprised.

In fact, at the first performance, we were. It went reasonably well. All the notes were in place—maybe not quite as brilliant as they had been in 1972, and maybe slightly lower in pitch, but there.

It was the second performance where he ran into trouble. He started his aria and aimed for the first high note, and it just didn't come out. All that came out was something strangled, a great big goose egg. I think everyone in the auditorium felt it in the pit of their stomachs. He didn't even try for the rest of the high notes. He sang them all down an octave, then went offstage and canceled the rest of the performance. Another tenor had to step in for act 2.

So of course what everybody remembered about that *Daughter* was that it was a debacle as well.

The next season I thought I had finally talked Luciano into something I had wanted for years. I thought I had finally convinced him to sing *Forza del Destino*. He had, after all, already recorded most of the big excerpts from it. And his voice was so perfect for Verdi roles. He agreed. We had the contracts for a big Met performance. But there was that superstition always at the back of his mind. *Forza* is a bad-luck opera. And superstition won.

He called me up one day and said, "I can't do it. I just can't do it."

Joe Volpe's response was, "What made me consider, or Jimmy think, that he'd ever do it, given that he couldn't even say the name of the opera, I don't know."

The Met had to switch to *Ballo in Maschera*, instead.

Luciano's whims were increasingly evident on every level. By this point, he was making theaters reconfigure their stagings of every opera he appeared in so he would have to move as little as possible. The duel in Giordano's *Andrea Chénier*, for example, which Luciano did for the first time at the Met in 1996, took place in a couple of sword thrusts, making Luciano's opponent look less a victim of bad luck than simply inept. In *Aida*, instead of having Radames take part in the Grand March, they had him seated, watching the parade. Everyone came in and laid booty at his feet. It looked like Christmas morning.

And glasses of water had to be hidden all over the stage in case Luciano needed a drink. It was better to set up the water than to leave it to Luciano to take action for himself. I'll never forget the time he was singing *Ballo in Maschera* at Covent Garden with Deborah Voigt—in her company debut, no less—and decided it was time for some lubrication. So he went offstage in search of it. The moment he chose to make his exit was while Debbie was singing her portion of their love duet. It was quite something to see the look on her face as, pouring out her passion for the tenor, she looked around and realized she was singing to an empty stage.

For Luciano, taking care of one's health and one's voice gradually meant making modifications in the actual singing. More and more, Luciano had a tendency to save himself for the dramatic moments in an opera. "Saving himself" can mean different things to different singers. In Luciano's case, it often meant hardly singing at all. Many singers "mark" in rehearsal, singing only in half-voice, taking notes an octave down. Luciano began doing this in performance. On opening night of *Aida* in 2001, he began singing Radames's aria in a kind of stage whisper. Joe Volpe went tearing backstage to find out what was wrong. Nothing was wrong. Luciano just wanted to make sure he had enough juice to get him through to the duet in act 4, which was something he did very, very well.

Luciano was so careful about taking care of himself that sometimes his health regimes got in the way of a performance. During one Met *Elisir*, he suddenly headed to the side of the stage, grabbing onto the proscenium to support himself. There was a murmur in the house, the curtain came down, and Joe Volpe and I were backstage in a flash. It turned out that Luciano had decided to go on yet another diet and taken what to most mortals would be a near-fatal overdose of diuretics. As a result, he was completely dehydrated. But, of course, Dr. Luciano knew the answer. He called for water—and salt pills.

"From being dehydrated," Joe said, "he's going to blow up like a blimp."

But he got through the performance.

RICHARD BONYNGE

The last time we worked together was an Elisir d'Amore *in Naples in 1997. He was telling the orchestra what to do. He was trying to run the rehearsal. He was doing nothing but standing there and explaining how the music was supposed to go. He was telling everybody how to sing, and so on and so forth. I finally told him to get off the stage, and he went off the stage. But what ultimately happened was that I left the theater. I don't like walking off, but I had no choice. And the theater had no choice, because of the commercial power a Luciano Pavarotti appearance had: there were television cameras from all over the world, and whatnot. So I left Naples, and I did not conduct the production. That was my last professional experience with Luciano and will remain so.*

To maintain a relationship with anybody over a long period of time, you have to be a little bit philosophical. It cannot all be good. That's simply not possible in this life. As a manager, you can't take all the glory without taking some of the crap, as well.

But I was starting to feel that I was taking more crap than ever. Working with Luciano was like coming under machine-gun fire. This was wrong, and that was wrong, and the other was wrong. Rat-a-tat. I'd make a suggestion, and that would certainly be wrong. And I noticed that Luciano was conducting more of his business dealings without me. His feelings about me seemed to have changed. He didn't seem as interested in what I had to say anymore.

It's very hard, you see, to know where you stand with Luciano. Luciano is like a building made up of three floors. He receives people on every one of those floors. But you don't know which floor is the one he tells the truth on. You're never sure if you're on that truth floor or on some other floor where he keeps up a false front but isn't really letting you in. It's difficult to judge.

Take Terry McEwen. Luciano and Terry had been through some ups and downs. You might have fairly said their friendship was no longer what it once had been. Terry and Luciano hadn't gotten along so well when Terry was in San Francisco; I think Terry felt Luciano had let him down a few times, and he had a certain amount of resentment about it. Terry also wasn't very well. As I said, he had retired to Hawaii. He was getting old, and he hadn't taken very good care of himself, and he had diabetes and couldn't do very much anymore.

Luciano would ask after him, out of the blue. "How is Terry?"

"Well," I'd say, "I don't think Terry is very good."

"Send him something," he'd say. "Send him ten thousand dollars."

So I would send Terry a check for $10,000. This wasn't an isolated occurrence. It happened several times, up until Terry died in 1998. Whatever Terry may have said or thought about Luciano in his late years, you would hope that Luciano's generosity would have been something of a factor.

It was hard to know what Luciano was interested in. He had basically stopped studying, and he wasn't challenging himself; he was just coasting along. Artistically, he had come to a complete standstill. All that seemed to animate him anymore was money.

Of course, everybody says that Herbert Breslin is in it only for the money, too. But I'm also in it for more than the money. I really do love music. And I felt I was getting less and less return on my work. I don't mean financial return. I mean inner satisfaction. The job was no less demanding. It took complete concentration, and commitment, and effort. But it felt like we kept repeating the same old thing.

I couldn't imagine Luciano was very satisfied, either. But I didn't know how to ask him.

"Why are you continuing?" I would ask him in my head. "What do you have to prove? Are you afraid to stop singing? Are you afraid to be alone? Do you feel you need the money?"

I may have let my thoughts be known a little bit. But I hardly ever asked him a question like that point-blank, aloud.

I never asked him about Nicoletta, either. She seemed to be running the show more and more. Her parents are bankers, and they took control of Luciano's money. Someone had to manage it, since Adua was obviously not doing it anymore. Adua came out fine in the divorce. She stood her ground for half his holdings, and I think she got it. Not that it was easy. Divorce is still a fairly new concept in Italy (it wasn't legalized until 1970), and it's complicated, and on top of that she had to deal with Luciano, a man who changes his mind every five seconds, so that once you've more or less agreed on one thing he decides that he wants something else. This can become a very tiresome process. The divorce wasn't finalized until October 2002. By then, there were rumors that Luciano and Nicoletta mainly lived apart, that Nicoletta had strings of other boyfriends, and I don't know what all. Those rumors ended, though, when Nicoletta announced that she was pregnant.

ADUA VERONI

He did everything by design. Even the separation. He's the one who pushed for it. I wasn't the one who went to a lawyer; it was him. We could have done it in a very different manner and spent a lot less money. But he insisted on a lawyer—for him it was very surprising, a lawyer. So I, to provoke him a little, said, "Fine, let's make some problems for him." So we were in it for the long haul.

The procedure is that you have these proposals that a lawyer draws up, and you have to say yes or no. And Luciano was always saying no, yes, no—you know how he is. One time he says fine and the next day no.

In my opinion, what happened is that after about twenty-seven proposals, Nicoletta finally said, "Basta. Enough." So what did he do? Our daughter Cristina had a baby. He called me up and said, "We should make peace. We've become grandparents, et cetera, and I want to come see the baby." And he arrived with his whole entourage and all kinds of beautiful, beautiful presents for the baby. It was also a way to soften me up toward him a bit. He had claimed he had rights to certain things I didn't want to give him. In the end, I just gave up and gave them to him anyway.

He had found another lawyer and told him, "Settle this, settle it, settle it." If the annulment didn't go through this time, we would have had to start from the beginning again and wait another six or seven years for a divorce.

After we saw each other in Modena, he had gone on to New York. I said, "If we want to settle this, you have to send signed papers to me from

the consulate because otherwise we can't trust you." We spoke about six
o'clock our time, so it was about noon in New York. And the next morn-
ing at nine o'clock the papers were there. Signed. Never in his life has
he ever been able to go to a consulate, send papers—his lawyers didn't
think for a second he would actually do it.

So we submitted all the papers, and we got the annulment.

Since Adua got the main house in the divorce, Luciano's base
of operations shifted to Pesaro, until he and Nicoletta got an
apartment in Modena, as well. Modena was his home. That's
what he always said in interviews to the press, for years and years:
"I'm Modenese." He said it, at least, until he began to run into
trouble with the tax authorities, after he started claiming resi-
dence in Monte Carlo. I don't remember exactly when he got the
apartment in Monte Carlo. It was another Hungarian named
Tibor—Tibor Katona—who helped make that happen. These
Hungarians kept rising out of the earth. People had a way of doing that when Luciano needed advice about money.

I don't know who was advising him. His European business
dealings remained obscure to me, and to be frank, I didn't want
to know about them. As long as I was getting my commissions
and staying out of trouble with the authorities, I was happy. The
American tax authorities can be pretty uptight. But they weren't
anything compared with what Luciano had to deal with from the
Italian tax authorities. Perhaps they were jealous of Luciano's new
allegiance to another country. After Luciano got his apartment
there, Monte Carlo evidently became very important to him in a
very short period of time.

"I am a citizen of Monte Carlo," he said in an interview. "I feel
myself to be a true Monégasque."

He expressed his touching devotion to his new homeland with
a series of concerts, the proceeds of which went to charity. He
does one appearance there every year, to demonstrate where his
home really lies. Luciano is a very charitable guy.

Anyway, the Italian authorities were ultimately not impressed with Luciano's displays of patriotism and allegiance to his new-found home. In fact, they questioned it outright. Perhaps they thought it odd that this Monégasque was still spending so much of his time in Pesaro and Modena. In 2001, there was a big investigation and Luciano had to cough up several million dollars. The Italians love making examples of big stars. They did the same thing to Sophia Loren.

Apart from money, retirement was a huge concern for Luciano. He began talking about it when he was in his midforties.

"I have eight, ten, maybe fifteen years of active singing left," he'd say. "I want to make the most of them."

Fifteen years later, he was a little less forthcoming on the subject of retirement, even if hearing him sing had a way of making people wonder about it. For a while, he allowed that he would retire in 2001, the fortieth anniversary of his professional stage debut. He said that until it got to be 2001. The anniversary was celebrated with a big gala in Modena, with Aprile Millo, and Alagna and Gheorghiu, and even Renata Scotto, who had suddenly become some kind of long-lost friend. It was all very touching. But it didn't signal the beginning of retirement. Luciano kept right on singing as often as he could, when he didn't cancel.

I think he was terrified of retiring. He didn't know how to face it. The problem was that Luciano hadn't figured out what to do after he stopped singing. In that, he was very unlike Plácido. Plácido just went from strength to strength. He kept on learning new roles, although he tried to find things that were more suited to his changing voice as it aged. He began a conducting career; he wasn't a very good conductor, but it kept him busy. He didn't need to be kept busy, though, because he also took over the running of two opera companies, in Los Angeles and Washington. He was still right in the thick of the opera world. Luciano, by contrast, didn't have a game plan.

When he heard Plácido was moving into conducting, he snorted. The next thing you knew, he wanted to try his hand at directing. So Luciano directed a production of *La Favorita* in Venice, with a little help from an assistant. All right, a lot of help. The production didn't exactly set the world on fire, and Luciano let the idea of directing drop. He thought he might be a teacher. He still talks about that, although, as I said, Luciano is not really a very good teacher. His idea was that he would teach only the very best students, who were already set for a career. That was smart, because when they're at that level you don't really have to teach them much. You just have to nudge them a little.

My idea was that Luciano should work in some kind of honorary capacity with opera houses as a way to attract subscribers. He could work together with the Met to come up with things he could do—attend a dinner where people would pay a lot of money to eat with him, or give master classes, or something along those lines. But he wasn't very interested in hearing that idea, even though I brought it up to him quite a lot.

And he certainly wasn't interested in hearing the word *retire*. In fact, he couldn't stand it.

"Luciano," I'd say, "maybe it's time for you to stop."

"You don't know what you're talking about," he'd say, for the four hundredth time.

Even Joe Volpe tried to broach the subject of retirement sometime around 2001. He went over to see Luciano at the Hampshire House and delicately—as much as the adverb *delicately* can be applied to Joe Volpe—tried to ask about the idea of a special farewell performance before his—

"Don't say it," Luciano said. "Don't say that word."

"All right, all right, fine," said Joe. "What would you like to talk about?"

JOE VOLPE

I always said, "I hope I retire before Luciano." Because I knew this was going to be painful. And it's going to be painful; there's no question about it. One way or another.

Maybe I'm as bad as he is. I go through it myself. I say, "What am I going to do when I give up this career?" It's scary to me. And you know, I don't walk off the plane and have hundreds of people chasing me for autographs. And I don't have to perform. I can stick around for a while. In his case, it changes his life. It could mean the loss of his manhood. The Italian mentality, you know. He won't be what he is anymore. And particularly now, with Nicoletta and their daughter, he's going to need to protect his manhood.

It's interesting, when you think about it, that Herbert is in the same situation as Luciano. Because without being involved in the music business, what's Herbert going to do? "I'm retiring." Oh, you're going to retire and do what? Write a book? Baloney. Give me a break. He's not retiring.

Luciano might have been slacking off in his own efforts, but he didn't want to feel that anybody else around him was doing any less work than they should be. But the fact is, it was getting harder for me to do the same amount of work for him. There weren't very many operas he would even consider, and there were fewer and fewer concerts. His ticket sales had begun to fall off. He couldn't draw 20,000 people to an arena anymore. He could draw 8,000 or 9,000, which is still very respectable, because there aren't many singers who can do even that. But it was a different ball game than it had been.

He didn't see it that way, though. From his perspective, what he saw was that I wasn't delivering.

"You're not doing the job anymore," he said. "You're not doing enough."

He said it over and over. Most of the time I just ignored him. I mean, what else are you going to do? It was another way of testing me. He had his lawyer write me a letter at one point. The letter said I was earning too much. From then on, I was supposed to get only 5 percent commission, across the board. I ignored that, too. I kept on charging a 10 percent commission on his opera contracts, the same way I always had, and I kept on getting it. Nobody ever brought it up with me directly, of course. As I've said before, Luciano never confronted anybody directly if he could find somebody else to do it for him, and if he couldn't, he wouldn't confront the person at all.

But this was not a lot of fun for me. The whole process was getting less and less pleasant, and I started to wonder why I was doing it.

In 2002, I was seventy-eight years old. I didn't feel it. Seventy-eight sounds incredibly old. I let everybody know that I was officially changing my age to sixty-four, because I didn't feel a day older than that. But on the other hand, I really was seventy-eight. I had scaled back my professional operations. I cut back down to a tiny little office—my fourth in the same building on West Fifty-seventh Street—which is just large enough to fit a couple of filing cabinets and my desk, and Hans's desk, and a desk for Christopher Ungerer, a young pianist who works for us. I still work, and I still go over to Europe whenever I can, and I feel just fine. But there were certain things I wasn't willing to do anymore.

After a while, you start to feel like you've had enough. I didn't need the hassle. I was sick of being pushed around. I was sick of being taken for granted. I was sick of having my feelings hurt by someone I gave so much time to. It's not worth getting upset about these things, but it reinforces the idea that I have a life of my own.

So gradually, I came to decide that it was time for me to stop working for Luciano Pavarotti. Given the way Luciano was riding me, it wasn't a very radical decision. You could even call it an inevitability.

I drew up a letter to Luciano, to say my formal good-bye. I had it written up on the computer. I was all ready to send it. But I didn't. I was waiting for the right time. I was waiting to see how things went. There was always a chance I wouldn't have to send it, after all.

One day we were on the phone, and he was on my case, as usual. The problem this time had to do with some concerts he was supposed to give in Mexico and South America. Someone had showed him an ad from one of the hotels in a town where he would be singing. They were advertising a package: you could book tickets to Luciano's concert and a room at a special weekend rate, that kind of thing. It's not exactly uncommon. That's how the hotel business works. But someone had gotten it into Luciano's head that he was being taken advantage of. He had decided that the hotels were using him for free advertising, and he was threatening to cancel.

It was very hard to know what to say. I mean, Luciano had sung in Las Vegas not long before, and all the hotels there had done exactly the same thing. All that made it different in this case was that he had gotten some kind of bee in his bonnet. And of course, it was all my fault.

"You're not doing the job anymore," he said. "You're not taking care of me anymore. You're not really working for me anymore." His old argument.

I suddenly said, "Well, you know, I'm going to stop working for you, and I have a letter I'm going to send you about it. I'm going to scale back my business, and I'm going to write a book."

He hemmed and hawed a little bit about that. He may have been a little surprised. On the other hand, I don't really know what he may or may not have felt. The bottom line is, he doesn't care about anybody but himself.

So I printed my letter out, and sent it off.

Dear Luciano:

I am writing as a follow-up to our recent conversation regarding our professional relationship. As I mentioned to you, I will terminate our professional relationship effective December 31, 2002.

I realize that your professional needs have changed in recent times. Over the years, I have tried to stay in tune with these needs and your shifting priorities. Throughout your career, I believe I have successfully maintained the type of organization needed to service your various ventures both in the United States and around the world.

Time is moving on for me and at this stage in my life I look forward to a different lifestyle to spend time with my family. This is only doable without the demands of a full-fledged business operation.

I will remain forever grateful for the history we have shared and proud of all the extraordinary accomplishments that we achieved together over the last 35 years. To do it all over again would be my pleasure. I know we will remain friends in the future.

I will service the following three engagements arranged and contracted for in 2002: two concerts in St. Paul, Minnesota, and Columbus, Ohio, and one opera performance of Tosca in Berlin.

I wish you well in the future and all very best wishes to you and the family.

Very truly yours,
Herbert H. Breslin

Luciano called me after he got my letter.

"Ha," he said, "I was going to send you the same letter myself."

"Well," I said, "two minds with the same thought."

The press jumped all over it. I was on practically every wire service in the world. Luciano still had that much renown. "Pavarotti Splits with Long-Time Manager." "Another Divorce for Pavarotti." I gave quite a few interviews. The story even made "Weekend Update" on *Saturday Night Live*.

"Asked for a comment," the newscaster said, "Mr. Pavarotti said, 'Ah—OK, I ate him.'"

I enjoyed that.

After that, it got much quieter around the office. Luciano didn't call again for a long time.

I may have stopped working for Luciano, but I'm not retiring.

I still go in to the office every day. There are quite a lot of things to do. I've scaled back, but I still have a couple of artists I represent.

And I have a number of other ideas. I want to get a piece of music written about Primo Levi, the Italian writer, who is a big idol of mine. I would like perhaps to act in some kind of consulting capacity for the Metropolitan Opera, which is having a terrible time selling tickets these days and seems to have no idea what it's doing. And then there's a small French record company that's putting out a series of recordings called *Nouveaux Interprètes*, with first-rate young artists nobody has ever heard of. I want to approach them about starting a concert series for those artists in the United States, under the same name. *Nouveaux Interprètes*. I think there could be a real future in that.

chapter XV

THE KISS OF TOSCA

Our Final Act

The last contract I got for Luciano was *Tosca* at the Deutsche Oper in Berlin. About a year before that, we had had a memorable experience with *Tosca* at the Metropolitan Opera. *Tosca* was far from being Luciano's first opera. He didn't even try the role until 1976. But it's certainly going to be his last.

Puccini's *Tosca* is based on a melodrama, celebrated in its day, that the French playwright Victorien Sardou wrote for Sarah Bernhardt. At the climax of the piece, Floria Tosca, the diva heroine, leaps from the parapet of the Castel Sant'Angelo to her death. One night, the story goes, Madame Bernhardt reached the parapet at this critical juncture, looked down, and discovered the stagehands had forgotten to place anything for her to fall onto; being a consummate actress, she refused to break character and jumped anyway, injuring her leg so badly that it ultimately had to be amputated. This story is often cited as a possible source of the ubiquitous theatrical wish "Break a leg."

By the date of that accident—which happened when Madame Bernhardt was seventy years old—Puccini had already written his operatic adaptation of the play, which remains a cornerstone of the repertory. *Tosca* has everything: doomed lovers, a villain, a picturesque setting (Puccini went to great pains to reproduce details of Rome, down to the actual tone of the bells from St. Peter's), and overblown tragedy. Sopranos love it—at least the ones who are capable of singing it. Audiences love it. Critics have traditionally tended to find it all a bit much. Joseph Kerman, the eminent musicologist, is well remembered for his dismissal of the opera as a "shabby little shocker."

Luciano's favoring of the opera in his late years had very little to do with how hard or easy the role of Cavaradossi is to sing. Of course, it doesn't hurt that it has two great arias for the tenor, but the main thing is that in *Tosca* Luciano can control his movement. He's worked out *Tosca* to a point where he hardly has to move at all. In *La Bohème*, Rodolfo has to do a certain amount of jumping around: he wanders around Montmartre with Mimì, he engages in all manner of spirited horseplay with his friends. But Cavaradossi, when you think about it, doesn't have to do very much of anything. At least not the way Luciano plays him. In the first act, which finds the hero painting in a chapel, Luciano paints sitting down; when his beloved Tosca enters, he expresses his ardor (if he's feeling particularly fit that night) by having her sit on his lap. In the second act, he has to walk onstage under his own steam, but then the guards lead him off to torture him and at his next entrance practically carry him back on, which is probably the least simulated thing that happens the whole evening. In the third act, Cavaradossi is a prisoner. When Luciano does the opera these days, he's already sitting out in the cold, at the spot where he's going to be executed, when the curtain goes up. This means that he doesn't have to move until it's actually time for him to be shot, which gives additional drama to that event, since everyone in the audience is on the edge of their seats to see how Luciano is going to manage to drop dead. Let's just say it takes a lot of padding, and even then Cavaradossi dies, shall we say, rather gingerly.

That's the Luciano Pavarotti take on the tenor role in *Tosca*. One wag christened it "Cadaver-ossi."

So it was pretty clear to everybody that *Tosca* was going to be Luciano's swan song. The only thing was that nobody could say it. As I said, he was allergic to the whole idea of retiring.

In January 2002 he did a *Tosca* at Covent Garden. In the spring of that year he signed up to do two at the Met. He wouldn't say they were his farewell performances. He wouldn't let anybody call them that. But everybody naturally noticed that he didn't have any upcoming contracts with the Met. The Met didn't exactly quell the rumors when it jacked prices up to special gala rates. For the final performance, on Saturday night, which was also the close of the season, they were asking upwards of $1,800 a ticket. Everybody, of course, rushed to pay in case it was the last chance they'd have to see Pavarotti. The people who are paying for those tickets care very little about whether Luciano is in good voice or bad voice or sings the role as well as he did twenty years ago. They just love Luciano and want to see him onstage one last time.

It's safe to say nobody who got tickets to those two performances will ever forget them. But not for the reasons we might have hoped.

Luciano flew in a couple of days before the performance. Joe Volpe was already a little bit miffed by that. It's Joe's contention that the only way for Luciano to get through an opera these days is for him to arrive a couple of weeks early and give himself time to get over jet lag, have some coaching, and feel his way back into the role. The problem is, Luciano's schedule doesn't usually accommodate that kind of lead time. For this *Tosca*, in fact, Luciano wanted the dress rehearsal to be held the day before the performance. Joe vetoed that idea. Luciano did show up early enough to do one of the staging rehearsals. Well, at least he did act 1.

"It was a little bit too much for him," Joe said, "to get through the whole thing."

The dress rehearsal, however, was perfectly fine. In fact, making allowance for Luciano's age, I thought he sounded terrific. At the second intermission, I went up to Joe and said, "Listen to how great he sounds. We should do a *Pagliacci* next year."

Joe, for some reason, didn't seem to share my enthusiasm.

"Yeah, it was good for him," he said, "because he got through it."

The dress rehearsal was on Monday, and the performances were on Wednesday and Saturday. By Wednesday, Luciano had developed a cold.

He wasn't sure how bad it was. He wasn't sure if he could sing or not. He had Gildo Di Nunzio over in his apartment, warming him up, trying to see if he could rise to the occasion. In a situation like that, there are all kinds of things Luciano will do to try to improve matters.

"I'll take a bath. I'll go to the toilet. I'll have some consommé."

This started in the morning. It went on all day. Of course, Joe Volpe was on the phone: "Can he sing tonight? Can you sing, Luciano?"

"We will see. We will see."

Luciano had sometimes managed to sing when he was sick. He got over his cold at his first recital in Liberty, Missouri. Once, in Vienna, he came down with a bad cold before a *Luisa Miller*, only to find out that his cover was sick as well. Giovanna nearly panicked.

"We go," Luciano said. "We sing tonight." He was hoarse. He had a temperature of 101. And he went to the theater, and he sang a terrific performance.

"How did you do that?" Giovanna said afterward.

"That," Luciano said, "is what you call technique."

We were hoping that technique could kick in for him now, for this *Tosca*. It was a very important event for Luciano at the Met. He certainly wanted to do it. He thought maybe he could do it. Then he thought maybe he couldn't. He dangled, and dangled, and dangled. And finally the answer came, around seven at night.

"No."

Joe had no choice but to pull out Francisco Casanova, a Dominican tenor who shares Luciano's girth but doesn't have quite as impressive a voice. Frankly, I don't think his weight helps. Anyway, Francisco went out and sang the evening's performance, and I suppose he did it well enough, but the audience, of course, was disappointed.

The next performance was on Saturday. Which gave Luciano three whole days to recover.

By now, excitement was building to a fever pitch. All the papers began following the Pavarotti story. Would he or wouldn't he? The *New York Times* had three people on the case. The *New York Post* ran a front-page headline about it the day before the performance.

"Fat Man Won't Sing," it read.

Not everyone believed it. The demand for tickets swelled to a hysterical clamor. The Met, which after September 11 had started to have a hard time selling tickets for the first time in its history, was delighted. They bowed to public demand and set up a screen in the plaza of Lincoln Center to broadcast the performance free of charge to an additional 3,000 people sitting outside on folding chairs—something that the Met had never done before.

Everyone thought he would pull it together. First he said he couldn't. Then he said he could.

JACK MASTROIANNI
(artists' manager)

I went to hear the Tosca *on Wednesday, with Casanova and Maria Guleghina, because Guleghina was one of my artists. And I thought, If the people who paid $1,800 for a ticket on Saturday see this, they're not going to be so happy.*

So I came home that night and wrote an e-mail to Joe Volpe saying, "This is just to let you know that Salvatore Licitra [the young Italian tenor whom I represent] is free."

I was going in to see Joe the next morning anyway, and Sally

Billinghurst, the assistant general manager, called me around ten and said, "We saw your e-mail, and we are very interested."

By the time I managed to reach Salvatore, it was about six-thirty in the evening in Milan.

"How are you feeling?" I said.

"Why?" Salvatore said.

I said, "I need you to get on a plane to New York."

"When?" said Salvatore.

I said, "Be ready in ten minutes."

"My bags are packed," said Salvatore.

We got Salvatore onto the Concorde from London, and he arrived in New York on Friday morning and went straight into a rehearsal at the Met. On Saturday, the day of the performance, he went to visit the Empire State Building. He has no nerves at all.

Later in the afternoon, I got a call from Joe. "Luciano's not doing it."

I called Salvatore's cell phone. "Where are you?" I said.

"I'm walking through Central Park."

"Get over here," I said.

Twenty minutes later I got another call from Joe. "He is doing it."

I called Salvatore again.

"OK," Salvatore said. "Then I'll stay in Central Park."

I got calls at four and at four-thirty. At five o'clock they called again.

"We don't know if he's doing it," they said. "You should be here at six."

At ten to seven, when we were at the Met, the final call came. He wasn't doing it.

So I went down with Salvatore to the dressing rooms, and there were Herbert and his wife, sitting outside the dressing room door.

I said, "Hello, Herbert, how are you?"

He said "Hello," and then something like, "Well, let's see if he does it."

And I realized: Herbert doesn't know. He doesn't know that Luciano's not going to sing.

So I brought Salvatore down to the end of the hall, to the last dressing room, and I called Joe.

I said, "Joe, Herbert's down here. He doesn't know."

"Oh, my God," Joe said; "I'll come get him."

So Joe came and brought Herbert and his wife up to his office and told them, and everybody waited till they were gone and then took Luciano's name off the dressing room door and put up Salvatore's. I didn't feel right about bringing my artist past them into the dressing room.

I went up to Joe Volpe's office and had a stiff drink and called Luciano. "You're not singing?" I said.

"No."

"At least come down to the Met," I said. "Come down and face your public. You have four thousand people waiting here to hear you sing. They just want to see you. You can say to them, 'My friends, I am terribly sorry that I cannot sing for you tonight, but I will be back. Mr. Volpe and I will organize my return, and I will be back to sing for you any way you want.' They'll understand. Just let them see you."

I really believed that that would have been the best thing to do. But of course he wasn't ready to do that. He was sick. He wouldn't come. And according to him, I, as usual, didn't know what I was talking about.

Joe had to go out and make the announcement to that gala crowd, which was all pumped up to see Luciano, that Luciano wasn't going to be coming. I'm sure he was flustered. It's a flustering thing to go out there in front of thousands of people and have to tell them something they really, really don't want to hear. Furthermore, in my opinion, he hadn't thought through what he was going to say. We were all so sure, you see, that Luciano would pull it together and sing. So there was Joe out onstage in front of this huge audience who had paid all this money to be there, and he was extremely annoyed, because he felt that this situation he was in was not his fault.

He said to the crowd, "I tried to convince Luciano to come over here and at least tell you in person how sorry he was. I said to him, 'This is a hell of a way to end this beautiful career of yours.' ".

Well, that was a very ill-advised thing to say. Because from Luciano's perspective, it looked like the Met was washing their hands of him. After all he had done for them.

Salvatore went out and gave a very decent performance. He has a fine voice, and he's young, and he can sing excitingly, and because of all the attention it was a big, big success for him. It looked like the beginning of a great career. Sony raced to get his solo CD debut out on the market as soon as possible. Still, he hasn't been able to parlay all of the attention into the next step he needs to take if he wants a career anything like Luciano's.

Anyway, Salvatore sang and got a huge, huge ovation. And Luciano went home to Italy.

There were a few consequences of that *Tosca*.

One was that Luciano told me—since I had not yet officially stopped working for him at this point—to get him some more *Tosca*s, in some major houses. He wanted to show everyone that he still could. So I sat down and wrote to the opera houses in Munich, and Paris, and Vienna, and Berlin, and I let them know that Luciano was available to do *Tosca* with them the following season. In the opera world, one year is very, very short notice. It's hard to pull a production of *Tosca* out of the woodwork if you weren't already planning to do one. Furthermore, the opera directors were very well aware that there was a big risk Luciano would cancel. So I can't say that the response I got was exactly overwhelming. But the Deutsche Oper in Berlin agreed to put on one performance of *Tosca*, as a gala, the following June. One out of four ain't bad.

Another consequence was that Luciano felt he had been ill-used by the Met, that Joe had not been properly supportive. So he wanted to go back and do *Tosca* at the Met immediately, in 2002–03. The problem was that the Met didn't have *Tosca* on the schedule in 2002–03. Luciano didn't see that this was a problem. European houses overhauled their schedules for him all the time.

But it was a problem for Joe. To do something like that, Joe would have to convince his board that the Met should go out of its way to put on *Tosca*, again, for Luciano, even after what had happened in May. The board had been dubious enough about the prospect the first time around.

"I'd be a laughingstock," said Joe.

Joe tried to find something else Luciano could do at the Met. He offered him *La Bohème*. He offered him a gala concert. A few months after the *Tosca* debacle, I went to talk to Joe about Luciano and his future at the Met.

"I think he'll come around," I said. "I think he's going to come back to the Met."

"I had a meeting with Luciano," Joe said, "after the incident of the spring, and I asked you to come to the meeting, with Luciano. And you didn't come. Why?"

"Well," I said, "because I don't think he wanted me there. He wanted to talk to you alone."

"He didn't want you there," Joe said. "He wanted to talk to me alone. So I go over to his apartment, and I sit in front of his desk, and he's sitting at his desk, and guess who's sitting over there?"

"Nicoletta," I said.

"Nicoletta," Joe said. "And we're discussing what he can do, and she's making suggestions. She said, 'Well, you know, Luciano could do Sundays next season, two *Tosca*s, two *Pagliacci*s, or maybe *Ballo*s, and two concerts.' "

(The Met, you see, doesn't normally have performances on Sunday. So as Nicoletta saw it, there should be no problem with sticking in a performance or two then. Union regulations, and overtime, and that kind of thing probably didn't enter her thinking.)

Joe continued, "But before she said that, Luciano said, 'No, no, no,' and gestured with his hand. 'Stop saying this.' "

" 'Stop saying this,' " I said, laughing.

Joe said, "So as we had this conversation, about ten minutes into this dinner, or whatever the hell we were having, she'd say something, or be about to say something, and he'd put up his hand for her to stop. And I said, 'Luciano, do me a favor. Don't put your hand up. She's going to get it in anyway. So you might as well let her shoot her mouth off and tell what she wants to say.' "

"Did you say it like that?" I said.

"Yeah!" Joe said. "I said, 'You might as well let her do it and forget about it, because you're not going to be able to stop her.' So after that, she was off and running."

"I'm sure," I said. "But I don't think he ever really listened to those ideas anyway. I don't think that was advice he took. I think she was just talking off the top of her head."

"Well," Joe said, "she was saying, 'Do the *Tosca*s that he wants, and do them on Sunday.' And I was saying, 'We're not doing that. We can't do that.' Meanwhile, Luciano clearly feels that, number one, I don't believe he can sing *Tosca*—he showed me reviews of the wonderful job he did at his last concert in Phoenix, to prove what good voice he was in; number two, I'm no longer a friend of his; number three, I don't like him; and number four, for those reasons I won't cancel performances this season, buy out artists, and put in operas for him.' "

So that was the situation between Luciano and the Met: a deadlock. But I think it bothered Joe considerably. He and Luciano had considered each other friends, more or less, for a long time. Therefore, it wasn't that surprising that eventually—sometime after I stopped working for Luciano—they reached a compromise. At least, I guess you could call it a compromise. The agreement was that Joe put Luciano on in three *Tosca*s in 2004. He bought out the artists he had already hired so he could engage the people Luciano liked.

In other words, Luciano got exactly what he wanted.

But all of that happened without me. My last *Tosca* with Luciano was the gala performance I had gotten for him in Berlin, in June 2003.

It was a funny time for Luciano and me. We weren't working

together anymore. We weren't talking very much anymore. He knew I was writing a book about my life and our relationship, and he didn't quite know what to think about that. All of this created tension between us. But the fact was that, even though we were no longer professionally involved, I had gotten him that contract. So I decided to go to Berlin. By coincidence, I happened to have planned a vacation with my whole family in France right after that *Tosca*, and I thought it would be useful to have my commission as spending money in my pocket.

When I got to Berlin, the first thing I did was ring up Jean-François Monnard, whose title is opera director of the Deutsche Oper.

"Hello, Mr. Breslin," he said. "How are you?"

I said, "Yes, well, what I want to ask is, can I get my commission from you? Because I'm going on vacation with my family, and I need some euros."

For some reason, Monnard seemed taken aback. Perhaps he was just distracted. He had reason to be, because Luciano, it emerged, had canceled that day's rehearsal. There would therefore be only one rehearsal, the dress rehearsal, for the whole performance. This was especially nerve-racking because the Deutsche Oper's *Tosca* production dated from 1969, and they hadn't put it on for a number of years. Things were likely to be a little rusty.

So my commission was not uppermost in Monsieur Monnard's thoughts. He suggested we discuss it in person at the dress rehearsal the next day.

The second thing I did in Berlin was go and find Luciano. He was in his suite at the Hotel Adlon.

The suite, of course, was enormous. Terri Robson, a former Decca executive who was Luciano's new press spokeswoman, ushered me in through a side door to a tiny bedroom where Edwin, Veronica, Thomas, and a chef were coming in and out, engaged in intense and sometimes heated debate about whatever happened to be that day's entry on the long roster of logistical headaches that are part and parcel of the job of looking after Luciano Pavarotti. I knew them all too well.

And in a huge room beyond, which was flooded with sun, sat Luciano, propped on pillows on a sofa, draped in towels. Pulled up nearly to his belly was a big white-clothed table bearing a deck of dog-eared playing cards, a crossword puzzle magazine, and a bottle of water. A giant silver refrigerator sat against the wall behind him, clinking gently when an assistant, at Luciano's bidding, went to get him a fresh water bottle. A grand piano stood in the corner. It was like entering the presence of an invalid. A sick king.

It had been a rough time for Luciano. The year before, both his parents had died—his mother right before the Covent Garden *Tosca*, his father right after the *Tosca* he didn't sing at the Met. That winter, Nicoletta had given birth to twins, one healthy, one stillborn. He had been through a lot.

But I was still a little shocked at his appearance. That morning, he had had a press conference to talk about his first Berlin opera performances in fifteen years, and his face was still thickly daubed with makeup. His eyebrows seemed painted on. He reminded me of the scene in Visconti's film of *Death in Venice*, when Aschenbach tries to conceal his age with makeup, and it starts to drip. And this pathetic figure was the person I had worked with for thirty-six years. The greatest tenor in the world. I was seized with a feeling of sadness. Also a feeling of nervousness. Luciano can be a very tricky person to be around.

"Hello, Luciano," I said. "How are you?"

"Agh," Luciano said. "Terrible. I have to sing in three days."

There you have it. If he doesn't sing, he's not happy. But if he sings, he's not happy. So he can't win. The Deutsche Oper was paying Luciano 25,000 euros for that *Tosca*. But it had to have cost Luciano a lot more than 25,000 euros to bring in all those people and put them up in the Adlon. The private plane alone probably cost more than 25,000 euros. If there's any financial logic here, I'm missing it.

"Well," I said brightly, "how is Nicoletta? You know, everybody keeps asking me, 'When are they going to get married?'"

"No, I am quite sure nobody is asking you," Luciano said. "But you want to know."

"In Italy, he can't get married in a church," Terri pointed out, "because he's divorced."

"I am married to Nicoletta in my heart," Luciano said. "Why do we need to go up in front of people to do this?"

In fact, they finally did get married. But not until six months later.

"How is Tibor?" I said. Tibor's devotion to Luciano is such that he built himself a house in Pesaro.

Tibor was well. For his age, Tibor was amazing. Of course, my age was the next topic of discussion.

"Seventy-eight," said Luciano in amazement.

"Well, you're right behind me, Luciano," I said.

"Eleven years," said Luciano, "is a big piece of life."

"What are you doing?" he added. "Whom do you represent now? You don't represent anybody."

"I'm writing a book," I said.

"You are not writing a book," Luciano said. "*She* is writing a book."

He gestured at my coauthor, Anne Midgette, who had accompanied me.

"Well, we are writing a book," I said, "and I wanted to talk a little bit about old times. Do you remember the first recital we did, in Liberty, Missouri?"

"Ah, yes," said Luciano. "You told me, 'Do a concert to see if you like the audience. Not to see if they like you.' I remember very well." For once, his tone seemed genuinely admiring.

"And remember, Luciano," I said, "I started you on Hermès scarves."

"No," Luciano said. "I did that myself."

"No, I gave you one as a gift," I said.

"No," said Luciano.

I said, "I gave you a blue—"

"Ah, ah, ah," said Luciano, "it is true. I remember. And then I went to Hermès myself, and I asked, 'How much is this?' At that time, how much were they? Fifty dollars. And I bought a stack like so." He indicated a pile several inches high with his hand.

"And do you remember the perfume I got you?" I said. "Impériale. From Guerlain."

"What?" said Luciano. "No. You didn't."

"*Profumo*," I said in Italian, to jog his memory.

"I think that was for my daughter," Luciano said.

"I gave you a huge bottle, like this," I said, gesturing to show him.

"Ah, yes!" said Luciano eagerly. He whistled and waved his hand, remembering the extravagance of the gift. "I remember. And I remember because those were the only two presents you ever gave me in forty-two years."

It seemed we had been working together even longer than I thought.

Luciano's mind was on other things. His daughter Giuliana was arriving from Italy. He was waiting as eagerly as a child to hear if she had landed. Once he learned from his cell phone that she had, he needed five-minute bulletins on her progress. The Italian president, Carlo Ciampi, also happened to be staying at the Adlon. Ciampi may not have commanded the best suite in the hotel, but he certainly commanded the best security, and the hotel garage was sealed off. Traffic was backed up for blocks. None of this exactly accelerated Giuliana's progress from the airport. I watched Luciano grab for his cell phone impatiently every two minutes and thought of an observation Adua once made that Luciano stopped growing up when he was about three and a half years old.

"Come," Luciano said, "we will make a surprise for Giuliana. She does not know that Herbert is here. We have to hide you."

"Hide me?" I said. "Where should I hide?"

"You sit over there," Luciano decided, "by the window, with your back to the door. So she will not see who it is when she comes in."

I obeyed and sat in a chair in the corner, by the window. It happened to be the same window Michael Jackson had dangled his baby from a few months before. Somehow it's not surprising that Michael Jackson and Luciano Pavarotti stay in the same suite when they're in Berlin. I could see out over the city—the Brandenburger Tor and the statue of the Friedensengel, or angel of peace, in the distance. I could also feel myself being watched.

"Look at that," Luciano said, from behind me. "Even from the back, you could not mistake Herbert for someone else. The pants the wrong color, the socks not matching the pants, the shoes matching the jacket."

Obviously, the effect I made wasn't pleasing him. He had Terri bring over a fedora for me to put on.

"The hat is good," Luciano said with satisfaction. "It makes you look like a very serious person. It distracts from everything else."

They wouldn't let me move until Giuliana came in. Then they didn't say anything and waited to see if she would notice. She kissed her father and then caught sight of me. It was a very satisfactory surprise. Her jaw dropped, and her eyes got completely round with delight. She came over and gave me a big kiss.

"Well, Giuliana, how are you? *Come stai?*" I said. I may have had a tear in my eye.

But there was too much to say, so we soon ran aground on small talk. In any case, it was time for me to go.

The dress rehearsal was called for ten o'clock the next morning, and when I arrived punctually at 9:45 and was walking across the courtyard by the stage entrance to the Deutsche Oper, I ran into Monnard, who had come out to wait for Luciano. Monnard looked somewhat sober, which is to be expected of any theater director who's dealing with presenting Luciano Pavarotti. It turned out he had other concerns, as well. Carol Vaness, who was singing Tosca, was sick. She would attend the rehearsal, but she couldn't sing that day and didn't know if she would be able to get through the performance.

From my point of view, finding Monnard was opportune because it gave me a chance to ask about my commission.

"You need to talk about that with Luciano," said Monnard. "We need him to sign a paper before we can give it to you."

"Oh, all right," I said. "Just forget it. I'll get it from him later."

Which I did. But not before having to put up with some of his resistance, which is what I had been hoping to avoid in the first place.

As I was talking to Monnard, Luciano's limo pulled up, and Luciano was extracted. Leaning heavily on Tino, he hustled inside and up to his dressing room, where he could sit down and recover from the exertion of moving from one place to another.

Monnard went into the suddenly crowded dressing room to advise Luciano that Carol was sick.

"Not as sick as me," said Luciano. "I am a very sick man."

Since Luciano was talking about a perpetual state rather than something that was immediately threatening to the performance, Monnard sought his input on other sopranos who might be acceptable to him. He suggested a few past winners of the Pavarotti competition. Fiorenza Cedolins? Cynthia Lawrence? Cynthia had sung with Luciano many times, but at the mention of her name, Luciano made a face. And he called for his sidekick.

"Get me Panoccia," he said.

So someone went into the hallway to get Franco Casarini, nicknamed Panoccia, Luciano's oldest and most loyal friend from childhood. Of course, Panoccia and his wife had come up from Italy for the performance. At the very least, Luciano needed a card partner in his entourage. Now Panoccia came into the dressing room to see what Luciano wanted.

"*La soprano è malata*," Luciano told him. "Find Madelyn Renée."

After their years apart, Luciano had recently given a couple of concerts with Madelyn. Madelyn was in no position to say no. Whatever had gone on between them in the past, there was nothing coming up on her calendar to compare with a concert with Luciano Pavarotti. And the concerts had gone rather well. The only hitch, in fact, was that Luciano had spoken sharply to her because at one point she had had trouble remembering some of her words. Luciano, you see, is the only singer who's allowed to forget his words. Everybody around him had better be perfect.

Panoccia scurried out on his errand, and then the dress rehearsal started, beginning with the last act and working backward. Tino ushered Luciano out to a bench, and Luciano got himself settled there, with a little table at his side with a thermos, and stayed there motionless for the whole act. Compensating for his immobility was Carol Vaness. She came bombing out onstage and emoted all over the place. The only thing was that, since she was sick, she wasn't making a sound. You had these two people onstage acting out a kind of dumbshow. Carol was pantomiming love and passion, and Luciano was pantomiming a prisoner who fortunately gets to have a leisurely cappuccino before he is executed. He didn't even move when the guards came on to kill him. He sipped at his cup and watched as they pointed their guns at an empty part of the stage where he was supposed to be standing. The only time he moved was when Carol came over to his bench and caressed him. Of course, he didn't want to get her cold. So he shifted away.

It was a fairly difficult rehearsal. Because the production was so old, the tech crew didn't quite remember how everything was supposed to go. Luciano didn't care how everything was supposed to go; he knew how he wanted everything to go. So he was constantly contradicting the stage director. Carol, meanwhile, was compensating for her inability to make a sound by investing the role with intense drama. In act 2, when the evil Baron Scarpia let her know that he would free Cavaradossi in exchange for, well, sex, she threw her scarf in his face, and Juan Pons got a mouthful of scarf and didn't like that, and there were evidently a few words. When I got backstage after that act, Carol was not letting her illness prevent her from making a considerable amount of noise in a full-blown diva episode directed at the hapless stage director.

Luciano wasn't sounding so great, either. His appearance stood in sharp contrast to the dress rehearsal for the Met *Tosca* a year before, where he had seemed fairly lively. He had also sounded better. Of course, it was hard to tell in rehearsal because he was marking and not singing full voice, but his voice seemed pretty ragged. If that was truly the current state of his voice, well, you had to make the best of it. But it would also be difficult to know why he was still singing.

After the whole thing was over, I made my way backstage through the crowd and went in to see Luciano. We closed the dressing room door and there we were, the two of us, for the last time.

I looked at the tenor I had worked with for thirty-six years, sitting there immobile, almost unable to walk, bad makeup running off his face, struggling his way through an opera he used to own, and I couldn't help myself.

"Luciano," I said, "are you happy?"

"I am very, very happy," he said.

"Well, you don't look very happy," I said.

"I am very happy," he said again. "In my life, there are only two people who are disappointing me. My wife and you."

Well, that shut me up for a minute. I mean, even to begin to parse that one would take hours. "How exactly did we disappoint you?" you could ask. "You mean, because Adua got some money out of you in the divorce? You mean, because I am writing a book?"

Luciano, you see, is not guilty of anything in this world. He's a paragon of virtue, and he's also a long-suffering victim, because everybody else does things to him. Like Adua and like me. There's no thought in his mind that he might in some way have disappointed us.

So there was nothing I could really say to that one. We said our good-byes, and then I left. A few hours later, I was on a plane to France. I stopped off in Paris and then went down to the south of France, where my whole family was waiting for me. Everyone was there, and everybody got along, and nobody fought for the whole two weeks, and we had a wonderful, wonderful time.

I didn't go to the actual performance in Berlin. I didn't need to see it. I could imagine very well how it would go. And I was right.

First of all, Carol Vaness canceled, of course, but she didn't cancel until the day of the performance, which made for a little extra drama behind the scenes. For some reason, Monnard had thought she would get better. He was probably far more concerned about the possibility of having to replace Luciano. In fact, he flew Salvatore Licitra in from Italy, just in case. It had to be very secret, because Luciano would not react well if he knew his replacement was already on hand. But Monnard was covered. Replacing the Tosca was not that big a deal. Madelyn, evidently, was not available, but Monnard flew in Eliane Coelho, a Brazilian soprano of rather average talents who sings a lot in Vienna.

Of course, the performance was sold out. I'm not saying it was an audience of real opera lovers. Luciano's performances, at this point, tended to attract two kinds of people: die-hard Pavarotti fans and people who didn't really know much about opera but had the idea that seeing one of Pavarotti's last performances was some kind of historic event. The sold-out house was the whole reason the Deutsche Oper agreed to put on the Tosca. They needed the money. Berlin has three opera houses and not enough state funding to support them, and they are all eager for every chance they can get. The last time Luciano had appeared at the Deutsche Oper, the ovation had lasted so long it set a Guinness World Record. That kind of response can be a shot in the arm for a struggling opera house.

I don't think the response to Luciano for this Tosca, though, set any Guinness World Records. From everything I heard about the performance, it was rather bizarre. Luciano, of course, made sure that there were glasses of water everywhere; at one point in act 1, he held his artist's palette up in front of his face to hide from the audience the fact that he was drinking. That was about as effective as a child hiding by putting her hands over her eyes; if anything, it drew attention to what he was doing. Luciano, though, was more concerned about helping Coelho through the performance, which he did with his usual subtle hand gestures.

Maybe that kind of thing distracted from the condition of Luciano's voice. Most of the evening's dramatic tension came from wondering whether he would be able to hit the notes. He missed a couple, drawing a murmur of concern from the audience, but at the key point in act 2, when he has to sing "Vittoria, vittoria" on a high A-sharp, he got the right pitches out, much to everyone's relief. After that, he began to mark. When he got backstage, he was worried that he'd given too much and hadn't saved enough energy for his big aria in act 3. His attitude seemed to be that the audience should be grateful for every pearl he was willing to give them and understanding of the other 60 percent of the notes in the score that he wasn't going to sing at all.

The scariest moment came at the beginning of act 3. Since Luciano had altered the plot a little to allow Cavaradossi to be onstage from the opening curtain, he was sitting out there hearing music that he wouldn't have normally heard when he was singing the part in the past. Not long after the curtain goes up, the orchestra makes a big statement of the phrase that, several minutes later, opens his aria, "E lucevan le stelle." Luciano heard the familiar music, and he automatically began to sing. He launched right into his aria, oblivious of the fact that he wasn't even supposed to be onstage, that it made no dramatic sense for him to be singing at this juncture, and that it was almost impossible to be heard over the surging orchestra. He cranked out two whole phrases before he realized that he was very much in the wrong place at the wrong time and shut up again until he was supposed to come in.

Did the audience notice? Probably not. They just wanted to see Luciano. That's the thing that's important to remember. He was so beloved that people just wanted to be in his presence. Audiences are very forgiving. They applauded him warmly. What they were really clapping for, of course, was not his performance. They were applauding what he had been.

This time, the fans didn't get to go backstage. Access to Luciano was restricted to theater employees, cast members, and people with a personal connection. In other words, the hallway outside Luciano's dressing room was still a zoo, as it is every time Luciano sings. Hordes of people were lined up with sheaves of things for Luciano to autograph—pirated recordings, old photos, you name it. Outside the door, Tino and Thomas and Panoccia and Terri and Giuliana and all the others waited patiently until it was time to go. Nicoletta was there, too. She had flown up from Italy for the performance. She was wearing a chiffony gown and thanking people who had sent gifts for the baby, Alice. Being Nicoletta, she had her eye on the practical. She was very curious about my book.

"Is it going to be a good book or a bad book?" she asked my coauthor.

"Well," Anne said, "it's going to be a very Herbert book."

"Ah, then it will be bad," said Nicoletta.

So that was basically the end of my work with Luciano Pavarotti. Maybe you think I was bitter. Well, I wasn't. Relationships change. You have to take what comes. There's absolutely no point in fighting against it. You can say things like, "After all I've done for you . . ." or "You should have treated me better." Those are the kinds of things Luciano says all the time. But to say things like that would diminish me. And I don't have those feelings. You may think I do, but I really don't.

Do I want to set the record straight? Possibly. But I'm a realist. I know that very few people understand what this business is really like. I've heard more misinformation about me and Luciano than you can imagine, and I'm not going to change anybody's mind now. As I said: let them talk. The only thing that irritates me a little is when people say I sold Luciano down the river for money. I did many things, good and bad, but I surely never did that. Frankly, I never had the power to do that. I don't know if anybody had the power, once this thing got going. As this career gained momentum, you could do things to feed it, but there was almost no way to change its course—certainly not for me, and maybe not even for Luciano. We just hung on for the ride. And, ups and downs, it was a great, great ride.

This book is really the story of two people who came from nowhere. I started out with nothing and worked my way to the very top of this little pissant business and helped change it and alter its limits and redefine the way people see it. Luciano started with nothing and became the most famous opera singer of a generation.

You may also say it's the story of the perils of money and fame and of what happens once you reach the top. Well, fine, perils, call them that or whatever you want. It's true: Luciano has tarnished his reputation. All that money had a very visible effect. His name used to be a synonym for excellence. Now he's become something of a figure of fun.

And that irritates me, too, because that's not the real story, either. The real story, the bottom line, is that this was a great, incredible, world-class career. Luciano Pavarotti had the greatest voice, and the greatest possibilities, and in many ways the greatest attitude I ever experienced in my life. We took that and we made it into something that the whole world noticed. It was thrilling to be a part of it. Those things, those great moments, are the things I won't ever forget. And somewhere deep down inside, I don't think he will, either.

THE FAT MAN SINGS

Luciano Pavarotti on Herbert Breslin

On June 27, 2003, Luciano Pavarotti graciously made time for an interview with Anne Midgette.

The memory of me and Herbert is very important. Because spending thirty-six years together is an important thing. Thirty-six years in which we were completely synchronized. We were both born under the sign of Libra; we are both very cautious but also really crazy.

I think that we were two people who went beautifully together, for the power that we had to take risks. And for the power that he had to protect me so people wouldn't take advantage of me, even when that meant being tough.

I have been in close relations with Herbert, professionally speaking and personally speaking. I feel he is a very intelligent and charming person. And if you are intelligent, you don't bother me. If you are intelligent, we will get along.

I met Herbert because he came to see me in Montreal, when Milan's La Scala was there for *Capuleti*. At that time, Herbert was not an agent; I was not a big tenor. We really started our rise together. I met Herbert because the head of London Records in America, Terry McEwen, talked to me one day.

He said, "Luciano, you are a beautiful singer. You are too, too charming. You are too vulnerable. You need to be represented by a very tough man, and I have the right name for you."

So that was how I met Herbert.

When you are a singer, you need a publicist. When you are really famous, everybody wants you. And when you are starting out and you have twenty very famous tenors in front of you, you need help in order to interest the rest of the world. Obviously, a press agent cannot do more than organize an interview. The kind of personality that comes out in the interview depends on what you say in the interview, not on the press agent. But still, you need somebody who lines up the best papers for you to appear in. For example, we did a beautiful interview in the *New York Times Magazine*, and that was a big beginning. It was called "Pavarotti, Mamma Mia," I remember.

After he had worked as my publicist, I decided to take Herbert as my manager because, as I told you, we are very much synchronized. Every time he offered me something to do, I generally liked it. I liked it very much when he came to me and said, "Luciano, it's time for you to go out by yourself and see if you like the audience." So I went to Liberty, Missouri, and I went to Dallas, and then I went to Carnegie Hall to do recitals with piano, and the experience was fantastic. I did like the audience. And the audience, evidently, did like me. From there began a kind of rapport and security that I did not have before, because when you go out in an opera you never know which applause is for you and which is for your colleagues.

I had done recitals before, many times. I did one in 1955, when I was a student, with Miss Freni; we did many recitals together. But it's one thing to do four pieces in a recital with someone else, and another thing to do twenty. It's one thing to do Bellini and Donizetti and Verdi and Puccini, and another thing to sing

Baroque songs or Tosti songs. When I went out the first time in front of the audience in Missouri, it was not completely new, because I had done it before. But it was definitely in a different dimension.

I saw Herbert completely devoted to one person, and I let him work with me, and I think it was very good work we did together. You can see it was not a problem that we had no contract, because we spent thirty-six years together. I think a contract is something that you have when you are not sure of a person. But when you are sure that you like the person and you are sure of the person, you don't need a contract. What would you need it for? I had managers all over the world. I had one in Berlin, who is still alive; I had one in London. But with Herbert, it was totally different. We were two brothers. We even gave each other advice in life. He is still giving me advice now. I was not close like this with anybody else.

Is his advice good? Advice is good if it works for you. I always make fun of the color of the things he's wearing and give him many other little pieces of advice. And we gave big advice, too. But, generally, no advice concerning the profession. The professional part was decided before.

We had the good fortune that at the beginning of my profession I had an incredible collaboration with Mr. Adler, in San Francisco. There, I did seven or eight new productions, all the most important operas of my repertoire. I did many, many, many things: *Trovatore*, *Favorita*, *Aida*, *Turandot*, *Gioconda*. Adler was a very intelligent theater director. Every time he booked me, say, in September for the following October, he would come visit me in the middle, in the summertime, to make sure I had not changed my mind.

After Terry McEwen took over, there were two reasons I did not appear as much in San Francisco. First, I was engaged in other theaters. The Met, especially, booked me almost constantly. And second, I had done everything there already. What should I do there? The opera I had not done was *Ernani*. I went there one year to do it, and my daughter fell sick and I canceled. *Mefistofele* is an opera we have recorded. Recorded very well, I think. And yes, I was thinking of doing it. But I never did.

I don't remember why there was a film of *La Gioconda* in San Francisco. No, it was not the beginning of a problem with Scotto. It was the beginning and the end of a problem. It was a huge misunderstanding that should not happen between friends.

I remember how the American Express ad happened, though.

I was watching television. And on television I saw Pelé. You know who Pelé is? He came out and he said, "Don't leave home without it." It was beautiful. Marvelous.

Fifteen minutes later, the telephone rings. And I pick up. It's Herbert.

"Luciano, they want to do something with you."

"What?"

"They would like you to do an American Express ad. But they don't pay much."

And I say, "Herbert, we should pay them. Because just now I saw my idol there on television. And they are making the comparison between me and him. They see me in my world as they see him in his world. It is a big compliment. Take the money they give; I don't care."

Why should I worry about becoming commercialized? You live in the world in which you live. Why should I stay out of the media? It's part of the profession. I don't want to say it's a huge part, but it's a good part.

Yes, Giorgio was something that I really should not have done. Now the whole thing makes me laugh. I remember, Herbert came from Metro-Goldwyn-Mayer and I said, "OK, read me the story."

He read me the story.

I said, "Herbert, the story stinks."

He said, "Well, but we have a very big director, Schaffner."

"Yeah, I know, I know. But this story!"

"Ah, we must do, we must do . . ."

"OK," I said, "let's begin to do this movie."

So we began in Hollywood, with a press conference announcing the movie in front of everybody. Everybody was there. Mention one person: he was there. And then we made this kind of, ah—I'm not going to say what it was, but this was the kind of movie we made. Herbert, as I said, is very intelligent. During the filming, he realized, like I did, that it was not going to work.

During the production, I was saying to the writer, "Why don't we make the movie funny?" It would be a good movie to make fun. But if you make it serious, the story of a guy who stays with the girl but is not married to the girl, with his wife, it's not very good. The movie was well made. The director was a very serious man. But it was the wrong story. I always said, "Herbert, you should not have done this to me."

But I thank him, too. Even without success, it was a great experience.

It's very difficult to tell you what I think about Herbert's reputation. For me, he has a maximum reputation. In the outside world, the only thing they may tell you is that they never saw him appear in a benefit concert. That is, he would not do anything without getting a salary.

I needed a tough guy at the beginning, to protect me, and he was the tough guy protecting me. And what are you like if you are tough? Well, that's what he's like. But this is normal. Sometimes, when somebody came to me to cry about him, I tried to make him a little sweeter. I tried to say, "Be a little lighter, Herbert." But most of the time I realized he protected me in the world of opera. He is disliked by my enemies. I don't think he is disliked by my friends. I don't think he is disliked by the people he represents in the business.

I remember when we began the arena concerts. Herbert did them before Tibor Rudas, with a certain success. But at one point Rudas wanted to do a concert in the open air, and Herbert said, "No." And we did not do it for a good three or four years. And the reason, I realized later—well, there were probably two reasons. First, if you do this kind of concert, your reputation will be affected a little. Second, if we do this, then Mr. Rudas becomes more important than Mr. Breslin. But I think to Herbert the most important consideration was my reputation. Many people even now say so, that I should have stayed only in the theater. We thought—well, I thought something else. I thought there should be opera for everybody, even on the moon someday when we are there.

At a certain point, after many years, we decided we didn't work enough together anymore. I think he is almost retired, and I am going more or less the same way, so we decided to stop.

Could I have had the career I had without Herbert? This is a question I will never be able to answer. I started out very well. I was already selling a lot of tickets. I was very much in demand as a young tenor. I don't know. Probably somebody else, Edgar Vincent or somebody, would have done my career. But certainly not been synchronized like me and Herbert were.

I played a role in his career, too. Before, he was not a manager, and he became a manager—and how. When you have this kind of living together for thirty-six years for the same cause, with the same center, I think it is a very important role for each other, absolutely. Herbert was my wife in the opera.

ACKNOWLEDGMENTS

No project of this nature could ever be accomplished without the help, support, love, and respect of many friends, and mostly admirers, who have acted as guides and advisers. They know full well what a tough assignment this was. To all of them we owe a deep debt of gratitude.

This book would never have come to be without Steve Rubin at Doubleday, who has accompanied the Pavarotti story from its beginnings (when he wrote the first story on Luciano for the *New York Times*) through to its end and who championed this project, brought its authors together, and offered both of us the profound benefits of his experience, knowledge, and friendship every step of the way. We cannot express the depth of our appreciation.

It was a privilege to work with Gerry Howard, our editor, who with acumen, patience, a keen critical eye, and dry wit played a major role in the conception and shaping of the book.

We are grateful to everyone who shared with us their memories and their time. Thank you, Richard Bonynge, Ian Campbell, Giovanna Cavaliere, Bruce Crawford, Judy Drucker, Kathryn Harrold, Marilyn Horne, Merle Hubbard, Joan Ingpen, Judy Kovacs, Bob Lombardo, Lotfi Mansouri, Jack Mastroianni, Randy Mickelson, Aprile Millo, Madelyn Renée Monti, Nicola Rescigno, Terri Robson, Sandy Sawotka, Michael Scott, David Patrick Stearns, Norman Steinberg, Sissi Strauss, Roman Terleckyj, Sir John Tooley, Christopher Ungerer, Adua Veroni, Edgar Vincent, Joseph Volpe, Olivier Wilkins, and those who preferred that their names not be used. A special acknowledgment to Alicia de Larrocha and to Dame Joan Sutherland, who, true to her lifelong dislike of interviews, had Ricky talk to us instead.

Thanks, too, to those who supported us in other ways: Anthony Baldino, Sarah Billinghurst, Charles Handelman, Brian Kellow, Rosette Lederman, Tibor Rudas, Maryann Santora, Robert Tuggle, Ronald Wilford, and Robin Heidi Kennedy for her help with the Italian.

We would like to remember some of the influential figures, no longer with us, who helped shape the events narrated herein: Ann Colbert, John Crosby, Agnes Eisenberger, Nathan Kroll, Richard Leach. And very special thanks to Robert Turnbull for generously making available the tapes of his unpublished interviews with the late, and unquenchable, Terry McEwen.

Thanks to Anthony Tommasini, Steven Erlanger, James R. Oestreich, Jack Schwartz, and other colleagues at the *New York Times* for their professional inspiration, encouragement, and a couple of really bad puns.

There might not be a book were it not for the company DriveSavers, which took a laptop computer that was destroyed in a house fire and retrieved all the data from it.

None of this could have happened without our wonderful spouses, Carol Breslin and Greg Sandow. This is not only because they read and commented on every word of the manuscript, several times, with professional and practiced eyes, but also, in Greg's case, because he was initially approached about doing the book himself and referred it to his wife instead.

And thanks, finally, to Luciano Pavarotti, who in spite of everything bravely agreed to speak to us, and allow us access, for this project.

HERBERT BRESLIN
ANNE MIDGETTE
New York, 2004

CLIENT LIST

This is a nearly complete list of my clients in publicity and management over the last forty-five years. Most of these relationships were very happy. Some were not.

FEMALE SINGERS

June Anderson
Victoria de los Angeles
Kathleen Battle
Hildegard Behrens
Teresa Berganza
Grace Bumbry
Montserrat Caballé
Cynthia Clarey
Fiorenza Cossotto
Régine Crespin
Natalie Dessay
Daniela Dessì
Susan Dunn
Rosalind Elias
Kallen Esperian
Maria Ewing
Lauren Flanigan
Renée Fleming
Mirella Freni

Elizabeth Futral
Cecilia Gasdia
Angela Gheorghiu
Rita Gorr
Markella Hatziano
Marilyn Horne
Soile Isokoski
Gwyneth Jones
Angelika
    Kirchschlager
Cynthia Lawrence
Pilar Lorengar
Christa Ludwig
Aprile Millo
Leona Mitchell
Jessye Norman
Maureen O'Flynn
Susan Patterson
Roberta Peters

Judith Raskin
Nina Rautio
Regina Resnik
Leonie Rysanek
Elisabeth Schwarzkopf
Renata Scotto
Natalie Stutzmann
Elena Suliotis
Joan Sutherland
Renata Tebaldi
Anna Tomowa-
    Sintow
Béatrice Uria-
    Monzon
Carol Vaness
Shirley Verrett
Elizabeth Vidal
Deborah Voigt
Elena Zaremba

MALE SINGERS

Alexandru Agache
Roberto Alagna
Fabio Armiliato
Carlo Bergonzi
Renato Bruson
Bruno Caproni
Fernando Corena
Plácido Domingo
Francesco Ellero-
    D'Artegna
Simon Estes
Geraint Evans

Dietrich Fischer-
    Dieskau
Jake Gardner
Nicolai Gedda
Marcello Giordani
Tito Gobbi
Jerry Hadley
Manfred Hemm
James King
Vincenzo La Scola
Cornell MacNeil
Robert Merrill

Sherrill Milnes
James Morris
Luciano Pavarotti
Paul Plishka
Hermann Prey
Juan Pons
Ruggiero Raimondi
Roberto Scandiuzzi
Neil Shicoff
Gérard Souzay
Martti Talvela
Jon Fredric West

CONDUCTORS

Marco Armiliato
Richard Bonynge
James Conlon
Sir Colin Davis
Lawrence Foster

Henry Lewis
Kent Nagano
Daniel Oren
Georges Prêtre
Julius Rudel

Gerard Schwarz
Leonard Slatkin
Sir Georg Solti
William Steinberg

INSTRUMENTALISTS

Pierre-Laurent
    Aimard
Vladimir Ashkenazy
Michel Beroff
Jorge Bolet
Myung-Whun
    Chung
Jean-Philippe Collard
Alicia de Larrocha
Rudolf Firkusny
Samson François

Horacio Gutiérrez
Lynn Harrell
Joseph Kalichstein
Julius Katchen
Wilhelm Kempff
Jaime Laredo
Yvonne Loriod
Moira Lympany
Arturo Benedetti
    Michelangeli
Itzhak Perlman

Carlos Prieto
Sharon Robinson
Janos Starker
Paul Tortellier
Rosalyn Tureck
Alexis Weissenberg

ORGANIZATIONS

American Opera Society
Boston Symphony Orchestra
Carnegie Hall–International
   Festival of Visiting Orchestras
Great Performers (Lincoln
   Center)
Luciano Pavarotti International
   Voice Competition

Lyric Opera of Chicago
Mostly Mozart Festival
Richard Tucker Music
   Foundation
Saint Louis Symphony

OTHER ARTISTS

Charles Aznavour (popular singer)
Barbara Cook (popular singer)
Natalia Makarova (ballerina)

Marcel Marceau (mime)
Olivier Messiaen (composer)
Pier Luigi Samaritani (designer)

SELECTED DISCOGRAPHY

The following are highlights of Pavarotti's discography as well as those of other artists who are referred to in the book. Recordings tend to float in and out of print, but most of these should be available, in one form or another, from Tower Records, amazon.com, or arkivmusic.com.

Renata Tebaldi: Puccini, *Tosca*, *Madama Butterfly*
Zinka Milanov and Jussi Björling: Verdi, *Il Trovatore*
Jussi Björling: *Jussi Björling Rediscovered*
Elisabeth Schwarzkopf: Richard Strauss, *Four Last Songs*
Joan Sutherland: *The Art of the Prima Donna*
Joan Sutherland and Marilyn Horne: Rossini, *Semiramide*
Marilyn Horne: *Just for the Record: The Golden Voice*
Alicia de Larrocha: Albéniz, *Iberia*
Alicia de Larrocha and Victoria de los Angeles: *The Concert at Hunter College*
Montserrat Caballé: Strauss, *Salome*
Montserrat Caballé: Donizetti, *Lucrezia Borgia* (a live recording of Caballé's American debut is available from the budget label Opera d'Oro)
Barbara Cook: *Barbara Cook at Carnegie Hall* (1975)

There are, of course, dozens of compilation recordings or solo recordings of Luciano Pavarotti on the market, mainly from Decca/London, his recording label. Among the best are *Pavarotti: Primo Tenore*, which he recorded in the early 1970s, and *Pavarotti Greatest Hits*, a collection of recordings from over three decades.

Most of Luciano's recordings with Joan Sutherland are still in print. Of special interest may be Donizetti's *Daughter of the Regiment, Lucia di Lammermoor*, and *L'Elisir d'Amore*.

Noteworthy recordings with Mirella Freni include the early *La Bohème*, with Herbert von Karajan; Mascagni's *L'Amico Fritz* (on EMI); and the poor-quality live recording of Pavarotti's only appearance in Massenet's *Manon* at La Scala (available on Opera d'Oro).

For a long time, Pavarotti's favorite role for the tenor was Riccardo in Verdi's *Un Ballo in Maschera*, which he recorded with Margaret Price and Sir Georg Solti (who later conducted his unforgettable *Otello*).

The charm that helped launch The Three Tenors as a global phenomenon is still audible in the recording of their first appearance together, in 1990, in Rome, *The Three Tenors in Concert*.

INDEX